MIXING IT UP

OTHER BOOKS BY JOHN SHELTON REED

The Enduring South: Subcultural Persistence in Mass Society
The Enduring Effect of Education (with Herbert Hyman and Charles Wright)
Southerners: The Social Psychology of Sectionalism
Southern Folk, Plain and Fancy: Native White Social Types
Glorious Battle: The Cultural Politics of Victorian Anglo-Catholicism
Holy Smoke: The Big Book of North Carolina Barbecue (with Dale V. Reed)
Dixie Bohemia: A French Quarter Circle in the 1920s
Barbecue: A Savor the South® *Cookbook*

COMPILATIONS AND ESSAYS

One South: An Ethnic Approach to Regional Culture
Whistling Dixie: Dispatches from the South
"My Tears Spoiled My Aim" and Other Reflections on Southern Culture
Surveying the South: Studies in Regional Sociology
Kicking Back: Further Dispatches from the South
1001 Things Everyone Should Know About the South (with Dale V. Reed)
Minding the South

EDITED VOLUMES

Perspectives on the American South, vols. 1 and 2 (edited with Merle Black)
Regionalism and the South: Selected Papers of Rupert Vance
    (edited with Daniel Joseph Singal)
Townways of Kent (by Ralph C. Patrick, edited with Dale V. Reed)
Cornbread Nation 4: The Best of Southern Food Writing (edited with Dale V. Reed)

MIXING IT UP

IT UP

A South-Watcher's Miscellany

JOHN SHELTON REED

LOUISIANA STATE UNIVERSITY PRESS   BATON ROUGE

Published by Louisiana State University Press
Copyright © 2018 by Louisiana State University Press
All rights reserved
Manufactured in the United States of America
First printing

Designer: Barbara Neely Bourgoyne
Typeface: Whitman
Printer and binder: Sheridan Books

Library of Congress Cataloging-in-Publication Data

Names: Reed, John Shelton, author.
Title: Mixing it up : a south-watcher's miscellany / John Shelton Reed.
Description: Baton Rouge : Louisiana State University Press, [2018]
Identifiers: LCCN 2018007297| ISBN 978-0-8071-6957-5 (cloth : alk. paper) |
    ISBN 978-0-8071-7000-7 (pdf) | ISBN 978-0-8071-7001-4 (epub)
Subjects: LCSH: Southern States—Civilization—20th century. | Southern
    States—Social life and customs—20th century.
Classification: LCC F216.2 .R4194 2018 | DDC 975/.04—dc23
LC record available at https://lccn.loc.gov/2018007297

To the memory of Beverly Jarrett Mills,
a great Southern bookwoman and my friend.

• • •

CONTENTS

ASPECTS OF THE SOUTH . . . 227

SURVEYING THE SOUTH . . . 271

PREFACE

When I published a book called *Minding the South* in 2003, I thought I'd pretty much finished collecting my essays and reviews. From time to time, though, I did look wistfully at a few pieces that hadn't fit into that volume, and I kept writing more, in a desultory kind of way, so some dozen years later I began to wonder if I had the makings of another collection. Certainly I had enough *words*, but did they hang together enough to make a book? True, all of them had something to do with the South, but otherwise—in subject matter, in style, in length—they were all over the place. That is so because I have taken to heart an observation by the great statistician John Tukey that I first encountered as an undergraduate. "Anything worth doing," he said, "is worth doing superficially."

I'm a sociologist by training and there is some sociology in this collection, both overt and covert, but there's also a good deal of survey research that probably doesn't attain the stature and gravitas of social science. I've practiced some political science without a license and I've committed a whole lot of journalism. I'm not a historian, but I've written about Sherman's March and Robert E. Lee. I'm no geographer, but I've tried to draw the boundaries of the South. If I claimed to be a litterateur, real litterateurs would laugh, but I have reviewed some novels. I have, in short, aspired to emulate Muhammad Ali, and float like a butterfly, sting like a bee. It's not for me to judge my sting, but I do think I've got the floating down.

I tried putting these pieces in various orders, various combinations, even rewrote some of the stylistic outliers, but eventually I came to realize that aside from being about the South, the principal thing that they have in common, maybe the only thing, is that I wrote them. I'm not a modest man, but even I recognize that perhaps that's not enough.

You're actually holding a book in your hands at this moment, however, because LSU Press thinks it might be. I hope they're right.

Given the miscellaneous nature of this collection, I originally called it "Southern Sundries," but Rand Dotson, my editor at LSU, thought that title carried implications of inconsequentiality that were unfortunate, from a marketing point of view, so we settled on the present title, which I've come to prefer for its ambiguity. *Mixing It Up* means blending stuff, of course, but it can also mean fighting, and many of these pieces began as contributions to old arguments. One or two might even start new ones. (That's fine; there's nothing wrong with disagreement—although not everyone agrees with that, either.) Oh, and another thing being mixed up here—a first for me—is a cocktail (see pages 201–203).

It may be hard to believe, but this isn't everything I had lying around. I have included a number of occasional pieces, individually trivial, that I hope add up to more than the expected sum but, trust me, I've not included others that I recognize would be a complete waste of your time and attention. I've also omitted a few reviews of books that aren't worth remembering, as well as some I dimly recall having written but can't track down. I haven't included articles I published in scholarly journals like *Social Forces*, *Public Opinion Quarterly*, and (no kidding) the *International Journal of Gynecology and Obstetrics*. Nearly all such articles even possibly of general interest have been collected in earlier volumes and the leftovers are of interest only to specialists, if to them. Some of them don't even interest me. (What was I thinking?)

I've even left out my very first journal article, an assessment written in 1968 of the Association of Southern Women for the Prevention of Lynching. It's so full of cringe-making grad student prose ("The present paper, however, attempts to assess . . .") that when I had to cut an unwieldy manuscript, it went. For various other reasons, so did an essay for the program for an Edinburgh production of Beth Henley's *Crimes of the Heart*; celebrations of my colleagues Guy B. Johnson and Hodding Carter III; potted histories of the sociological study of the South, the Institute for Research in Social Science, and the journal *Southern Cultures*; a melancholy reflection on autumn for *Southern Living*; and a Lee's Birthday address requested by the Military Order of the Stars and Bars.

I have wrangled the remaining pieces into a few ragged groups on the basis of provenance, style, genre, or subject matter. (Inevitably, some groups hang together better than others.) Headnotes provide such information as when and why the things were written. I've also taken this opportunity to expand, correct, update, or otherwise make minor changes in some of them.

Finally, I admit that you will find some favorite lines and quotations used more than once. There's even some substantial overlap between some of these pieces, and between them and others previously collected, that would be called plagiarism if I were borrowing without attribution from anyone other than myself. But I believe that a good turn of phrase, like a good suit, should see you out.

WHAT'S UP DOWN SOUTH?

These three essays are "State of the South" overviews, a genre for which, I'm happy to say, there seems to be an inexhaustible demand.

SOUTHERN CULTURE—ON THE SKIDS?

This began its life as a paper called "Dixiology's False Dichotomies," read to a symposium at the University of Bonn in 1997. (The proceedings were published as Regional Images and Regional Realities, *edited by the conference organizer, Lothar Hönnighausen.) Four years later, with some new material and a new title taken from the name of a Chapel Hill rock band, this version appeared in a special issue of* Atlanta History *on "The American South in the Twentieth Century."*

• • •

If you had to choose one state to represent the entire South, which one would you choose? The answer is not obvious.

Not long ago Mississippi would have been a plausible choice, not because it was "typically" Southern (whatever that might mean), but because it was *ultra*-Southern. For 150 years or more, most generalizations about the South went double for Mississippi. When the South was rich, Mississippi was richest; when it was poor, Mississippi was poorest. The South was mostly rural: Mississippi was even more so. The South is biracial: Mississippi had and still has the highest percentage of African Americans in the country. White Southerners were committed to white supremacy: eighteen of the forty martyrs commemorated on the Civil Rights Memorial in Montgomery were killed in Mississippi. And so on.

In short, for a long time Mississippi was the most Southern of the Southern states, and "Southern" referred to the economic, cultural, political, and demographic legacy of plantation agriculture and slavery. Mississippi was at the core of *Dixie*, the land of cotton. It and the other Deep South states were where what sociologist Charles Johnson called "the shadow of the plantation" fell darkest and lingered longest.

Dixie has had many lives. It was the Old South, the plantation South, the Cotton Kingdom—the South of both *Gone with the Wind* and *Uncle Tom's Cabin*. From 1861 to 1865 it was the Confederate States of America. For decades after the 1890s it was the "Solid South" in politics—solid for the Democrats, the party of states' rights and white supremacy. Well into the twentieth century it was, in Franklin Roosevelt's phrase, "the nation's number-one economic problem."

Only yesterday Dixie was still a powerful reality, and perhaps an even more powerful myth. It still survives here and there, and the ongoing conflict over the Confederate battle flag suggests that old times there are not entirely forgotten. But if it is a little early to write Dixie's epitaph, that version of the South is clearly on its deathbed—and most Southerners don't live there any more. Mississippi is no longer the most Southern of the Southern states because the South has changed. (So, for that matter, has Mississippi.)

Urbanization, industrialization, and the end of de jure segregation have produced what we can call (for reasons I'll get to) *the Southeast,* a vibrant, dynamic, industrial region, a magnet for migration and investment from other parts of the nation and increasingly from abroad. The Southeast occupies much of the same territory as Dixie, but that shouldn't blind us to the fact that it is an entirely new development—indeed, in many respects an entirely different region.

So what state is the most Southern state now? Well, when a Southern Focus Poll conducted by the Odum Institute at the University of North Carolina in 1994 asked, "If you had to say, what one state best captures your idea of the South?" the most frequent choice by far was Georgia, chosen by over a quarter of both Southerners and non-Southerners.

To be sure, Georgia was part of Dixie. Atlanta was the scene, after all, of the great Cotton States and International Exposition of 1895, the great race riot of 1906, the premiere of *Gone with the Wind* in 1939, and the funeral of Martin Luther King Jr. in 1968. But I suspect that history is not the reason people these days say Georgia "captures the idea of the South." No, they choose it because Georgia's capital city has become the capital of the entire Southeast.

Consider: Atlanta is where regional trade associations have their annual conventions, where regional corporations are likely to be headquartered, where national corporations have their regional offices. It's where the television networks, wire services, and national publications have their Southern bureaus. The *Wall Street Journal*'s Atlanta office now publishes a regional supplement, and the *Journal-Constitution* is the nearest thing the South has to a national newspaper. Atlanta is at the center of the South's transportation grid as well: its airport is by some reckonings the busiest in the United States, giving rise to the Southern joke that even if you're going to hell you'll have to change planes in Atlanta.

The Southeast that Atlanta serves is the South of the future. It barely existed before World War II, but it's all around us now. And it seems to be unstoppable, as its booming economy and surging population are translated into political power (primarily through the medium of the Republican Party, Dixie's old adversary).

But there's a reason to call it the South*east*. We can see plainly now a development predicted more than sixty years ago by the sociologist Rupert Vance: The post-agricultural South has split down the middle. Grant's work at Vicksburg has been completed: the Trans-Mississippi has been lost. More precisely, it has become a region in its own right—essentially Greater Texas. Dallas and Houston don't report to Atlanta. The western South has its own regional institutions, its own magazines and corporate headquarters, even its own editions of the *Wall Street Journal*.

This distinction between Southeast and Southwest is increasingly evident in business and trade association names, and that's no accident, because these regions are primarily economic entities, not cultural ones. As Lew Powell was the first to observe, we speak of commercial activity in the Southeast, but not of Southeastern religion, Southeastern music, the Southeastern gentleman, or Southeastern fried chicken.

So we have Dixie, the old, agricultural South, rooted in the plantation economy and the institutions that grew out of that—fading fast and soon to be of interest primarily to historians. And we have this new metropolitan Southeast—a mere quadrant, culturally speaking, a region of interest primarily to economists and industrial recruiters. Is there anything left that is recognizably *the South*?

When Rupert Vance predicted the emergence of the Southeast and Southwest, he remarked that the South's continuing existence represented the triumph of history and culture over economics and geography, and it is to a shared culture that we must look if we are to find the South in the twenty-first century. Yet many argue that the South's culture has become virtually indistinguishable from that of the rest of the United States. Others argue that the South is so varied internally that it makes no sense to speak of it as a single entity. Some confused souls seem to accept both of these arguments, although it's not clear how Georgia and Kentucky can be greatly different from each other if they both look like Michigan.

Let's try to sort this mess out. Is there something we can call "Southern culture"? If so, how is it different these days, if at all, from that elsewhere? If there are differences, are they decreasing?

The question of whether there is a single, dominant, widely shared Southern culture has been on my mind of late, because I now find myself coeditor of a journal called *Southern Cultures* (note the plural). I preferred *Southern Culture*, but my colleagues in this enterprise fought for the plural with a dogmatic zeal worthy of the Council of Chalcedon. For them, it was plainly not just a harmless gesture to political correctness but somehow a statement of objective truth.

And of course it is true that there are many cultures in the South. For starters, there are striking geographic differences. When Chapel Hill's Howard Odum compiled his encyclopedic survey in 1938, he called it *Southern Regions of the United States* (again, note the plural), and distinguished even then between the Southeast and the Southwest.

And of course there are subregions within subregions. You can't understand the politics of any Southern state without a grasp of the differences between uplands and lowlands; mountains, piedmont, and coastal plain; sandhills, piney woods, and wiregrass. And each part of each state is a conglomeration of localities with more or less distinctive cultures, and economies, societies, and interests, too.

Dwelling on these distinctions may be a Southern trait, our notorious "sense of place," but it does keep cropping up. To take just one example, both John Hiatt's great song "Memphis in the Meantime" and Peter Taylor's lovely novel *Summons to Memphis* are basically about the difference between Nashville and Memphis. If we hear less than we used to about geographic variation it's not because there's less of it, but because the new multiculturalism concerns itself with more fashionable diversities—in particular, the Holy Trinity of race, class, and gender. But those, too, delineate different Souths. And it can't hurt to be reminded that although the South may have been a white man's country, the white man's story isn't the only one that has played itself out in our parts. But put all this together and you might wonder if there's any reason to talk about *the South* at all—and Jack Temple Kirby, in an article called "The South as a Pernicious Abstraction," once suggested that we stop.

Fortunately for Jack's career and mine that pernicious article was little noted nor long remembered, but it does represent the reductio ad absurdum of this line of thought. Absurd, because although there are many Souths, many cultures in *the* South, most of the many Souths do have something Southern about them, and for some purposes that is what's interesting. Some students of the South want to document its diversity, but others want to examine the effects of the regional context on one or another of the diverse populations in it. For example, to summarize the results of one old article of mine, Jews in the South can be viewed as either Southern Jews or Jewish Southerners. In a Southern context, they look culturally Jewish; in a Jewish context, they look culturally Southern. Take your pick.

Similarly, we need to recognize the growing Asian and Hispanic presence in our region, but studies have found that Vietnamese immigrants in North Carolina and Mexican Americans in Texas differ from their compatriots in California in stereotypically "Southern" ways. To make this observation is not to disregard or to disparage diversity. Quite the contrary, surely.

Even across the historic black-white divide, there has been an emerging, tentative recognition and exploration of the obvious fact that the two races have copied one another, shared with one another, stolen from one another, influenced one another to such an extent that we can speak in some respects of a biracial Southern culture. If you doubt this, see Jimmy Lewis Franklin's recent presidential address to the Southern Historical Association, "Black Southerners, Shared Experience, and Place"—or, for that matter, just about any Southern cookbook.

Those who've remarked on the Southernness of black folk include Albert Murray, Ralph Ellison, and Martin Luther King a generation ago; Andrew Young, Randall Kenan, Alex Haley, Margaret Walker, Charlayne Hunter-Gault, Eddie Harris, Eugene Rivers, Glenn Loury, Anthony Walton, and a score of others more recently—to mention only *black* folk who've spoken to this point.

I think W. J. Cash got it just about right fifty years ago, in *The Mind of the South*. "If it can be said there are many Souths," he wrote, "the fact remains that there is also one South." That there are many *kinds* of Southerners isn't the only truth about us. And, by the way, how is discussing the characteristics of Southerners different from discussing those of Italian Americans or Hispanics or Asians—or, for that matter, African Americans or workers or women— rather than the many different kinds of each?

How you look at any social category depends on your purpose. Some of us are lumpers, others are sorters. What Cash thought Southerners had in common was more relevant to his purposes than what divided them. Same for me, when I took Cash's observation as an epigraph for my book *One South*.

Cash also knew the argument that Southerners are not "really" different from other Americans. He acknowledged those folks—"usually journalists and professors," he said—who contended that the South is just "a figment of the imagination." But he refused to take them seriously, and maybe that's the right response. Certainly survey research suggests that most Americans other than journalists and professors believe that Southerners are a special kind of American, and in some important respects they are right about that. Southerners have been different from the run of the American mill in ways that observers from Jefferson and Tocqueville to C. Vann Woodward, V. S. Naipaul, and John Hope Franklin have identified.

Many of these folks have argued that the South is the least "American" part of America. John Crowe Ransom, for instance, in *I'll Take My Stand,* argued that the South was European in its disdain for the values of commerce and industry. In "The Irony of Southern History," C. Vann Woodward put a different spin on the same theme: the prosperity, success, and innocence of the *non-Southern* United States is (or was) what's unusual. Sheldon Hackney has even written of the South as a "counterculture." On the other hand, Howard Zinn, in his book *The Southern Mystique,* argued that the South is the *most* American part of America—and, writing from the political left in 1964, he didn't mean that as a compliment. Whatever the angle, though, the South has been used, again and again, to construct, in Woodward's phrase, an "American counterpoint."

Survey research can be used to measure some of these differences, and in many respects it *is* true what they say about Dixie. Southerners really do tend to be more religious, more conservative, more polite, more "touchy." They're more likely to hunt and fish, stop their cars for funerals, and eat black-eyed peas on New Year's Day. Whether these differences are big enough to signify is a judgment call, but the last time anyone looked (Norval Glenn, in the 1960s) he concluded that cultural differences between white Southerners and white non-Southerners were bigger than differences between blue-collar and white-collar workers, bigger than differences between the sexes or the generations, between high-school graduates and those who hadn't completed high school, or between urban and rural folk. Regional differences among white Americans were about the same size, on the average, as cultural differences between black and white Americans. To be sure, Glenn looked at a rather arbitrary set of cultural indicators, but his results do suggest that if *any* cultural differences in the United States are important, regional ones are.

One interesting stream of research looks at the South as the Protestant, Anglophone, northern tip of a pan-American plantation region; leave that aside, however, and most really significant studies of the South have given at least implicit attention to how it differs from the rest of the United States. There's a good reason for that. The South is a complex, modern society; setting out to study it differs only quantitatively from setting out to study the world. As David Potter observed some time ago, focusing on those differences provides, if nothing else, a principle of selection.

But just as an emphasis on the many Southern cultures ignores what they have in common as *Southern* cultures, emphasizing how Southerners and non-Southerners differ ignores what we have in common as Americans. Those who question the significance of regional differences in the United States do have a point: some countries much smaller than the United States show a regionalism even more vigorous, and an interesting question for research, or at least speculation, is why a continental nation like ours doesn't have even *more* differences, and larger ones. But my point is that sometimes it is useful to focus on differences, sometimes on similarities, and we need to keep in mind that there are plenty of both.

Another perennial question is this: Are the cultural differences between South and non-South going away? This question is often confounded with the question of the relative importance of continuity and change in Southern culture, but we have to untangle the two. Perhaps because I once wrote a book called *The Enduring South,* I usually find myself put in the continuitarian camp, especially by people who've heard of the book but haven't actually read it. At a symposium in Memphis some years back, I had the disconcerting experience of hearing myself congratulated by a sociologist from Mississippi State for having shown that nothing of importance has changed in the South, that the fundamental realities of racism and class hegemony are much the same as ever. When it came my turn to speak I couldn't resist observing that one thing at least has changed: you didn't used to run into Marxists from Mississippi State.

Ironically, one constant in Southern history has been the experience of change—never more rapid than in the past few decades, I started to say, but no doubt historians would remind me of the dynamism of the early nineteenth century, not to mention some rather abrupt changes in the 1860s. Anyway, economic, demographic, and political changes both produce and reflect cultural change. So of course there has been change in Southern culture, W. J. Cash and my Mississippi State friend to the contrary notwithstanding.

But to allow that Southern culture has changed, is changing, does not mean that it is disappearing as a variant on the American norm (whatever *that* might be). We can be sure that the culture of the twenty-first-century South will be different from that of the last century, just as the twentieth-century South differed from the nineteenth. Like other living organisms, cultures change as they age. But there is no reason to suppose that the change will produce a culture identical to that elsewhere in the United States.

One reason it will not is that the South is inhabited by people who identify with it, to the extent of calling themselves "Southerners," and they won't let it. Southerners sometimes do things in "Southern" ways because those things link them to their community and their heritage. In this, they are no different from the many other identity groups that make up our increasingly multicultural society.

That fact suggests that we might want to turn our attention from the specifics of cultural difference to the mechanisms that sustain group identity. In particular, we might want to look at the workings of what might be called the "Southern culture industry"—magazines, associations, journals, conferences, academic programs, and the like that nourish regional identity, whether by studying it explicitly or simply by assuming that it is somehow a fact of nature. When we go looking for such institutions, we see that whatever the current state of Southern culture may be, the *study* of it has never been in better shape. Maybe this is just a result of overproduction of PhDs in the humanities and social sciences. Or perhaps, as George Tindall once suggested, it's the cultural equivalent of having your life pass before you as you're drowning—drowning, in this case, in the American mainstream. But, for whatever reason, the

Southern culture industry is booming. Witness the publication you hold in your hands.

Let me close by giving my own answer to the question I started with. If I had to choose one state to represent the entire South, I would pick Tennessee, not just because I grew up there (although I did), but because it displays both the legacy and the inventiveness of Southern culture. Start with Bristol, in the eastern mountains, where Ralph Peer recorded Jimmie Rodgers and the Carter Family in 1927 and the Bristol Motor Speedway now hosts NASCAR's Sharpie® 500. Go west to Nashville, Athens to Atlanta's Rome, home of the Grand Ole Opry, the Vanderbilt Agrarian authors of *I'll Take My Stand*, and the Vatican of the Southern Baptist Convention (insofar as that fractious and decentralized body has one). Wind up in Memphis, a city of shrines: Beale Street, embalming Dixie's heritage of the blues; the National Civil Rights Museum in the Lorraine Motel; Mason Temple and the headquarters of the 6-million-member Church of God in Christ; and—one word—Graceland. Need I say more?

EVERYTHING THAT COULD
BE HAPPENING, IS

This was originally a paper presented to a 2004 symposium at the University of Mississippi on "The American South, Then and Now." I recycled it when Paul Greenberg of the Arkansas Democrat-Gazette *asked me to put together an orientation program for Yankee journalists visiting Little Rock in 2008 for a meeting of the National Conference of Editorial Writers.*

• • •

It may have escaped your notice, but lately we've seen the rise—more accurately, the announcement—of something called the "New Southern Studies," which promises, among other things, to attend to "the richness of the intersection, the overlap, the fortuitous simultaneity." (You can tell that professors of literature are involved.) As a longtime practitioner of Southern Studies Classic I have mixed feelings about this development. I feel about Old Southern Studies (*good* old Southern Studies, as I like to call 'em) sort of the way I feel about Old Glory, Old Yaller, and That Old-Time Religion. But there's no question that what we can call, for convenience, "the South" has changed in fundamental ways in the half century I've been talking about it and that many of the old questions about our region are pretty much played out.

Take the one about whether the South is disappearing. People have been asking some version of that question for as long as there's been a South to ask it about. What might be called the modern era, though, dates roughly from the publication in 1958 of a book by the late Harry Ashmore called *An Epitaph for Dixie.* In the decades since then right many of us have eaten pretty well by writing and talking about whether Southern culture is still distinctive. John Egerton and I got into the act in the early seventies, when he published *The Americanization of Dixie* and I published *The Enduring South* in the same year, and we must have debated that question a dozen times since then.

Yes, some of us have been beating this dead mule for a long time now. And the corpse has given us a surprisingly good ride. But maybe it's time to acknowledge that the beast is not just dead but decomposing, time to dig a great big hole and bury it. Because the truth is that we all realize—anyone who's thought about it for more than thirty seconds realizes—that you can't really talk about what's happening to Southern culture *in general.*

Southerners like to quote scripture. My text for today is Isaiah 22:5: "For it is a day of trouble, and of treading down, and of perplexity." For the student of Southern culture the emphasis is on perplexity, because, in one respect or another, everything that could be happening, *is* happening

The model of regional convergence that most people had in mind, whether with hopeful anticipation or sorrowful resignation, was one in which the South would, as the saying went, "rejoin the Union"—in other words, stop being the regional odd man out and begin to look American (that is, like New York or California). And, to be sure, some of the old Southern stigmata are disappearing. Incomes, occupations, literacy, urbanization, even the racial attitudes of white folks—in all of these respects the differences between Southerners and other Americans have decreased dramatically in the past half century, and are now so small, by historical standards, that they hardly matter at all.

In a few cases we've gone overboard. Some ancient regional differences have disappeared altogether, only to reemerge as differences in the opposite direction. We converged with the rest of the country and then kept on going, coming out the other side: from a higher birthrate to a lower one, for instance, and from net out-migration for blacks to net in-migration. Moreover, from time to time, we import things from abroad, from places like New England and Japan, make them our own, and almost forget where they came from. Think of kudzu, college football, and the Republican Party, just for starters.

But some ancient cultural differences are persisting. Attitudes toward the role of women, for instance, have been changing, but they have been changing everywhere, and the South remains relatively conservative on this score. Some regional differences are even getting larger: Southerners are more economically conservative than a generation ago—and more Baptist than a century ago. Believing in the devil and saying "fixing to" and "might could" are also more common in the South and more distinctively Southern than they used to be.

In other respects, however, regional differences are indeed getting smaller—but because the rest of the country is starting to look like the South. That's true for homicide rates, for tastes in music and sports, and for some aspects of diet. Young Americans outside the South are losing the distinction between "pin" and "pen" in speech, and are even starting to say "y'all." We've exported country music, NASCAR, and the Southern Baptist Convention so successfully that they may not be "Southern" institutions much longer. They may soon go the way of Coca-Cola, Walmart, and Holiday Inns, once-regional institutions that became symbols of *American* civilization, and are now teaching the world to sing, save, and slumber.

Finally, to complicate matters even further, new technology and new affluence mean that Southerners keep inventing new and unpredictable ways to be different. I mentioned country music and stock car racing: We need to remind ourselves that both of those were twentieth-century innovations, made possible by technologies that didn't exist before. So, for that matter, were key lime pie and ice tea, which required sweetened condensed milk and reliable supplies of ice, respectively.

Where is all this taking us? That's good question. We're not where we were, that's for sure. And we're not yet where we're going. But I don't know what that destination is. If I were any good at prophecy I'd be living off my investments somewhere, so I'll leave that sort of thing to Isaiah. But I would bet the farm, if I had a farm, on two propositions. One is that people will still be talking about the South a hundred years from now. And the other is that the South they'll be talking about will be a very different place, maybe as different from the South we're in right now as our South is from the South of a century ago.

One large and consequential difference is the astonishing growth of the South's Hispanic population. As a student of Southern culture and society, *Estoy estudiando español.*

Just one story, to close. My wife and I spoke recently at a dinner for the cook-off judges at Charlotte's annual "Blues, Brews, and Barbecue" festival. What could be more "Southern" than barbecue, right? But wait a minute: There were judges from Pennsylvania, Kansas, and Oregon—and a visiting

couple from Hertfordshire. As a Southerner, I'm delighted to see all this interest in a national dish of the South, but we need to watch out or it'll get away
from us. Already the barbecue competition rules are established by someone
in Kansas City. And there's more: These good folks were going to be eating
barbecue all the next day, so our hosts, the Levine Museum of the New South,
didn't want to feed them barbecue for supper, too. Instead, they got dishes
from four local restaurants: Cantonese char shu bao, Vietnamese báhn mì,
Salvadoran papusas con curtido, and tacos al pastor from the Mexican state
of Hidalgo—all barbecue-like treats now available every day in Charlotte.

There's been a lot of chatter in foodie circles about "New Southern Cuisine,"
but keep your eye on these developments. Fifty years from now, I wouldn't be
surprised to find Southern cookbooks treating cilantro as a traditional food-
stuff of the Old South.

PREACHING IT THE OTHER WAY

This address to a meeting of the North Carolina Press Association in 1998 starts by explaining why I'd been invited. The commencement speech it refers to was much the same as the "Last Lecture" beginning on page 264.

• • •

I was invited to talk to you today because of one line in an address I gave at the December 1997 commencement exercises of the University of North Carolina at Chapel Hill, an address that many of your papers were kind enough to report, and several even reprinted in part. I talked about Chapel Hill as a great *Southern* university, pointing out that studying the South is one thing—maybe *the* one thing—that we do better than anyone else in the world. (A commencement ceremony is no place for institutional modesty, after all.) After bragging on Carolina I went on to brag on the region that we serve, pointing out, with lots of examples, that the South seems to be taking the lead these days in America's political and economic life.

Now, *that's* the news. We haven't seen that for a long time. But I felt obliged to remind folks that we still have some old problems and that progress brings some new ones. I said I could have given that speech instead—that I could have preached it either way. A couple of days later my phone rang, and I was asked to speak to you all today. "Why don't you preach it the other way?" my caller said. "Oh, and by the way," he said, "be amusing."

Well, it's not easy to be amusing about things like malnutrition and illiteracy. (It can be done, but it's usually in poor taste.) It's also not easy to find anything new to say about the South's problems. They've been documented over and over again, and analyzed at tedious length. So what I'm going to do here is more in the way of reminding than informing. Let's start with that division between new problems and old ones.

The big Southern story of the past half century has been that economically and politically and demographically, in most respects we're looking more like the rest of the country all the time. This means that increasingly we have the same problems as the rest of the country: problems of an urban, industrial society—problems of crime, and urban decay, and congestion, and environmental degradation, not to mention more rarified problems like anomie, angst, and melancholy.

But what gets special reports written about the South are not these new problems, not problems we share with the rest of the developed world, but our old ones, problems that are and have been, in the American context, "Southern" problems. (Never mind that they're problems we've shared with most of the developing world.) Every six years since the mid-seventies a new Commission on the Future of the South has been convened by the Southern Growth Policies Board. Every six years the Commission has labored and brought forth a report. And every six years it has pointed to pretty much the same problems. That's because they're real problems, and they aren't going away. For the most part they stem from the South's legacy of rural poverty. They're pretty much the same problems that UNC sociologist Howard W. Odum wrote about in his book *Southern Regions of the United States,* published in 1936. Two years later, Franklin Roosevelt called the South "the nation's number-one economic problem"—and he drew on the research of Odum and his colleagues for that conclusion.

Thank God, those problems aren't what they were in the 1930s. The hard work, and entrepreneurial efforts, and political skills of a couple of generations of Southerners have borne abundant fruit. That's what I was talking about at that commencement. But the benefits of economic development haven't been spread around universally, or even indiscriminately. As Charles Evers put it a few years ago, there's still a lot of shade in the Sunbelt, so much so that one of those Commission reports spoke of the emergence of "Two Souths," a booming metropolitan economy in a region of small towns and rural areas very largely bypassed by the boom.

Incidentally, I said it's hard to be funny about these things, but my friend

Doug Marlette, the Pulitzer Prize–winning cartoonist, has done it. A musical comedy based on his comic strip *Kudzu* is set in the little town of Bypass, North Carolina, and concerns, among other things, the town's efforts to attract Japanese investors. There's a wonderful opening number called "Why Pass Bypass By?"

Anyway, we can locate these continuing problems pretty precisely *within* the South. Look at the maps in *The State of the South*, a report issued in 1996 by MDC, a North Carolina think-tank, written by Ferrell Guillory of the UNC journalism school. Or look at the maps in a report called *The Southern Black Belt*, prepared for the TVA by Ron Wimberley at North Carolina State University. The same pattern appears over and over again. Someone described the economic South a few years ago as something like "patches of green in a vast brown swamp." These days it would probably be more accurate to say that there are patches of brown in a flourishing green forest. But whatever indicator of deficiency and pathology you're looking at—poverty, or ill-health, or unemployment, or the lack of education—you see four major patches of it in the United States, and three of them are in the South, if you count Texas as part of the South.

The non-Southern one is less a patch than a sort of archipelago of western counties that turn out, on closer examination, to be mostly Indian reservations. Another concentration of poor rural folk appears in south Texas, along the Mexican border, in a string of counties with Mexican American majorities. A third brown patch can found in the Southern Appalachians, principally in the coalfields of the Cumberlands, in Kentucky and West Virginia, where the poor are almost entirely native white people. Finally, the fourth, and the largest in both population and territory, is a band of counties reaching from Southside Virginia down through eastern North Carolina and most of South Carolina, across the Deep South into east Texas, with extensions north and south in the bottomlands of the Mississippi River. This is pretty much the old Cotton Kingdom. It's Dixie—"the land of cotton," remember?—and most of the poor folk here are black. What the distinguished black sociologist Charles S. Johnson sixty years ago called "the shadow of the plantation" still falls on Dixie.

Four concentrations of rural poverty, ethnically distinct—one white, one black, one Mexican American, and one Indian—and, as I said, three of the four are in the South. Most Southerners aren't poor or rural anymore, but if you're looking for poor, rural Americans, the South is still a good place to start. Else-where in America poverty is largely a phenomenon of the inner city, of large metropolitan areas. In the South, our poorest citizens are likely to be rural. And this isn't likely to change any time soon. It's true that the South, with something less than a third of the nation's population, has been generating about half of the nation's new jobs lately. But nine out of ten of those new jobs have been in metropolitan areas. From the Research Triangle, or Charlotte, or Atlanta, or Nashville—from places where most visitors to the South hang out and most native analysts of the region are likely to live—it's easy to forget that many of the South's people and most of its acreage haven't seen much in the way of economic development.

North Carolina is a relatively prosperous Southern state. The piedmont region is witnessing explosive economic growth and population increase. In our mountains and in some coastal counties, there's been an influx of rel-atively well-off retirees who have certainly raised *average* incomes, thus at least masking persisting rural poverty. But Ron Wimberley shows that sixteen counties in eastern North Carolina are among the poorest quarter of counties in America—as it happens, almost exactly the same sixteen counties that have populations more than 40 percent black. Some of these counties and their neighbors have been losing population for decades, and most aren't seeing many new jobs. They're struggling to hang onto the ones they've got. And what's true of a few of our counties is true for a great many more in Louisiana and Alabama and Kentucky, not to mention Mississippi and West Virginia.

When it comes to dealing with social and economic problems, we in the university have done a pretty good job of documenting their nature and extent. The UNC Press and our University Library and the Institute for Research in Social Science have been in that business since the days of Howard Odum and Frank Porter Graham. Our new Center for the Study of the American South simply recognizes the research and scholarship of literally hundreds of faculty members and graduate students over the years—scores of them right now. Thanks to that work and that of our colleagues at other institutions, anyone who's seriously interested either already knows or can easily find out what the South's problems are. What's more, sometimes we academics can give some research-based guidance about which proposed solutions won't work, which might, and at what cost. And we have the skills to do more of that sort of program evaluation if we were asked to do it.

But what's really lacking is not this sort of *information*. What's really lacking is the collective will to do something about these problems. And it's not the job of those of us in the university to provide that. All that we academics can do *as such* (leave aside our role as citizens), all that we *should* do as academics, is to keep reminding people that the problems are still there, and to provide the data for informed advocacy, and informed decisions. Whether to do something and who is to do it are inherently political decisions, not academic ones. Mobilizing public opinion—building a consensus about who is to act, who is to benefit, who is to pay—that's the business of our politicians, and of people like yourselves.

WRITING ABOUT THE SOUTH

When I got tired of writing about the South I could usually arrange to write about people who were writing about it. In the nature of things, a good many of them were my friends, but it's only hard to review books by friends when they're bad books. Fortunately none of these were.

THE SOUTH THE PLANTATION MADE

Published in the American Journal of Sociology *in 1976 and slightly revised here to bring it up to date, this is an appreciation of the work of Edgar Thompson (1900– 1989), an old-fashioned Southern gentleman with surprisingly radical ideas about how the South should be studied.*

• • •

The most common approach to the study of the American South has seen it as an aberrant corner of the United States, compared it with the rest of the nation, and addressed its peculiarities. Edgar Thompson's approach was different: he viewed the South as "the northern part of the Gulf Caribbean region," sharing with the rest of that region and with other large-unit, cash-crop agricultural systems certain characteristics not evident elsewhere. You don't have to believe with Thompson that "whatever is 'different,' whatever is special about the South appears to go back to the plantation" to recognize that the region was shaped early and lastingly by that institution and that the momentous results can be illuminated by studying the South in the context of similar societies elsewhere. And no one has ever been better qualified to conduct that study than someone who combined wide-ranging erudition with a plantation upbringing and firsthand experience in Hawaii, South Africa, East Germany, and beyond—a combination almost unique, I would imagine, to Thompson.

Unfortunately, Thompson never wrote the big book that he could have written, but in 1975 his essays were collected in *Plantation Societies, Race*

Relations, and the South: The Regimentation of Populations. The book opens with an introduction that defines the plantation by distinguishing it from other agricultural establishments like the family farm, the hacienda, the manor, and the "military agriculture" that produced opium in pre-Communist Manchuria. Two chapters then compare the plantation to the mine and to the mission school—both instructively similar to it and instructively different; a third treats the climatic theory of the plantation; and a fourth examines the institution as a setting for the emergence of the South's traditional system of race relations. Six papers follow that deal with various aspects of race relations, starting with Thompson's once (deservedly) well-known "The Plantation as a Race-Making Situation" and including excellent discussions of the connection between linguistic patterns and race relations, of school desegregation (viewed comparatively), and of the problems and the potential for social theory of the small mixed-blood groups found in most multiracial societies. The book concludes with seven papers all having something to do with the South but otherwise disparate; they include one on the planter as a social type, one on religion in the old and the new South, and a first-rate treatment of the relation of sociology to regional studies, which could clarify many similar discussions of black studies, women's studies, or almost any interdisciplinary enterprise.

Thompson treats the plantation under four aspects: (1) "as a way of settling and concentrating a population of mixed origins on a frontier," (2) "as a way of producing an agricultural staple for a metropolitan market," (3) "as a way of disciplining a population for labor under the authority of a planter," and (4) "as an institution which develops in time through collective activity a distinctive style of life or culture." The last emphasis is the strongest and, to my mind, the most interesting.

In 1934 (about the time the first of these papers appeared), Carl Carmer wrote in *Stars Fell on Alabama* that "the Congo is not more different from Massachusetts or Kansas." One of Thompson's successes is to show the fundamental sense in which Carmer's observation is not fatuous—not in emphasizing how peculiar Alabama was under the plantation regime, but precisely in showing that neither it nor the Congo is at all peculiar, that certain consequences follow from trying to realize certain goals in particular settings. Thompson also helps readers to understand the institution not just intellectually, as an inevitable development from a set of givens, but, so to speak, from inside. He uses documents adeptly to convey a sense of the sheer ordinariness of everyday plantation life for its participants (surely the first requirement of a going social system), quite a feat at a time when many aspects of that life look bizarre, not only to Carmer's readers but even to many who live on or near what may still be called plantations. These essays are not only contributions to sociology and history; many are literary achievements.

While emphasizing regional differences within the United States may too often stress the merely odd, Thompson's approach has its own drawbacks. Taken as a whole, these papers seem to me to underemphasize the fact that the South has been bound, inextricably after 1865, to the rest of the United States, which looks not at all like the Congo, and consequently to treat the South without much attention to the terms of its trade with the national market or to the reaction of the rest of the country to its emergent culture and institutions. But the South has had not just an economy and a resulting culture but, rather, a *colonial* economy and a *minority* culture, fateful qualifications.

Nevertheless, four decades after its publication, twice as long since the earliest paper was written, and a quarter century after Thompson's death in 1989, this book is as timely as ever. The Southern plantation may be gone with the wind, but its legacy is still with us, now transplanted in part to our cities, and similar agricultural systems in many parts of the world can be studied profitably in the light of the Southern example. Moreover, the kind of comparative institutional analysis Thompson did so well (if not the clear and vigorous prose in which he did it) has lately experienced a rebirth in the guise of "New Southern Studies," and his work is finding a larger and more appreciative professional audience now than it did when this book was published. Witness the fact that his 1932 doctoral dissertation was published in 2010 by the University of South Carolina Press; titled simply *The Plantation*, it is introduced by anthropologists Sidney Mintz and George Baca as "a pioneering approach to the study of early capitalistic experiments in overseas export-oriented tropical agriculture that used forced labor on land taken from native peoples, with capital, plants, and technology coming from Europe and Asia."

THE USES OF SOUTHERN HISTORY

This review, written in 1999 for the Oxford American, *examined a book by Jim Cobb, of the University of Georgia. A few years later Jim won the Fellowship of Southern Writers' Woodward-Franklin Award for the Writing of Southern History.*

• • •

I don't know why historians these days don't seem to be as far gone in theory, jargon, and disciplinary solipsism as their literary and social-scientific colleagues, but it seems to me that most aren't ashamed to produce books and articles that might engage their faculty colleagues in the next building. Even bad historical writing is usually just trivial or tendentious, not unintelligible or nonsensical, and some of it might even interest the average college graduate. Indeed, many of the very best historians have gone out of their way to write popular surveys, essays, and reviews in the highbrow press, and op-ed pieces for newspapers.

James C. Cobb is a historian's historian, a scholar who has written prize-winning books on Southern industrial development and on the Mississippi Delta (*The Selling of the South* and *The Most Southern Place on Earth*, respectively) and has served as president of the Southern Historical Association. But, like some other past presidents of that organization—notably C. Vann Woodward and George B. Tindall—over the years Cobb has leavened his monographs with lively, learned, and witty essays, many of them collected in *Redefining Southern Culture: Mind and Identity in the Modern South.*

Some of the opening essays in that volume just summarize and evaluate what historians who study the late nineteenth- and early twentieth-century South have been up to. "Beyond Planters and Industrialists," for instance, examines the long-standing argument about who ran the first, postbellum "New South": the Old South's planter class returned or a "new class" of bourgeois entrepreneurs—or old planters who thought like bourgeois entrepreneurs, or bourgeois entrepreneurs who thought like old planters, whatever. Many have thought that the answer to this question could explain some important differences between the South's industrialization and that of the Northeast and Midwest. After ably summarizing the controversy, however, Cobb executes a neat finesse, suggesting that it probably made little difference who was in charge, given the constraints placed on them by national—indeed, global—forces beyond their control.

This sort of précis is a painless way for interested amateurs to get up to speed with historical thinking, but even more rewarding, to my mind, are Cobb's wry, historically informed observations of the contemporary South and his speculation about where it's headed. Anyone interested in how the South's past is being deployed to shape its future will find much to think about in several free-wheeling essays that discuss everything from the changing politics of country music to the implications of the restaurants to be found near Cobb's Georgia hometown, from the meaning of the meaninglessness of the Atlanta Olympics' sorry mascot to the popularity of Southern "smart-ass groups" like the Austin Lounge Lizards, who sing "Jesus Loves Me (But He Can't Stand You)."

As the book's subtitle suggests, many of these essays circle back to the question of identity, of what it means to be "Southern" these days. For white Southerners, at least, regional identity was long a matter of contrast—to be a Southerner was to be *not* a Yankee—and of grievance (at Northern condescension, if nothing else). Yet, as Cobb observes, "white southerners were witness within hardly more than a decade (late 1960s–early 1980s) to the decline, disintegration, and virtual disappearance of their figurative regional nemesis, the old morally and economically superior North." So what does it mean to be defined no longer by what one *isn't* but by what one *is*? And what might that be? One reason so many white Southerners have been attached to the Confederate battle flag as a symbol of unity and pride, Cobb suggests, is because they feel there's so little else left to work with. (And, I would add, the flag does tend to bring out that old, reassuringly familiar Yankee annoyance with us.)

Meanwhile, just as regional identity in some white circles is becoming more uncertain, ambivalent, or ironic, Cobb observes in an essay entitled "Searching for Southernness" that there seems to be a growing tendency among black Southerners to claim that identity. As the label "bama" undergoes a revaluation similar to what happened to "redneck" a decade ago, will the black and white versions of Southern identity remain separate, albeit increasingly equal? That will depend, Cobb suggests, less on blacks' and whites' "ability to agree than on their willingness to tolerate disagreement about an identity that, to preserve, they must first learn to share."

THROUGH THE SOUTHERN LOOKING-GLASS

The English do like to hear about the American South—a fact that I've parlayed into several delightful visits to their country. This review was commissioned by the (London) Times Literary Supplement.

• • •

A *New Yorker* cartoon matron probably spoke for many readers when she declared, standing in a bookstore, "I'm sorry for Mississippi, but I just don't like to read about it." We Southerners can't expect others to share our apparently endless fascination with ourselves, so any new compilation of literature from or about the South must somehow distinguish itself from its many predecessors to deserve attention. Fortunately, *The Oxford Book of the American South* does.

The editors, Edward L. Ayers and Bradley Mittendorf, have organized it chronologically (nothing novel about that) with sections devoted to the antebellum South, the Civil War and its aftermath, the hard times that persisted until quite recently, and the present era, which has been one of economic boom and civil-rights revolution. Within each period, however, we hear first from witnesses or participants writing at the time; then from others, looking back; finally, from present-day writers who have treated the period in literature. This often allows for an interesting sort of triangulation, as we see how events and situations looked at first hand, then how they look when filtered through a modern sensibility.

The editors serve up a rich gumbo of letters, diaries, memoirs, and fiction, producing a pleasantly literary volume worthy of a region that boasts such writers as William Faulkner, Eudora Welty, Thomas Wolfe, Zora Neale Hurston, Flannery O'Connor, Ralph Ellison, Erskine Caldwell, and Walker Percy—to mention just a few of the best-known of the fifty-eight represented here. Only a couple of the selections are shopworn, and there are some delightful surprises (my favorite is "Why I Like Country Music," by James Alan McPherson, a black writer from Savannah).

But the greatest surprise of this book lies in what has been omitted. The phrase "The Silent South" used to refer to marginalized groups like Southern blacks and white liberals; here, in a curious inversion, those silent are the conservative white men who pretty much ran the place for its first three and a half centuries. The section on "The Old South," for example, gives us the voices of black abolitionist Frederick Douglass, fugitive slave-girl Harriet Jacobs, insurrectionist Nat Turner (his own confession and William Styron's imaginative rendition), and twentieth-century white liberals W. J. Cash and Katherine Du Pre Lumpkin (looking back). In defense of slavery we hear only from Daniel Hundley, an Alabama-born lawyer, who observed simply that the South's peculiar institution seemed to be part of the divine plan, not from far more powerful pro-slavery theorists like John C. Calhoun and the largely forgotten likes of George Fitzhugh, James Henley Thornwell, and Louisa S. McCord.

One can imagine another book that is almost a mirror image of this one: not Alice Walker but the moonlight-and-magnolias plantation novelist Thomas Nelson Page; not W. E. B. Du Bois but Thomas Dixon, the racist author whose novel *The Clansman* was turned into the movie *Birth of a Nation*; not Maya Angelou but the Southern Agrarian poet Donald Davidson; not the fierce critic of segregation Lillian Smith but someone like Henry Grady, the Atlanta newspaperman and tireless booster who popularized the phrase "the New South"; not Martin Luther King but James Jackson Kilpatrick, author of *The Southern Case for School Segregation*. That would be a valuable book, too.

It's not that these views "deserve a hearing"; it is rather that the dominant voices of the South, not the dissenting ones, are now the most alien, the hardest for most modern readers to understand, and thus, in some ways, the most challenging. Still, if this book offers a sort of alternative-universe South, one in which the defenders and beneficiaries of slavery and segregation are seen largely through the eyes of the victims and opponents of those Southern institutions, that's not only fair enough (for a long time it was the other way around), it also makes for a useful corrective. This may not be the only book or even the first book to read about the South, but it should appeal to anyone willing to read about it at all.

PLUS ÇA CHANGE, Y'ALL

This is an expanded and updated version of a review of a book about the South's changing political landscape, originally published in the Weekly Standard *in 2005.*

• • •

A while back my wife and I were eating lunch in a greasy spoon in a small South Carolina county seat. A black guy in work clothes (name embroidered over his shirt pocket) came in to pick up a takeout order. He was chatting up the white waitress (tattoos, short cropped hair) and when he asked her for a date I started eavesdropping more intently. She said no, but he persisted. She said no again, and he asked why not. I braced myself for her reply. I know it's a New South, but this town seemed to me the sort of place where maybe they hadn't got the memo. She said, "I don't date *men.*"

My, my. As Big Jim Folsom said when the fighter plane crashed, kiss my ass if *that* ain't a show.

The times they are a-changin' in Dixie. Certainly when it comes to politics they are. But change doesn't always mean convergence. The South used to be the most Democratic region of the country, but after the Republican breakthrough in the 1994 off-elections, it became the most Republican part (except for some of the mountain West—but nobody lives there, so who cares?). What's more, change doesn't mean loss of continuity. In *The Hand of the Past in Contemporary Southern Politics*, James Glaser argues that the dramatically changed surface of Southern politics conceals, even reflects, some enduring themes. His point is not just that conservative white folks still usually call the shots (although that, too); he also examines the persistence of time-honored traditions like populist rhetoric and appeals to localism, as well as the continuing effects of run-off primary systems adopted in the days of the one-party Democratic South. (All but two of the thirteen Southern states oblige the top two vote-getters in a primary election to run in a second primary if no one gets a majority in the first; no non-Southern state does this.)

Glaser's examination reveals other continuities that he points out less explicitly. The dominant party in the South is still doing its best to redistrict the minority into near-oblivion, for instance, although that dominant party is now Republican. (Republicans learned how to play hardball well from all those years of seemingly hopeless opposition.) Similarly, the "majority-minority" congressional districts imposed on the South by the Justice Department have precedents that go back to the days of white supremacy: then, as now, concentrating black voters in a few districts strengthened the hands of conservative white candidates in other districts and gave them little political reason even to notice the interests of black voters.

Glaser summarizes the major arguments of the three heavyweight books that should be read by anyone seriously interested in understanding Southern politics, V. O. Key's classic *Southern Politics in State and Nation* (1949) and two by the brothers Earl and Merle Black, *Politics and Society in the South* (1987) and *The Rise of Southern Republicans* (2002), but his own aims are modest and so was his "methodology" (to use ironic quotation marks of the sort that, by the way, he is a bit too fond of for my taste). He picked five races for open congressional seats in 1996 and 1998, hung out with the candidates and their entourages, spoke with voters and local journalists, read up on the histories of the districts, and reports what he observed and what he takes it to mean. When he does venture briefly and somewhat incongruously into logistic regression and related arcana he actually comes back with a couple of interesting findings about run-off primaries. It appears that they attract more candidates—possibly a good thing—and apparently "come-from-behind" candidates who win run-offs after finishing second in the first primary tend to fare better in general elections than those who win first primaries outright or, especially, those who win run-offs after leading in first primaries.

Glaser's campaign narratives are scrupulously evenhanded and dispassionate, even when candidates engaged in repellent negative campaigning (as some of these did), but an unspoken subtext of his book is the question of whether Democrats can still win congressional races in majority-white Southern districts. He shows that they can, but the circumstances must be very special, and even when they do win they need to watch their backs.

In 1996 Democrat Max Sandlin won, for example. It helped that his east Texas district had a long history of populism, to which Sandlin appealed (his argument that government should be kept out of decisions on abortion sounded less pro-choice than antigovernment), but a personal fortune that allowed him to outspend his opponent by better than three to one also helped, as did the fact that his opponent bore an unfortunate physical resemblance to Groucho Marx. Glaser's narrative ends with Sandlin still in Congress, but in 2004 the Republican state legislature redistricted him into a race against a Republican incumbent from a neighboring district, and he got only an embarrassing 38 percent of the vote.

Just so, in Mississippi's Fourth District in 1998, Democrat Ronnie Snows began with a demographic head start: The vast majority of the district's black population would vote Democratic if they voted at all, and since the district was 41 percent black, Snows needed only to turn out these voters and pick up a fifth or so of the white vote. Glaser shows how Snows used black churches and radio stations to deliver subtly different messages to black and white audiences. He also played the homeboy card against the Republican nominee, a wealthy Catholic tax lawyer, and he won in 1998. Four years later, though, when redistricting changed the composition of *his* district and put him in a race against a Republican incumbent, he lost. (This despite an American Conservative Union rating of 65.)

Southside Virginia in 1996 presented a story with a somewhat different outcome, though no more encouraging for Democrats. Democrat Virgil Goode, a man as down-home as they come, faced a Republican opponent who had moved from California not long before. Goode made the most of that, and campaigned vigorously and personally in the best Strom Thurmond tradition. Observers complained that it was hard to tell where he stood on the issues, but when it was clear, he was so clearly conservative that Republican efforts to link him to Bill Clinton were unavailing. He won handily, but after that he became Congress's most conservative Democrat, less aligned with Clinton than four of Virginia's five Republicans (and tied with the fifth). After voting to impeach the president in 1998 he became an independent. In 2002 he ran and won as a Republican, and even as a Republican he anchored the right wing of his party.

The other two districts Glaser examined were even more comfortably Republican. In 1998, in the North Carolina district that includes Charlotte, it was Republican Robin Hayes who had the common touch, despite being an heir to the Cannon Mills fortune. His opponent made it easy for him. ("Why does he tell people he went to school at Harvard?" one of his aides complained.) Hayes's folksy appeal to the district's small-town and rural voters and the fact that Charlotte's suburban growth was filling the district with new country-club Republicans made a GOP victory appear to be such a foregone conclusion that the hapless Democrat had trouble raising money. Glaser thinks he might have run a much stronger race if he'd had the resources, but we'll never know. Hayes's district was redistricted to his disadvantage by North Carolina's legislature (still Democratic), but he survived in 2002, 2004, and 2006, largely thanks to his mastery of the classic conservative Democratic formula of conservative social policies and liberal pork-barrel spending.

Finally, the 1998 contest in the Greenville-Spartanburg area of South Carolina shows how things work in a district where the only elites with Democratic leanings are union leaders and trial lawyers, and the real contest, if there is one, is between conservative Republicans backed by the Christian Right and conservative Republicans backed by the Chamber of Commerce. After a tough fight in the Republican primary against a retired NFL quarterback advised by Ralph Reed, formerly of the Christian Coalition, Jim DeMint coasted to victory in the general election, holding his Democratic opponent, a Krispy Kreme doughnut franchisee, to 40 percent of the vote (which was better than expected). DeMint kept his promise to serve only three terms in the House of Representatives. In 2004 he won Fritz Hollings's old seat to become South Carolina's junior senator.

In short, Republicans now have the upper hand in most of the region. Democrats who get lucky with their district's racial composition, personal wealth, or weak opponents can sometimes give them a good race, especially when the top of the ticket is strong. Goode and Hayes both lost to Democrats in 2008. The new Solid South isn't as solid as the one V. O. Key described in his classic account, where (a few mountain areas aside) whites didn't vote Republican and blacks were rarely allowed to vote at all. But even Democrats who win can seldom relax and enjoy their incumbency. For the foreseeable future, the South is the Republicans' to lose.

Glaser doesn't put it this way, and might not, but I will: That's because the parties have changed even more than the South has.

MY PEOPLE, MY PEOPLE!

In 2005 I reviewed a book about Alabama history by Alabamian Wayne Flynt (see "A Good Thing from Auburn," on page 97) for the Gulf South Historical Review. *My title came, as I explain, from his fellow Alabamian Zora Neale Hurston. Wayne is another winner of the Fellowship of Southern Writers' Woodward-Franklin Award.*

. . .

Like the state it portrays, Wayne Flynt's *Alabama in the Twentieth Century* is teeming with oversized personalities. The obvious public figures are here, of course: governors like "Kissing Jim" Folsom and the less lovable George Wallace, black leaders in the struggle for equal rights (Booker T. Washington, Rosa Parks, and Martin Luther King, just for starters), their white allies like Judge Frank Johnson and Justice Hugo Black, and their formidable adversaries like Eugene "Bull" Connor. But less predictable characters also make appearances: Hank Williams, Helen Keller, Bear Bryant, Ralph Ellison, Bobby Allison, Werner von Braun, Tallulah Bankhead, Hank Aaron, W. C. Handy, Harper Lee, architect Samuel Mockbee, photographer William Christenberry, entomologist E. O. Wilson. . . . This baker's dozen of the nationally recognized, chosen almost at random, indicates how widely Flynt has cast his net in this masterful overview of his native state. He also introduces us to a great many less well known Alabamians who deserve wider recognition, or notoriety. Indeed, it looks to me as if the only eminent, infamous, or accomplished twentieth-century Alabamian who doesn't appear in this six-hundred-page book is Ray Wilson Scott, the Godfather of competitive bass fishing. (Gotcha.)

But this isn't just an Alabama *Who's Who*. Flynt is an award-winning historian who has spent much of his career studying the South's poor whites, and he puts to good use the letters and diaries of common folk who would otherwise be all but "perished, as if they had never been" (to borrow from the scriptural epigraph to *Let Us Now Praise Famous Men*—a book Flynt discusses at some length). Nor is *Alabama in the Twentieth Century* merely a collection of colorful anecdotes. Flynt is a great Southern storyteller, and Alabama gives him a wealth of great stories to tell, but threaded painlessly throughout the stories of remarkable individuals are telling statistics and sound generalizations about economic, demographic, and cultural trends.

The book begins with a chapter on Alabama's constitution, "the oldest, longest, and one of the most complex in the nation," adopted in 1901 and still in effect, albeit with more than seven hundred amendments that make it now forty times longer than the U.S. Constitution. On his first page Flynt claims that "most if not all the state's formidable problems had their origins in [this] document," a bold assertion that he goes on amply to support. Chapters on Alabama's politics and the state's economy are next, followed by chapters on social class, education, Alabama women, African Americans, twentieth-century wars, sports, religion, and culture both high and low. Within each chapter, the narrative is basically chronological, a structure that lets chapters be read as stand-alone essays, read in just about any order, or skipped altogether (although that would be a mistake). It does make some repetition inevitable, although it is not obtrusive and can even be informative. That race, religion, and football keep cropping up in chapters other than their own tells you something about the importance of these topics for understanding Alabama.

In *Dust Tracks on a Road* Zora Neale Hurston (born, Flynt observes, in Notasulga, Alabama) wrote a chapter with the exasperated title "My people, my people!" Flynt often seems to feel the same way about his people. As an active and conspicuous advocate of constitutional and tax reform, sometimes he can barely conceal his scorn for the politicians and power brokers who have, time after time, failed to rise to the occasion. Indeed, reading his book, one is struck that a people so passionate about politics should have a government so useless. Alabamians, it seems, love politics, hate government, but get a lot

of it—often of the wrong kind. I cannot resist quoting at length his summary
of the achievements of one recent governor:

> Fob James, while regularly denying that the state had an image problem,
> did more than any governor after George Wallace to create one. James re-
> instituted chain gangs in state prisons, imitated a monkey at a State Board
> of Education meeting to demonstrate his opposition to textbook treatment
> of evolution, declared that the Bill of Rights did not apply to Alabama,
> sought to eliminate judicial review of legislative acts, purchased 900 copies
> of *Darwin on Trial* for state science teachers, threatened to use National
> Guard troops to prevent removal of a courtroom plaque containing the Ten
> Commandments, removed what he claimed were demonic portraits from
> the governor's mansion, and endorsed messianic prophecies of apocalypse
> beginning in Israel.

It goes without saying that *Alabama in the Twentieth Century* will be of
particular interest to Alabamians who want to know more about their state,
and I guarantee that they will know more when they've read it. Outsiders like
me will learn even more, of course, and learning has never been more plea-
surable. Flynt has a keen eye for irony and absurdity, and he finds plenty of
both, whether it's the Greater Birmingham Convention and Visitors Bureau's
slogan "Birmingham: It's better than you think" or a Mountain Brook Pente-
costal megachurch based on "the new Christian revelation that the task of the
church was to serve members, not the other way around." My favorite one-
liner is occasioned by the fact that the presidents of Auburn and the University
of Alabama, threatened with budget cuts, brought their football coaches to a
press conference, the implication being "that in order to have college football
it was necessary to have colleges."

SURVEYOR OF THE BOZART

Hal Crowther is another friend whose book I reviewed, in the journal Southern Cultures. *It was a good one, so I didn't have to wound a friend, or lie. Hal wasn't so lucky, as you'll see. I called my review, and him, "Surveyor of the Bozart." Some readers will catch the reference; others can do some research, or ignore it.*

• • •

Hal Crowther is an award-winning North Carolina journalist whose column in the (Raleigh) *Spectator* used to evoke angry letters from that weekly's conservative readers. When he moved across the Triangle to Durham's *Independent* his column evoked angry letters from the left-leaning readers of that publication. He might be described as politically liberal and culturally conservative, but there are a great many exceptions to each of those generalizations. He is, in other words, a man who toes nobody's party line, thinks for himself, and makes his readers think, too, if they're capable of thought in the first place. A collection of his Southern-themed essays, *Cathedrals of Kudzu*, won some of those awards, and I looked forward eagerly to more of the same in *Gather at the River: Notes from the Post-Millennial South.*

When reviewing a book, I make a point of not reading the front matter until the end, so I can form my own impressions before being told what to think. Imagine my dismay when I discovered that the foreword to this volume, by the great scholar of Southern literature Louis Rubin, not only used the same quotations I had flagged but said everything I had intended to say in my review, only better. If this were the review I had mentally outlined people would think I cribbed it, which would be wrong, this time. Tell you what: Buy the book (trust me on this) and read what Rubin has to say. He's right. As for me, I'll just summarize what these essays are about.

The first, "The Tao of Dixie," examines the persistence of Southern self-consciousness and distinctiveness, and links it to the sort of casual slander of the South that permeates American intellectual discourse. Crowther describes himself elsewhere in this volume as "a middle-class hillbilly raised by Unitarians" (born, incidentally, in Canada, to a military family), but he illustrates the truth of Sheldon Hackney's observation that there is a "sense of grievance at the heart of Southern identity" when he remarks that someone's equating the Confederate battle flag with the swastika "brings out the Rebel even in mild mongrel Southerners like me." No wonder that "among blooded, old-growth Confederates, it brings out the emotional equivalent of Pickett's Charge." (By the way, when he writes of the new "vital, urban South, where unemployment is low and ringworm unheard-of," I'm sure he means hookworm. That he could write it that way, and that his editors at LSU Press could let it pass, suggests just how much things have changed since the days when that parasite ranked with pellagra as a public health problem and an element in the stereotype of Southerners.)

Most of the essays that follow examine and celebrate various of Crowther's enthusiasms, among them Key West and miscegenation. Many are appreciations of appreciable Southern writers, including Thomas Wolfe, Elizabeth Spencer, Marshall Frady, James Still, Wendell Berry, Denise Giardina, and Larry Brown. The volume's very last essay treats that scourge of the Southland, H. L. Mencken, whom Crowther acknowledges as a master and, in some respects, a model. Crowther is not generally given to understatement, but his observation that Mencken was "somewhat deficient in empathy" is a beaut.

Crowther also appreciates some Southern musicians, notably Dolly Parton, Tommy Thompson of the Red Clay Ramblers, and all the contributors to the sound track of *O Brother, Where Art Thou?*, which provoked his "first rush, in a long, logic-hobbled life, of something that felt like chauvinism." He's more ambivalent about the Coen brothers' movie, but one film he likes very much is King Vidor's first talkie, *Hallelujah*, which is, to say the least, unfashionable these days. He also has good words for baseball player Shoeless Joe Jackson, the slightly unhinged folk artist Reverend McKendree Long, and Marine Lance Corporal Brian Anderson of Chapel Hill, who died in a war that Crowther detested. One of the best of his essays here is a eulogy of his college friend Kirk Varnedoe, a curator and art historian who championed Southern artists Jasper Johns, Cy Twombley, and Robert Rauschenberg, and was himself "the closest thing to a rock star that art history has ever produced."

He is less enthusiastic about postmodern literary criticism, although in "Faulkner and the Mosquitoes" he provides a remarkably balanced and restrained critique of what our nation's English departments are up to. He also has serious reservations about the recent efflorescence of memoir, expressed in a review of his friend Lewis Nordan's *Boy with Loaded Gun*. It's hard to be honest when you don't like a friend's book, but Crowther tells us the truth: He thinks the book wouldn't have been redeemed even by Nordan's original title, *Don't Cry for Me, Itta Bena*. He also didn't like a couple of other books that sound as if they really deserve the wry put-downs he delivers: Pamela Petro's *Sitting Up with the Dead: A Storied Journey through the American South* and Suzi Parker's *Sex in the South: Unbuckling the Bible Belt*. Of the first he observes: "We are no Samoans; she's no Margaret Mead. She is, arguably, the most clueless Outlander to write about the South since V. S. Naipaul's *A Turn in the South*. But she's no V. S. Naipaul either." Of the second—well, read him.

It's politicians, though, who really get him wound up. Some of his targets are predictable (Trent Lott, Jesse Helms), but others are less so. For example, a visit to the ruins of the Koreshan compound outside Waco prompts him to observe that "Janet Reno may not be Satan's mistress, but she was ever a gutless and feckless public servant, and the teddy-bear cemetery at Mount Carmel is a ghastly memorial she could have avoided." If you agree with Crowther you'll really enjoy it when he gets a good rant going. If you don't agree with him you won't enjoy it at all—but, then, being flayed alive isn't supposed to be fun. You can still admire his style in vitriol.

I have only one complaint about this book, which is that Crowther repeats as a simplistic morality play the story of a brouhaha at a North Carolina community college where a member of the Sons of Confederate Veterans was accused by a young newspaper reporter of teaching that slaves were happy with their lot. The charge echoed through the media, the man was pilloried in the press worldwide, and he died soon afterwards. Jerry Bledsoe makes clear in his book *Death by Journalism?* why this little episode was more tragedy than melodrama, and Crowther, who is usually scrupulous when things are more complicated than they appear, should have given the story its due or simply omitted it.

Still, as Rubin says in that foreword, "there's not a plodding sentence or an inane comment in *Gather at the River*." These essays run the gamut of pity, scorn, fury, condescension, fond affection, sober appreciation, and awed admiration, all admirably expressed, adding up to (Rubin again) "as vigorous and adventuresome a set of pieces, mostly about the South, as anyone with a taste for good sense and sharp insights set forth in lustrous prose might ask."

OUR CELTIC FRINGE

This is a slightly updated version of a review published by the Weekly Standard *in 2005. After it appeared, James Webb went on to grander things, like the U.S. Senate.*

• • •

C. Vann Woodward, the eminent historian of the American South, once spoke of the regional differences among his graduate students at Yale. The Southerners, he said, wanted to tell stories about their region, while the Yankees wanted to advance some thesis or other. Appropriately for someone who grew up all over (in a military family), James Webb does both in *Born Fighting: How the Scots-Irish Shaped America.* In fact, he has written almost two separate books.

The first book, the storytelling one, is a memoir and family history, and it's a corker. The son of a self-made Air Force officer, Webb went to Annapolis, then as a Marine infantry officer to Vietnam, where he was wounded twice and received the Navy Cross for valor. In 1972 he left the service and enrolled in law school at Georgetown, where at the time a warrior was, to say the least, not understood. (The experience obviously still rankles.) While a student he wrote a book on U.S. strategy in the Pacific, and began a legal campaign to clear a fellow Marine wrongly convicted on charges of war crimes—a campaign that eventually succeeded, but only three years after the man's suicide. In 1978 he published *Fields of Fire,* a highly praised novel of the Vietnam War and the first of his six bestsellers. He served in the Reagan administration as assistant secretary of defense and secretary of the navy, resigned to protest cuts in naval strength, and turned his hand to journalism, business consulting,

and screenwriting and producing ("Rules of Engagement"). In 2006 he ran
as a Democrat for the Senate in Virginia, and served one term before stepping
down (to pursue, among other things, a quixotic campaign for the presidency).

Webb comes from a long line of fighters, both in and out of uniform. His
people have been fighting their nations' enemies, their own, and occasionally
each other for hundreds of years, and some of their stories are as compelling
as Webb's own. Why are these people so scrappy? Well, Webb has a theory
about that, and that's the second book.

Webb's ancestors were for the most part Scots-Irish (more commonly,
if perhaps less correctly, "Scotch-Irish"), part of the great wave of eighteenth-century immigrants from Ulster to Pennsylvania, who then moved
south down the Shenandoah Valley to settle the Southern backcountry, moving on from there to Texas, Missouri (where Webb was born), and points north
and west. Webb believes that the Scots-Irish have a distinctive culture that
includes aggressive response to insult, attack, and attempted intimidation:
"Physical courage fueled this culture, and an adamant independence marked
its daily life. Success itself was usually defined in personal reputation rather
than worldly goods." Moreover, as his subtitle "How the Scots-Irish Shaped
America" indicates, he believes this culture's "legacy is broad, in many ways
defining the attitudes and values of the military, of working-class America, and
even of the particularly populist form of American democracy itself," in fact
that it "has become the definition of 'American' that others gravitate toward
when they wish to drop their hyphens and join the cultural mainstream."

If I find this argument appealing, it's possibly because the Scots-Irish are my
people, too. I grew up less than ten miles from Moccasin Gap, Virginia, where
Webb begins his book, searching for his great-great-grandparents' graves, and
given how things were in the early years of Virginia's "Fighting Ninth" congressional district we're probably cousins, although most of my ancestors were
Unionists and Republicans and most of his Rebels and Democrats.

Webb sees this belligerent culture as "bred deeply into every heart," "passing with the blood," even "in the Scots-Irish DNA" (although I think he's
speaking figuratively). He argues that it has been shaped and reinforced by
the group's experience, and a potted (and occasionally padded) history of
Scotland, Ulster, and eighteenth- and nineteenth-century America amply illustrates his point that the Scots-Irish have a long record of invasion, oppression,
and resistance. Again and again, they have found, or put, themselves in the

position of, well, *insurgents*. This history of incessant conflict, together with the Scottish clan structure, the Protestant Reformation, and rural isolation, has "ingrained" certain attitudes and values in the Scots-Irish and the other groups they have influenced and absorbed:

> The culture in its embryonic form stood fast against the Roman and Norman nation-builders who created a structured and eventually feudal England. The unique emphasis on individual rights and responsibilities that sprang from Calvinism and the Scottish Kirk caused it to resist the throne and finally brought down a king. The fierceness of its refusal to accommodate the Anglican theocrats in Ulster created the radical politics of nonconformism, and this attitude was carried into the Appalachian Mountains. Its people refused to bend a knee to New York and Boston either before, during, or after the Civil War, standing firm against outside forces that would try to tell them how to live and what to believe. And even today . . . it refuses to accept the politics of group privilege that have been foisted on America by its paternalistic, Ivy League–centered, media-connected, politically correct power centers.

I think he's on to something here. During the conflict over the Mississippi state flag I was struck when a reporter for the *Irish Times* found the whole controversy eerily reminiscent of Ulster, where they also "do battle over the right to flaunt symbols of division in the name of irreconcilable versions of history."

But Webb's argument was presented more succinctly in a *Wall Street Journal* op-ed piece he wrote just before the 2004 elections ("Secret GOP Weapon: The Scots-Irish Vote"), and it has been presented more thoroughly and systematically by David Hackett Fischer in *Albion's Seed* (which Webb cites often), and Grady McWhiney in *Cracker Culture* (which, oddly, he doesn't cite at all, although he did take a chapter title, "Attack and Die," from another of McWhiney's books on the South's "Celtic" heritage). Anyone seriously interested in Webb's thesis would do well to read Fischer and McWhiney, as well as a fascinating and underappreciated book called *Culture of Honor: The Psychology of Violence in the South,* by Richard E. Nisbett and Dov Cohen. One should also read the extensive literature critical of these books, because this is a highly controversial field of scholarship, although you wouldn't know that from Webb's presentation.

And that's the problem with this second book of his. Webb draws extensively from W. J. Cash's 1940 classic *The Mind of the South* (which he describes as "perennially well-regarded"—not exactly so, but I don't want to turn this into even more of a bibliographical essay). Like Cash, Webb paints with broad, bold strokes, and one can only admire the sweep and dash of his treatment. But, also like Cash, he has a way of treating as fact what is actually conjecture and hypothesis. Like his ancestors, Webb wades fearlessly into battles—in this case, historiographical ones, some of them recent (like the importance of the "Celtic" heritage), others (like the causes of the Civil War) ones that have been raging for decades. I pretty much agree with him on most points, but then, as a Scots-Irishman myself, I would. A good many serious historians do not, and by no means are all of them prisoners of political correctness (a phrase which should probably be retired, although Webb is fond of it).

Also, predictably for an academic, I have an overpowering urge to pick nits that are individually trivial, but that add up to make me uneasy. To say that John Calvin is "the founder of the modern Christian evangelical movement" and that Scots-Irish culture still has an "emphasis on Calvinist theology," for instance, simply ignores the culture war in the antebellum Southern uplands between Calvinists and Arminians (the "free will" ancestors of modern evangelicalism), a war the evangelicals won. Similarly, as a measure of the unimportance of slavery to Southern yeomen, Webb mentions, twice, that only 5 percent of antebellum white Southerners owned slaves. This is technically correct, but a more meaningful figure is that between a quarter and a third of white Southern *households* owned slaves (and a much higher percentage in the cotton states).

In short, Webb has an interesting and important argument, although it's not as novel as he apparently believes, and he doesn't really make the best possible case for it. Even if he's right, it raises as many questions as it answers. Why, for example, do contemporary Scotland and Ireland (Ulster perhaps aside) no longer display some of these "Celtic" traits? And how it is that so many other Southerners and Americans—in particular, those who trace their ancestry to West Africa—happen to have many of the same values? These questions are not unanswerable in Webb's terms, but they do suggest that the story is more complicated than the simple "passing in the blood" version that we get here.

It's also not entirely clear what Webb wants us to do. Plainly, he wants to alert politicians and the media to the presence, grievances, and influence of this largely neglected and ignored American ethnic group, and who could object to that? (Well, Charles Krauthammer, for one. When Howard Dean said that he wanted the votes of "guys with Confederate flags on their pickup trucks," Krauthammer accused him of going after the "white trash vote" of "rebel-yell racist rednecks." Webb observed at the time that Krauthammer "has never complained about this ethnic group when it has marched off to fight the wars he wishes upon us.") But apparently Webb also wants to raise the consciousness of Scots-Irish Americans themselves. If you had asked them, Webb's ancestors would have said they were "Americans" or "Southerners" or (usually) both, but almost certainly not "Scotch-Irish." As Webb describes it:

> In their insistent individualism [the Scots-Irish] are not likely to put an ethnic label on themselves. . . . Some of them don't even know their ethnic label, and some who do don't particularly care. They don't go for group identity politics any more than they like to join a union. Two hundred years ago the mountains built a fierce and uncomplaining people. To them, joining a group and putting themselves at the mercy of someone else's collective judgment makes about as much sense as letting the government take their guns. And nobody is going to get their guns.

In other words, when it comes to identity politics it looks as if many of us Scots-Irish just don't *get* it. How else to account for the fact that, as Webb reports, 38 percent of the population of Middlesborough, Kentucky, told the 2000 Census that their ethnicity is "native American"?

Personally, I'm glad that that there is no Scots-Irish Anti-Defamation League. Certainly we Scots-Irish have been defamed ever since the English American Virginia aristocrat William Byrd visited North Carolina in 1733 and wrote scornfully about the inhabitants of "Lubberland," and Webb points out the irony of lumping the Scots-Irish with "WASPs," their historic adversaries: "In this perverted logic, those who had been the clearest victims of Yankee colonialism were now grouped together with the beneficiaries. All WASPs were considered to be the same in this environment, as if they had landed together on the same ship at Plymouth Rock and the smart ones had gone to Boston while the dumbest had somehow made their way to West Virginia." But not only have most Scots-Irish resolutely refused to see themselves as victims, some of us have even made contemptuous jokes about those who do. The Southern comedian Brother Dave Gardner's proposal for a National Association for the Advancement of White Trash is just a starter.

Webb believes that "the final question in this age of diversity and political correctness is whether [Scots-Irish Americans] can learn to play the modern game of group politics." He tells the story of Phyllis Deal of Clintwood, Virginia, who was asked by a *Washington Post* reporter if her traditional Appalachian foodstuffs were being marketed through local food cooperatives. "No," she answered. "There's a traditional resistance to cooperatives in our area. We're not very cooperative." Webb comments: "Dear Mrs. Deal: I admire your independent spirit. But it's time to get more cooperative." I like her attitude, too, but I'm not sure I want to see her change.

WE, THE NATIVES

This book review for Chronicles *magazine was written back when travel books sold for fifteen dollars and "sound as a dollar" wasn't said ironically.*

• • •

"There is no frigate like a book," Miss Dickinson wrote, in lines that used to send seventh-grade boys into paroxysms of suppressed giggles—"to take us lands away." When I confess that I'd rather read even a bad travel book than most best-selling novels these days, I don't know whether that reflects poorly on me or on the novels, but there's no question that with the price of travel what it is, travel books are a comparative bargain, even at fifteen dollars and up.

Here's a test. Consider two books: (1) an account of a small-boat trip down the Mississippi by an Englishman who has been a Mark Twain enthusiast since childhood and recently wrote a fine travel book about the Middle East; (2) an op-ed piece from the *Washington Post* on regional diversity in the United States, expanded to 427 pages by its author, who flew around the country for a year on an expense account, popping in here and there to talk to folks. Which is the better book?

You're wrong (and I was, too). *Old Glory: An American Voyage,* by Jonathan Raban, is a disappointing exercise in self-indulgence, and *The Nine Nations of North America,* by Joel Garreau, is good, solid reporting, with a provocative thesis that's well worth thinking about.

One of the delights of travel books comes from revisiting exotic places where one has actually been before. Good books can evoke familiar smells and tastes as well as scenery; bad ones give the reader the more subtle pleasure of one-upping the author. Almost as satisfying, to me at least, are books about places I haven't been—perhaps especially when they persuade me that I'm not missing anything. Paul Theroux's *Old Patagonian Express*, for instance, has guaranteed that I will never go out of my way to visit Latin America, and Eric Newby seems to specialize in this genre: *The Big Red Train* will convince any sensible reader that Siberia is best left unseen, and *Slowly Down the Ganges* has to be the most excruciatingly tedious travel book ever written. Books like that, which not only make the reader feel he's "been there" but cure him of any desire to go again, are a blessing to those of us with world-class wanderlust and bush-league budgets.

My fondness for travel books is in direct proportion to the extent to which I can identify with the authors. When I can't put myself in their place (as I can't, for instance—despite trying very hard—with T. E. Lawrence), I may read their books with pleasure, but I read them for information, not for vicarious experience. This is almost always the case with books written by natives: I'll give them a respectful hearing, figuring they know more about it than I ever will (whether they choose to tell me or not), but I don't come away with the feeling that I've visited the places. On the other hand, when Theroux traverses the Orient in *The Great Railway Bazaar,* when V. S. Naipaul goes *Among the Believers* of the non-Arab Islamic world or his brother Shiva does an Evelyn Waugh number on Guyana and California in *Journey to Nowhere,* I can imagine having the same experiences. The author and I are amused, puzzled, irritated, pleased by the same things; we are both outsiders, just passing through, and nothing *matters* as much as it would to a native.

I liked Jonathan Raban's *Arabia* very much. It wasn't the greatest travel book since the *Odyssey,* as some of the reviews implied, but it was good journeyman work: evocative description, amusing anecdotes, interesting conversations, occasionally a sharp observation. I looked forward to *Old Glory.* I should have known better.

A different sort of problem comes up when outsiders (Raban, as I said, is English) write books about *our* society. Here *we* are the natives. When the author is amused, puzzled, irritated, or pleased, we're the reason. And here the presumption of knowledge is with the reader, who (in my case, at least) reads these accounts with some anxiety: Does he understand? Did he get it right?

Sometimes, of course, even a bad book—one that gets many things wrong—

can be interesting because of *how* it gets them wrong. *Separate Country,* an otherwise unremarkable book by an Englishman named Paul Binding, earned a place in my heart and on my bookshelf for one passage alone. Binding arrived in Atlanta by train, in early morning, and set out to walk downtown from the station (and who but a foreigner would *walk*?):

> I had walked for some time down a pleasant but uninteresting suburban road before, standing at the crest of a downward-sloping avenue, I saw—as if placed there for my benefit only instants before—downtown Atlanta. I think there can be no urban landscape in the world more dramatic than Atlanta seen from a short distance. It is a dense, sudden, strange cluster of skyscrapers, diverse in shape and height but all at a casual glance seemingly made of polished glass. . . . [The] rising sun shone through that abrupt and soaring forest of buildings and made the most extraordinary of them all—the round, gigantic, dominating Peachtree Hotel—a burning column of green and orange.

Well, like most conservative Southerners, when I look at Atlanta *I* see what two hundred thousand Confederate soldiers died to prevent, but I'll never see it again without realizing that there is one Englishman out there who thinks it looks like the Emerald City of Oz.

My pleasure in these odd new angles, however, is usually offset by irritation that someone can presume to write about *us* on the basis of a quick and superficial tour. Of course, it's gratifying, in a way, to be thought interesting enough to be the subject of a book, and Southerners probably have this experience more often than other Americans. With the possible exception of Southern California, the South is the part of America that New Yorkers and other foreigners seem to find most exotic. Maybe a great travel book could be written about Nebraska (after all, Newby wrote about Siberia), but I have yet to hear of one. Nebraska for the Nebraskans seems to be the general view. Sometimes, though, a Southerner can envy Nebraskans their normality, their boringness, or whatever it is that keeps visiting firemen away. One can get tired of reading about his homeplace and wondering where the author got *that* idea.

Southerners and Midwesterners alike will often find themselves responding that way to *Old Glory,* although sometimes, unfortunately, it's perfectly evident where Raban got his ideas: they're about what you would expect from the Smith College professor that he once was. At one point he seems to sympathize, almost, with an Iowa businessman who protests that Easterners are always treating Iowans as yokels, but usually he can't resist putting down Midwesterners himself. (I can't either, but I'm not writing a travel book.) One doesn't expect Raban to like everything, but one wishes his likes and dislikes weren't so predictable.

As he told the Iowan, this book is not the inside story on America, but rather the inside story on Raban (which gives an unexpected and almost certainly unintended twist to the title, *Old Glory*), and perhaps that's the trouble. Raban's opinions and personal problems lead him into activities he cares about, but when he expects his readers to care, he expects too much. One particularly wearisome episode sees our narrator laying over for some weeks in Memphis to fight for truth, justice, and the American way in the context of a mayoral election. He may have been, as he believes, on the side of the angels, but what is an English travel writer doing on any side at all? He didn't meddle in Yemen's politics when he was writing *Arabia*—or if he did, he didn't insist on telling us about it. The self-indulgence that dictated Raban's itinerary shows up again and again, and long before the journey was over I'd concluded that however pleasant it was to visit the Middle East with him, Raban is not the sort of chap I'd choose for company on a boat ride from Minneapolis to New Orleans. To make matters worse, he has a tendency to pick up unpleasant companions and not to drop them fast enough. One woman in St. Louis, in particular, gets tiresome some dozen pages before Raban wearies of her.

Maybe I'm too hard on the boy. Maybe I'm jealous because nobody paid me to take that trip and write about it. Let's be fair. There are the makings of a good two-hundred-page book scattered through this four-hundred-pager. Raban is not the book's real hero: that is Old Man River, who does indeed just keep rolling along. There are some marvelous passages about the river—as good as anything Raban's beloved Twain ever wrote. Those readers who've seen the Mississippi only from the bridges and hotel windows will never see it the same way again. And Raban didn't miss *all* of the interesting people en route. My favorites, inevitably, are Southerners: a good old boy from Tiptonville, Kentucky; a Negro undertaker and a thoroughly assimilated Lebanese merchant in Vicksburg; an indomitable formerly grande dame in a Natchez old-folks' home; an Irish-Choctaw-Scotch-Mexican riverboat captain—*Old Glory* is at its best when Raban just lets some of these people talk. Here is a group of card-players at Erjie's Bar and Cafe in Lockport, Louisiana. Raban asked about a place to stay:

"Hey," called a fat man from his bar stool. "You want a place, I can show you a place. Out there in the bayous. . . ." He swiveled around. "Know what's there? A cave. A cave full of froomids. You know what a froomid is?"

"No."

"He's shooting his mouth off. Keep quiet, Louis."

"Froomids is . . . paradise. They is . . . men and women all mixed up together. [Some anatomical description follows.] That's froomids. They'll eat you alive. But with the froomids, it's like heaven, know what I mean?"

"Hermaphrodites," I said.

"Froomids!" he said. "Listen to what I'm saying to you!"

"Louis Beauregard," said the man next to me, "after you come here, this place done go to the dogs."

Louis Beauregard glittered contentedly. "Well . . . all *you* got to do is: barbecue them dogs."

Raban can listen, and if he'd stuck to describing the river and playing straight man to Cajuns, I'd be more enthusiastic about his book.

• • •

You'd think that trying to prove an explicit thesis would pretty much sour a travel book, but in *The Nine Nations of North America* Joel Garreau doesn't let it. He states the thesis forthrightly on page one:

Consider . . . the way North America really works. It is Nine Nations. Each has its capital and its distinctive web of power and influence. A few are allies, but many are adversaries. Several have readily acknowledged national poets, and many have characteristic dialects and mannerisms. Some are close to being raw frontiers; others have four centuries of history. Each has a peculiar economy; each commands a certain emotional allegiance from its citizens. . . . Each nation has its own list of desires. . . . Most important, each nation has a distinct prism through which it views the world.

Right or wrong, Garreau's framework serves him well. He means to say some important things about what is happening to America, but he believes that to put the question that way is misleading: different things are happening to different parts of America. If you look at *Ecotopia*—well, maybe Charles

Reich was right. But *The Foundry* isn't being greened, and its problems are completely different from those *of Dixie*, which differs in turn from the dry but resource-rich *Empty Quarter* (named after the original, in Saudi Arabia). The "United States" (after reading Garreau, you want to put it in quotes) is being nibbled away at from the South, and it just doesn't make sense to talk about Miami in isolation from *The Islands*, which it serves as unofficial capital, or to treat El Paso apart from the rest of *MexAmerica*. But that's not Minnesota's problem, and anyway *The Breadbasket*, like *New England*, is encroaching on the territory of "Canada"—an even worse idea than the United States, as many natives of *Quebec* have been saying for some time.

All this may sound rather too schematic, but there is obviously a grain of truth here, if not a whole carload. The incredible diversity of our continent has never been in doubt in some quarters, but in others (Washington, for instance, where Garreau works) it can't be emphasized too often.

In general, Garreau seeks out and approves of things that make his "nations" different from one another and scowls at those that make them similar. This is not just a matter of liking things that support his thesis. Unlike Jonathan Raban, who was ready enough to acknowledge that the America he boated through was different from the one for which he was apparently writing, but usually saw those differences as either quaint or appalling, Garreau clearly tends to delight in diversity per se. (So do I. The appropriate scriptural metaphor, we rednecks might say, is the Coat of Many Colors, not the Tower of Babel, but I confess—and Garreau might, too—that this judgment is as much aesthetic as political.)

The persona that emerges from Garreau's book is that of a curious, perceptive, and witty reporter, a good companion for the kind of voyage the book offers and one with whom the reader can identify. Having brandished his conceptual axe at the outset, Garreau grinds it only inconspicuously through the next nine chapters, each a visit to one of the "nations." For the most part, he appears to do simply what I wish Raban had done: travel around, seek out telling scenes and interesting people, watch and listen and report. This is artful, of course, but we've been warned. Garreau's opinions are evident, to be sure, but they are seldom intrusive and not always predictable. He has some fun with the "Ecotopians" of the Northwest, for instance, whose treasured "quality of life" presupposes an economy stoked by defense contracts.

Garreau intended something more than an updated (and superior) version of *Inside U.S.A.*, though, and *The Nine Nations of North America* at least raises the interesting question of whether (and if so, why) the United States is immune to the centrifugal tendencies lately evident in almost every other industrialized state. Garreau thinks we're not, and you could draw the same conclusion from reading Alvin Toffler's *The Third Wave,* a work of pop sociology that has good news and bad news for nearly everybody, most especially conservatives. Jonathan Raban caught a glimpse of the same vision by watching television commercials in an Iowa motel:

> The families who populated this bland fiction of American middle-class life looked and sounded like a pack of fancy weirdos. They were skinny fast-talkers, jabbering about laxatives and cake mixes and automobiles. They were as foreign to the America that I was living in as I was myself. . . . I thought how tamely we had all succumbed to the theory that television automatically draws the world together. Surely it had just as strong a tendency to pull the world apart. It was television that fueled [the] hatred of the "beautiful people," the Washington outlaws, Angelenos and New Yorkers. . . . [One] switched on his set in order to be reminded of their beastliness.

Time will tell, of course, whether these prophecies of decentralization (my less-Calhounian friends might say disintegration) will be fulfilled. Meanwhile, we can enjoy *The Nine Nations of North America* as a good *travel* book, combining most of the various pleasures I mentioned above. There are parts of North America (I'll leave them unnamed) where I no longer want to go; other parts I enjoyed visiting, or revisiting, and seeing through Garreau's eyes. I think he even gets the South pretty much right: his boundary-drawing exercise is right on the money, his resolution of the problem of what to do with Miami is a great relief, and his account of how Dixie is shaping up these days is right up there with Fred Powledge's *Journeys through the South*—and Powledge is a native. A good traveler's account of journeys around North America is no small achievement, even if it was not Garreau's principal intention. I don't shudder to think of foreigners reading *Nine Nations*—unlike *Old Glory.* But I notice that even Garreau doesn't have much to say about Nebraska.

THE WAR AND ITS LEGACY

I'm no historian, just an interested amateur, but I've occasionally written about the Late Unpleasantness, when asked, and also about its contemporary echoes. Here are some examples.

BRINGING THE JUBILEE

The Wall Street Journal, apparently assuming that someone who writes about the South would want to read about "that devil Sherman," asked me in 2008 to review a book about the devil's notorious March.

• • •

If you're the kind of Civil War geek who reads every word of sentences like "A two-gun section from Battery H, 1st Illinois Light Artillery, Captain Francis De-Gress commanding, operated throughout the day, joined for a period by a section from Battery H, 1st Missouri Light Artillery, Lieutenant John F. Brenner in charge," Noah Andre Trudeau's *Southern Storm: Sherman's March to the Sea* is the book for you. For others it will often seem a lot like what the March was for the troops who undertook it: a weary slog, intermittently enlivened by assorted diversions. Like Yankees soldiering through mud and swamps and freezing rain, readers will find themselves trudging through page after page of unmemorable detail—pretty much a catalogue of which units were where, doing what, each day.

But at least most readers will know where they're going. That wasn't the case for Sherman's sixty-two thousand soldiers. When they turned their backs on a burning Atlanta and headed east in November 1864, their destination was a secret even from President Lincoln. Of course, as every schoolchild once knew, five weeks later Sherman famously presented Lincoln "a Christmas gift" of Savannah. Behind him was a swath of destruction "sixty miles of latitude, three hundred to the main," in the words of "Marching Through Georgia," a popular song (in some quarters) written the next year.

Sherman's men broke up the monotony by burning buildings, wrecking railroad lines, feasting on looted chickens and hogs, bullying civilians, and occasionally engaging Confederate cavalry. Footsore readers will find diversion in episodes like the citizens of Monticello turning in a hiding Confederate officer they found arrogant, property-owners in Sherman's path playing whatever cards they had to get protection (Masonic regalia often did the trick), or a spunky teenager named Zora Fair blacking up as a Negro, sneaking into occupied Atlanta on her own to spy, and mailing her findings to the governor of Georgia in a letter intercepted by the Union army. Trudeau's narrative is also peppered with trenchant observations from Sherman himself. Undoubtedly the most quotable general officer in a very long time, Sherman was a realist, his lack of sentimentality perhaps matched only by that of Nathan Bedford Forrest (whom he admired), whose dictum that "war means fighting, and fighting means killing" was matched by Sherman's own: "War is cruelty. There is no use trying to reform it. The crueler it is, the sooner it will be over."

And just as all that marching turned out to have a point—it broke the back of the Confederacy—readers who persevere will be rewarded. The fifty-odd pages of Sherman's own brisk account in his memoirs give the big picture, but to really understand the March, there's no substitute for taking it one step at a time, all the way to Savannah. Trudeau does a splendid job of that, which is what he set out to do.

So it's mere carping to wish that his book, at seven-hundred-plus pages, did anything more. But only in his last twenty pages does Trudeau address any consequences of the campaign other than the military ones. He points out almost as an afterthought, for example, that, on the extensive evidence he has provided, the March was not what generations of Americans, on both sides, have believed it to be—neither as jaunty and carefree for its participants as "Marching Through Georgia" portrayed it, nor as unremittingly brutal as white Georgians have ever after recalled it. (It was bad enough, but by today's standards they got off easy. There was, for example, only one documented case of rape.)

In general, this book could also have used a little more—well, human interest. Trudeau mentions that the 1st Alabama Cavalry (U.S. Volunteers), a regiment made up mostly of white Unionists from the hills of north Alabama, was one of the few units censured for excesses against civilians. He doesn't point out, though, that Sherman chose this regiment for his personal escort. That choice, like those excesses, probably reflects the fact that the desperados of the First Alabama were fierce fighters: for them, the war was often personal (one paid a call on his hostile Rebel uncle and stole a horse) and if captured, they faced serious trouble from their fellow Southerners.

Trudeau also tells his story almost entirely from the Union point of view. There are good dramaturgical reasons for this, and it probably reflects the abundance of sources as well: Union soldiers wrote a lot of letters and diaries. It does mean, however, that the reactions of black and white Georgians to the March are largely seen through the eyes of Northern observers. Just so, although Trudeau skillfully describes the Confederate military response (largely a story of missed opportunities, faulty intelligence, and weak and divided leadership), we get little sense of how Sherman's inexorable advance was experienced by those in arms against it.

This last omission may also be a drawback from a marketing point of view. Most of the avid Civil War buffs I know are on the Confederate side, and they'll find the lack of that perspective a disappointment. But those Yankees who are interested in how their people fought that war will find this book well worth their attention.

A FLAG'S MANY MEANINGS

This is another Wall Street Journal *piece, an op-ed about the significance in the year 2000 of the Confederate battle flag, which had become an issue in that year's presidential primaries.*

• • •

Last Monday fifty thousand people rallied in Columbia, South Carolina, to protest the flying of the Confederate battle flag over the South Carolina state capitol, and, with the South Carolina primaries coming up, the presidential candidates have found themselves obliged to take a stand on what had been heretofore a local issue. Not surprisingly, both Al Gore and Bill Bradley, running in a Democratic primary where a majority of voters will be black, have said it should come down. Republican candidates, on the other hand, with a virtually lily-white constituency, assert that it is up to states to decide how to decorate their statehouses. Even John McCain, who originally called the flag "a symbol of racism and slavery," has now "clarified" his position. (Standing up to Iowans on ethanol subsidies is one thing, but the man's not crazy.) Meanwhile, opponents of the Georgia state flag, which incorporates the battle flag in its design, are even threatening protests at the Super Bowl. Now, that's serious.

What's this all about? Didn't we settle this in 1865?

The beginning of wisdom when it comes to the Confederate flag is to recognize that it means different things to different people. Unfortunately, that wisdom is in short supply among Southerners, many of whom find it extraordinarily difficult to recognize that any other view is even possible, let alone legitimate. Three major meanings stand out. (Think of it as something like a Rorschach test.)

The flag has, notoriously, been deployed by groups ranging from the Dixie-crats to the Ku Klux Klan as a symbol of white supremacy, and for a racist fringe of Southern whites it still has that meaning. Ironically, they share that understanding with the flag's opponents, most of them African Americans, who also see the flag as a symbol of segregation and slavery.

Many white Southerners, on the other hand, see the flag as representing what they sincerely believe to be an honorable legacy of duty, valor, and sacri-fice. Some (I among them) question whether it is appropriate for state-spon-sored display, but that doesn't mean they see it solely or even primarily as a rac-ist symbol. When defenders of the flag print tee-shirts and erect billboards that say the flag stands for "Heritage, Not Hate," they're not being disingenuous.

To other Southern whites the flag symbolizes a less historical sort of rebel spirit and pride, exemplified in the good-timing, hell-raising music of Lynyrd Skynyrd and Hank Williams Jr. This interpretation is shared, oddly, by a good many young Europeans, but we can ignore it here.

"Southern heritage" groups recognize that they have a problem. In 1989 the Sons of Confederate Veterans (SCV) passed a resolution denouncing "extrem-ist political groups and individuals who seek to clothe themselves in respect-ability by misappropriating the banner under which our southern ancestors fought for a cause which was as noble as much latter day use is ignoble." The SCV declared that the flag's "misuse" by those "espousing political extremism and/or racial superiority degrades [it] and maligns the noble purpose of our ancestors who fought against extreme odds for what they believed was just, right, and constitutional." There have been some confrontations between groups like the Sons and racist groups they see as misusing the flag, and there has even been a peculiar attempt to find or to invent a significant black pres-ence in the Confederate army.

These efforts are well-meant, and the impulse behind them is admirable in its way, although they're probably too late to do much good. The NAACP, for its part, is having none of it. That organization has denounced the flag as "an abhorrence to all Americans and decent people," "the ugly symbol of idiotic white supremacy, racism and denigration," and "an odious blight upon the universe." Not much room for dialogue there.

Obviously, many of those who care about the flag care passionately. Neither side will give up without a fight, and even if there were some sort of middle ground, there is little reason to seek it. So long as the conflict continues, whatever happens, one side has a victory and the other a grievance, and either can be useful, from an organizational point of view. (Membership in the Sons of Confederate Veterans has doubled in recent years, largely in response to attacks on the flag and other Confederate symbols.) Partisans on both sides simply talk past each other.

Black demonstrators in Columbia responded to the "Heritage, Not Hate" message with signs that said "Your Heritage Is My Slavery." And of course they have a point. If "heritage" refers to the South's political and economic history, that history—like that of most peoples—is indeed a sorry saga of conflict, division, oppression, and exploitation. Slavery was an important part of that history, and undeniably part of what secession was about, as any honest reading of the secession debates in the various Southern states will attest. (This is not to say that individual Confederate soldiers were fighting for slavery, which is where the SCV has a point.)

But if "heritage" means food, music, speech, religion, humor—what the sociologist Edgar Thompson once called the "idiomatic imponderables" that make up a culture—the irony is that black and white Southerners share a great deal. The challenge is to find symbols of the South's cultural history, which has from the start been a story of borrowing, copying, blending, and producing a flavorsome creole stew. If Southerners can ever get over the political history that divides them and simply enjoy a culture whose making they have shared, and still do—if they can "forget the bad and keep the good" (as a country song by Tanya Tucker puts it)—the South might really rise again.

Maybe it's possible. It's true that when the University of North Carolina's Southern Focus Poll asked residents of thirteen Southern states in 1994 whether the flag is "more a symbol of racial conflict or of Southern pride," only 26 percent of blacks chose Southern pride, compared to 75 percent of whites. But in response to another question a third of white respondents and half of black ones said that they "don't care much about [the flag] one way or the other." I suspect that many Southerners of both races are profoundly bored with the subject and would welcome even another celebrity murder trial or presidential sex scandal if it would get the flag off their front pages and television screens.

BLACK REBELS

This was written as another op-ed piece about the Confederate flag, but it never found a publisher, I suspect because its conclusions are unwelcome in some quarters.

• • •

In April 2001, Mississippians went to the polls to decide whether to change their state flag. A blue-ribbon committee appointed by the governor had proposed that the old design, which prominently incorporates the Confederate battle flag, be replaced by an anodyne pattern of stars and stripes. To no one's surprise in Mississippi, roughly a half-million citizens voted to keep the old flag, while only half as many wanted the change.

To a considerable extent the vote followed racial lines. A *Jackson Clarion-Ledger* poll taken several weeks before the referendum showed that almost four out of five whites with an opinion favored the old flag and nearly as high a percentage of black voters wanted to change it. An AP poll showed a racial divide almost as large. Most whites told pollsters and anyone else who would listen that they cherished the battle flag as a symbol of their history and heritage. To the former commander of the state Sons of Confederate Veterans, for example, the flag self-evidently stands for "courage, devotion to duty, devotion to family, honor, valor, and a lot of other qualities that we should aspire to in life." Many Mississippians also apparently resented being told what they should do—not just by the NAACP, but by the *New York Times*, *USA Today*, the *Birmingham News*, and even the *Clarion-Ledger*, which supported the change, along with nearly all of the state's political, religious, economic, and civic elite. As former Republican governor Kirk Fordice told the *New York Times*, Mississippians "resent the heck out of the constant drumming on the part of the media and others, day after day, that something's wrong with you if you support the old flag."

In contrast, most black Mississippians, remembering all too well how the Confederate flag was deployed by opponents of the civil rights movement in the 1960s, saw it as a symbol of white supremacy and racial hatred. Unita Blackwell, the mayor of Mayersville, Mississippi, spoke for many when she said, "When I think about the flag I think about the Ku Klux Klan and when they came along here burning crosses in my yard—they had that flag." Even the most generous of the flag's black opponents saw it as a symbol of *white* heritage, which excludes them. The actor Morgan Freeman voiced that view when he said, "Personally, I have every appreciation for those Mississippians who say the flag represents their heritage. But it's not everybody's heritage." (Freeman played a Union army sergeant in the movie *Glory*.)

But what about those who broke ranks with their racial group? We heard a great deal from and about whites who favored the change. They were active and vocal, filling the letters columns of the state's newspapers, frequently interviewed by the reporters who flooded the state, and outspending the flag's defenders by more than 35 to 1, largely to finance radio and television ads. We know what they thought and why they thought it. Most didn't share the NAACP's view that the Confederate flag is a racist symbol (many took pains to make it clear that they did not), but recognized that most black Mississippians and a good many non-Mississippians see it that way. Given that, they argued either that Mississippi's public relations and economic development would benefit from a less controversial flag—the *Mississippi Business Journal* ran an editorial headlined simply, "Bad for Business"—or simply that the flag should be changed to, as author John Grisham put it, "something not offensive to 35 percent of our population."

As for the black Mississippians who voted to keep the old flag, they were clearly a minority of the black community, but they weren't a *negligible* minority (like the one that voted for George W. Bush). The *Clarion-Ledger* poll found that 20 percent of black adults who were aware of the referendum opposed the change and another 15 percent had no opinion. The AP poll showed "almost 3 in 10" black Mississippians opposed to the change and another one in five undecided. Put another way, the *Clarion-Ledger*'s data suggest that something like 12 percent of those who planned to vote for the old flag were black. When the votes were tallied, Sharkey and Quitman Counties, both 69 percent black, returned majorities against the change, as did Issaquena County, which is 63 percent black; in Coahoma County, 69 percent black, the new design won with less than 52 percent of the vote.

Part of the explanation is that black turnout may have been lower than white (which needs explaining, too), but that can't be the whole story. African Americans make up a third of the state's population: if they were anywhere near that proportion of referendum voters, the number of black Mississippians who voted to keep the old flag must have been fifty thousand or more. What could they have been thinking?

A handful of black Mississippians expressed essentially the same views as the Sons of Confederate Veterans; in fact some African Americans—an estimated two dozen, nationwide—*are* Sons of Confederate Veterans. In Mississippi, a young black man named Anthony Hervey, head of something called the Black Confederate Soldier Foundation, dedicated to memorializing blacks who fought for the Confederacy, was conspicuous in the weeks leading up to the election, with his view that the battle flag stands for his heritage, too, and that defending the flag is akin to "standing up for home." (Unfortunately, Hervey was later accused by Bob Harrison, a black Confederate reenactor, of running a con game, bilking white Southerners eager to demonstrate that the War was not about slavery.)

Another black Mississippian expressed support for the old flag of a less historical sort. Even before the state flag was an issue, the Reverend Walter Bowie of Jackson's Koinonia Baptist Church told the black conservative publication *Issues & Views* that "the so-called Rebel flag is the flag of the South, the symbol of many good things about our culture and history that are dear to the hearts of southerners, white, black and red. It becomes racist only in the hands of a racist." But Bowie, like Hervey, was expressing what was a distinctly unpopular view among black Mississippians. The president of the Columbia County branch of the NAACP called blacks who talked that talk "house Negroes," and Anthony Hervey even claimed that somebody took a shot at him.

Maybe that's why so few African Americans who voted for the old flag spoke for the record—although it's also possible simply that no one asked them to. *The Clarion-Ledger* did run an article about blacks who didn't vote at all, in which a twenty-year-old woman from Anguilla denied that the flag has a racist history. "I didn't vote," she said, "because there was no reason for it because they have had the flag for generations. . . . I think everybody is comfortable with the old flag instead of the new one. That's why the old flag won." And the mayor of Rolling Fork pointed out that, for many black Mississippians, "this flag decision wasn't a really big issue. They have a lot of higher priorities and they are facing other problems that are more important to them. Deciding whether or not we have a cross or some stars on a flag is not one of the graver issues that people are struggling with every day."

And here we have a clue about what may have led some African Americans to vote for the old flag. One of the few who told a reporter why he did complained that the leadership of the state NAACP is unresponsive to what he saw as *real* black concerns, which are economic rather than symbolic. This man, a county economic-development official, said his vote was a protest vote. You don't have to agree that symbols are unimportant (people die for flags, after all) to see his point, and other black Mississippians may have shared his opinions. When the pollsters asked folks why they planned to vote the way they did, the responses weren't broken down by race, but we can speculate. The most common reasons for supporting the old flag were tallied as "Part of Mississippi history" (38 percent said that) and "Proud of my heritage/Southern heritage" (35 percent). No doubt some who said those things were black, but I suspect that most black supporters of the old flag fell in the third most common category, "Other," which included the 20 percent of old-flag loyalists who gave such reasons as "Waste of money," "Don't like change," and "Issue is stupid."

The conservatism and stubbornness and downright contrariness of Mississippians has long distinguished them even among Southerners, and those traits clearly played a part in the vote on the flag. But the referendum results suggest that it's not only *white* Mississippians who don't like being told what to do.

WHY HAS THERE BEEN NO RACE WAR IN THE SOUTH?

Daniel Chirot, a friend since grad school days, asked me to write this piece for a conference on ethnic conflict that he and the psychologist Martin Seligman organized, held, appropriately, in Derry/Londonderry, Northern Ireland. I lifted portions of my paper from an article Merle Black and I had written earlier for New Perspectives, *a publication of the U.S. Commission on Civil Rights.*

• • •

We American Southerners are not accustomed to having our region thought of as a good example. Certainly not when it comes to race relations. But the question posed by my title may lower the bar sufficiently. We did have one race war, of course, a protracted one against the American Indians, culminating in what was euphemistically called in the 1830s the "removal" of some sixty thousand to Oklahoma. But that was a long time ago, by American standards—ancient history. So long ago that most Americans now think of the South as having always been essentially a biracial society, black and white. And that's the race war that may not have happened. Let me sketch a cursory history of black-white relations in the American South, emphasizing the violent conflict that did occur; then we can decide whether something needs to be explained.

The Slavery Era, 1661–1865
After slavery was legally recognized in Virginia in 1661 it soon spread to the other North American colonies, especially to the plantation colonies of the

South. By the turn of the seventeenth century the wholesale importation of enslaved Africans was well underway, and for the next 260 years blacks in the American South were ruthlessly and efficiently subordinated, first under slavery, then under the system of law and custom known as "Jim Crow." When legal importation of slaves ended in 1807, roughly a half-million blacks had been brought to what became the United States. By 1860, the black population of the South had increased to more than 4 million, over 90 percent of them enslaved, most as agricultural field hands, especially on the cotton plantations of the Deep South, where many counties (and the states of Mississippi and South Carolina) had black majorities.

Slave rebellions and conspiracies were far from rare in the South: there were at least 250 of them, but most were small, and all were suicidal. The bloodiest and best-known was that led by Nat Turner in Virginia, in 1831: Turner's rebels killed some 60 whites; the 60 or 70 insurrectionists and at least 120 unimplicated blacks also died. The demographics I mentioned earlier largely explain why there weren't successful slave revolts in the American South. At emancipation most black Americans were at least three generations removed from Africa, and the age and sex distributions of the black population were more balanced than elsewhere in the Americas. They lived in families, for the most part, not as gangs of young men. Also unlike elsewhere, slaves in the South were dispersed, usually outnumbered and always outgunned by whites. When blacks had the opportunity to resist successfully, they seized it: during the Civil War more than two hundred thousand joined the invading Union army. And when their segregated units faced Confederate troops we did see something like a race war, with all the usual atrocities. Confederates seldom took Negro prisoners.

Reconstruction and Jim Crow, 1865–ca.1958

With the defeat of the Confederacy came emancipation, and a brief period of experimentation and uncertainty about the future of race relations—in some states even a period of black political rule—but also a period of extensive and systematic violence directed against blacks and white Republicans. If this wasn't a race war, it often looked like one. The year 1866 saw massive race riots in Memphis and New Orleans, and soon the Ku Klux Klan and dozens of similar organizations sprang up in every Southern state, acting as a secret paramilitary arm of the Democratic Party to intimidate Republican voters and politicians, and to kill hundreds of them. Weariness in the face of this deter-mined and protracted resistance certainly contributed to the shift in Northern public opinion that led eventually to the removal of federal troops from the South and the restoration of white Democratic rule. After 1878, conservative Southern whites moved swiftly to reestablish their control of the black popula-tion, and by 1900 Southern blacks were as effectively subordinated as they had been under slavery. Most were sharecroppers, in a condition of near-peonage. Stripped of the vote, segregated by custom and increasingly by law, without effective legal protection or even the protection slaves had as property, they were reduced to dependence on the goodwill of whites.

It should be emphasized, however, that the black population as a whole was an indispensable component of the Southern economy. Although the situation of individual blacks was precarious, the jobs to which most were relegated by segregation—especially field labor—were essential, as planters' later opposi-tion to the activities of Northern labor recruiters attests. Under such a regime, violence was hardly necessary to maintain white supremacy, and too much violence could have had dire economic consequences. There was a good deal of it, however, especially in Southern cities, where most black institutions were concentrated and where African Americans had established the greatest measure of independence from white control. The decades around the turn of the century witnessed dozens of large-scale urban race riots (and not just in the South: more than twenty cities across the United States experienced them in the summer of 1919). In 1898 one of the worst, in Wilmington, North Carolina, decimated that port city's flourishing black middle class—and how to commemorate its centenary in 1998 presented an interesting civic problem for Wilmington. (Atlanta faced a similar problem in 2006: its history in these matters does not always square with its carefully constructed image of racial moderation and goodwill.)

That the segregation era saw virtually nothing in the way of violent black resistance except in immediate self-defense surely speaks both to the effec-tiveness of the white majority's domination and to the obvious futility of such resistance. As the national success in 1915 of the racist film *Birth of a Nation* attested, black Southerners could not look outside the South for politically consequential white allies. White Northerners by and large shared Southern white views of appropriate race relations, or at least believed in allowing white Southerners to implement their views without Northern interference. Individual acts of defiance did occur, but they were dealt with brutally. (Lynching peaked in the 1890s, but continued after the turn of the century at a rate of 50–100 a year, reaching a total of more than 3,700 before waning in the 1930s.) A far more common black response was emigration. Millions of blacks left the South in one of the great migrations of human history. In 1900, 90 percent of black Americans lived in South; by 1965 only 40 percent did. In the 1950s one out of every four Southern-born blacks lived outside the South, and more than half of the non-Southern black population was Southern-born.

The Civil Rights Movement

At midcentury the segregationist regime of the South seemed to most observers simply an immutable fact, one that would have to be reckoned with by anyone concerned to improve Southern race relations. As late as 1942 only 2 percent of white Southerners had told a public opinion poll that black and white children should attend the same schools. It appeared to be true, in the words of historian Ulrich B. Phillips, that a determination that the South "be and remain a white man's country" was "the cardinal test of a Southerner." (For Phillips and others, "a Southerner" was simply assumed to be white.) As the civil rights movement picked up steam around 1960 it appeared to be headed straight into a solid wall of white opposition. Reporting on a study conducted in 1961, political scientists Donald Matthews and James Prothro concluded that "only a significant change in white racial attitudes, awareness, and expectations [could ensure] the prevention of a racial holocaust and the preservation of political democracy in the South."

Well, a few decades later, there has *been* a significant change in white attitudes. Support for racial segregation simply evaporated. Only about 5 percent of Southern white parents object to sending their children to school where "a few" of the children are black, a figure no higher than that for the rest of the country. In most respects, white Southerners' racial attitudes are no longer appreciably different from those of other white Americans in communities with significant black populations.

The poverty rate for black families in the South—twice as high as that elsewhere as late as 1970—is now comparable to that for the rest of the country. In fact, the Southern rate has now fallen below that for the North Central states. In 1960, a mere quarter of the eligible black voters in the South were registered to vote. (In Mississippi only 6 percent were registered five years after that.) The Voting Rights Act of 1965 changed that, and one consequence is that blacks are now more likely to hold elected office in the South than in any other region. In 1965, of the tens of thousands of elected officials in the South, precisely 78 were black. Thirty-odd years later, two-thirds of America's 8,015 black elected officials were in the South, nearly 1,500 in Mississippi alone. Perhaps the most impressive statistics are those that show, since about 1970, more blacks moving to the South than leaving it, reversing a population flow that once seemed a given in American demography. Once again a majority of African Americans live in the South.

Andrew Greeley has argued that the change these statistics reflect is "one of the most impressive social accomplishments of modern times." (Certainly the collapse of white Southern support for segregation is at least one of the most complete turnarounds in the history of public opinion polling.) Moreover, in historical and comparative terms, this change happened very quickly, and it can be argued that it came about at remarkably little cost.

That last statement would strike many Americans as bizarre. The civil rights movement lasted for roughly a decade, from the Montgomery bus boycott of 1955 to the Voting Rights Act of 1965, and Americans remember these years as violent ones, a collective memory periodically reinforced by historical melodramas like the movie *Mississippi Burning.* Among the most conspicuous examples of violent opposition to the movement were the riots at the University of Mississippi in which two people died; the deaths of four young black girls in the bombing of a Birmingham church; the assassination of Medgar Evers of the NAACP and later that of Dr. King himself; beatings and killings in connection with the Selma, Alabama, voting rights march; and the Mississippi Summer Project of 1964, which witnessed 80 beatings, 35 shootings, 35 church bombings, 30 house bombings, and 6 murders. We should not forget these events, nor should we forget the courage it took to confront this sort of thing.

But we must recognize that, as historian Richard Maxwell Brown has pointed out, the violence deployed against the civil rights movement, though brutal and terrifying (as it was meant to be), was seldom fatal. Brown estimates that the massive structure of Jim Crow law, designed to fix the shape of Southern race relations forever, was utterly destroyed at a cost of forty-four people killed during the entire course of the civil rights movement. Those deaths should not be forgotten or minimized, but they must also be assessed by comparison to the thousands of earlier deaths by lynching and in race riots, not to mention the ghastly toll exacted by intercommunal violence elsewhere in the world.

Something to Be Explained

Here, if anywhere, is what needs explaining. Matthews and Prothro were not the only observers who feared "racial holocaust" in the South, yet it is simply a fact that the basic structure of Southern society was changed without anything near that description. How did this happen? Part of the answer surely lies in the political and strategic genius of the civil rights movement's campaign of nonviolent civil disobedience. Organized and run largely through black churches, the most powerful independent institutions in the black South, the movement was able to enforce a remarkable level of discipline on its adherents. Its powerful ideology and charismatic leadership no doubt helped, too. That campaign resulted not only in concrete, immediate concessions, but (more importantly, I believe) in long-term sympathy from white Northern public opinion.

Of course, to produce that result, Southern whites had to respond with enough violence to alienate non-Southern public opinion, which they—perhaps I should say "we"—obligingly did. The interesting question is why they did not respond with crushing counterforce, as their ancestors had occasionally done in the Reconstruction and Jim Crow periods.

One answer is that non-Southern public opinion, shaped by television coverage of the movement and translated into political support, guaranteed that when Southern white opponents of the movement confronted armed resistance it came not from black militias or guerillas but from federal marshals, "federalized" National Guardsmen, or the United States Army. This may largely explain why violent resistance came from such a small minority of the opposition, compared to the violence that had worked ninety years earlier to end Republican rule. Few segregationists were willing (as those in the movement were willing) to risk their lives, their freedom, their jobs, or even their comfort on behalf of their views.

But that's not the whole story. Why did the violent minority not receive the unqualified and near-unanimous support from the white community that the equivalent, and much larger, minority did in the 1870s? The political importance of ambivalence, resignation, and indifference should not be underestimated. As one observer noted during Little Rock's troubles, 124,500 of the city's 125,000 citizens went about their business, then went home at night and watched the other 500 on television. What produced this balance?

An American Dilemma, and a Southern One

All I can do here is to speculate, but let us return to the strategic wisdom of the civil rights movement's leaders. It is clear, in retrospect at least, that their appeal to basic Christian and American values not only won support outside the South, it persuaded a few Southern whites and immobilized a good many others. Social psychologist Paul Sheatsley wrote in the mid-1960s that most white Americans knew "that racial discrimination is morally wrong and recognize the legitimacy of the Negro protest." "In their hearts," he concluded, "they know that the American Negro is right." It seems unlikely that most white Southerners knew anything of the sort, but enough did, and enough others suspected as much, that the facade of white racial unity was less solid than it had appeared.

A generation earlier, Gunnar Myrdal had written in *An American Dilemma* of the gross contradiction between the values embodied in America's founding documents and official creed and the nation's—especially the South's—treatment of its black citizens. This contradiction was not immediately self-evident to many Southern whites; they had persuaded themselves and each other— they sincerely believed—that black Southerners did not object to segregation, even that they preferred it. (Sheatsley reports, for example, that in 1963 only 35 percent of white Southerners believed that "most Negroes feel strongly about [the] right to send children to the same schools as whites.") The movement's activities made it much more difficult to see support for segregation as a matter of endorsing a polite biracial consensus; it became more clearly support for the naked imposition of inferior status on an unwilling people. Some Southern whites did not shrink from that view of what they were about, but others did.

In addition, and perhaps even more importantly for the South, the movement appealed explicitly to the shared Evangelical Protestant heritage of black and white Southerners. Cultural similarity is obviously not sufficient, and may not even be necessary, for harmony, but of the many similarities between black and white Southern cultures, this one proved especially important. When the civil rights movement's opponents tried to paint it as alien to American and Southern values—in particular, when they tried to tar it as Communist-inspired—they got no help from the movement itself, which was led by Protestant clergymen, its rhetoric filled with biblical imagery, its songs (without exception, as far as I know) gospel songs. If nothing else, by quoting Jefferson and Moses and asking only for what almost everyone understood to be the rights of American citizens and those made in the image of God the movement put its opponents at a distinct rhetorical disadvantage.

Competing Values and Conventional Attitudes

A second factor is that most white Southerners, though committed to white supremacy and racial segregation, were not committed *only* to white supremacy and segregation. For many, commitment to other values—to law and order, to the good repute of their communities, to economic development—competed for primacy. In particular, I believe, the movement benefited from an American value fully as widespread in the South as elsewhere, that of materialism. Economic development isn't everything, but it's closer to being everything in the South than anywhere else I know, and much of the region's economic growth in this century has been fueled by outside investment. Cities identified with racial strife like Little Rock in 1957, or Birmingham in 1963, demonstrably paid an economic price for that identification. Atlanta, which proudly billed itself as "the city too busy to hate," is only the best-known case of a city whose business elite determined to make whatever concessions were necessary to avoid racial "trouble" because it would be bad for business. Another is Charlotte, North Carolina, whose motto was once (I'm not making this up) "Charlotte: a good place to make money." You can't imagine the satisfaction many North Carolinians felt when Charlotte's school desegregation plan was held up as a model for Boston, Massachusetts.

For other Southern whites, fatalism may have had the same result as avarice. A common cultural value among both black and white Southerners, fatalism has been most common among rural, poorly educated, older people: in those sectors of the population who, if white, were most likely to oppose desegregation. Confronted with the prospect of change, many segregationists believed their cause was lost whatever they might do. They may not have been happy about what was going to happen, but did not believe they could prevent it.

Moreover, it is clear with hindsight that the segregationist attitudes of many white Southerners were merely conventional—that Thomas Pettigrew was right when he argued in 1959 that many were simply conforming to community norms, endorsing existing arrangements and institutions. The rapidity of the subsequent change suggests as much: if attitudes are deeply rooted, embedded in a supporting ideology or serving important psychological functions, change does not take place readily. To be sure, the destruction of an established and taken-for-granted social order is a disconcerting prospect, but it can be a relief simply to have matters settled. Once desegregation had taken place, its opponents were the ones who wanted change, and whatever contribution temperamental conservatism had made to the defense of segregation it now made to the defense of a new status quo.

It helped, of course, that desegregation was simply not as bad as many Southern whites had feared. That many had been genuinely frightened by the prospect—which meant an end, after all, to the South as they knew it—is indicated by the fact that the Supreme Court's 1954 school-desegregation decision apparently produced a measurable deflection in the white Southern birth rate. Given that, perhaps it is not surprising that many of the most vociferous opponents of desegregation withdrew in the wake of its accomplishment to private schools, private clubs, and the like—which, of course, allowed the process to proceed more smoothly. (In some communities that withdrawal has now proven to be temporary, although in others of course it appears to be more or less permanent.)

In any case, I believe that all of these factors contributed to the frequent finding in the survey data from the 1960s that those Southern whites who had actually experienced desegregation were the least likely to oppose it.

Are There Lessons for Others?

Without glossing over the very real problems of race relations that remain, I believe we must conclude that we have a higher class of problems than we used to. We can treat the recent Southern experience of relatively peaceful social change and racial adjustment as something of a success story. Can that experience be replicated? A number of factors came together in the American South in the 1960s, and unfortunately I don't see many examples of that happy concatenation elsewhere in the world—or in human history, for that matter. But let me try to avoid simply concluding with a variation on the tiresome theme of American exceptionalism—a conclusion that the American South was uniquely lucky—by listing a few of the factors that helped to produce the result I have been describing:

(1)   Important civic and religious values shared by the movement and its opponents, to which the movement could plausibly appeal to justify its activities.

(2)   Opponents who held values that could be brought into conflict with their opposition (perhaps especially bourgeois materialism: as Samuel Johnson said once, "A man is seldom so innocently engaged as when he is making money").

(3)   Aims that when realized proved to be less unpleasant for opponents than they expected.

(4)   "Safety-valves" that allowed the most determined opponents to avoid some of the consequences of its success.

(5)   A movement for social change with leadership that recognized the futility of violence (in this case: I wouldn't care to argue that violence is always futile).

(6)   An organization capable of enforcing discipline, keeping its members committed to nonviolence in the face of egregious provocation, while isolating and immobilizing potentially violent dissenters.

(7)   Potential outside allies for the movement who could deploy over-whelming deterrent force, without the movement's having to do so itself.

This last condition is particularly important, not only to prevent the escalation of violence in the course of the movement, but in its implications for whatever process of reconciliation takes place subsequently. But that's another paper.

WHAT MAKES GOOD LOSERS?

The conference in Ulster that evoked the previous paper was followed by a meeting in Philadelphia to talk about setting up a database for the comparative study of ethnic conflict. Marty Seligman asked me to talk some more about the Southern experience, so I took a closer look at a question I hadn't really addressed. (In the event, the database project didn't secure funding and died a natural death.)

• • •

Today I'm going to talk mostly about the American South—partly because I can't speak with any authority about much else, but also because I do believe that its history offers a particularly instructive case for an "ethnic conflict-conciliation database." At the conference in Ulster, my assignment was to discuss the question, "Why has there been no race war in the American South?" (See the essay above.) If you're skeptical about the premise, you're not alone. As I said in Londonderry, whether there has been one or not depends on what the meaning of "race war" is.

Nevertheless, there is something about the South's recent racial history that needs to be explained: In the 1960s there was an astonishing change in Southern race relations, brought about at surprisingly little cost, at least in comparative terms. That's what I talked about in Ireland. But the struggle for civil rights was unusual in another way that I only suggested: Even the apparent losers of the conflict now believe that the South is a better place.

Many other societies have undergone abrupt and dramatic transformations, but usually somebody (sometimes everybody) has thought the changes were

for the worse. But in the South today hardly anybody—nobody of any consequence—would like to undo the changes the civil rights movement produced.
That raises the general question I want to ruminate about today: Looking
at the subset of conflicts that end with more or less decisive victory for one
side, we can ask: When do the beaten stay beat? When do losers accept their
loss—and not just that, but come to see their defeat as a good thing, perhaps
not even a defeat at all? Here's where the South is an interesting case, because
this has happened to white Southerners twice: in the 1960s at the hands of the
civil rights movement and its allies, and a century earlier at the hands of the
Union army.

That earlier loss came at a much greater cost in blood, and it took the losers
longer to get over it, but eventually the outcome was similar. Thirty-some years
after Appomattox, white Southerners were flying American and Confederate
flags side by side, and former Confederates were wearing Yankee blue in Cuba
and the Philippines. By 1900 the United States—by then, as Shelby Foote
pointed out, a singular phrase—the United States was well along the road to re-
union (to steal the title of Paul Herman Buck's book on this subject). Secession
was the "Lost Cause," and it has stayed lost. Survey research these days shows
white Southern support for an independent South in the single digits—not
much higher than the expected percentage who misunderstand the question.
Ernest Renan once remarked that the existence of a nation requires that a
great many things be forgotten. Well, "old times there" may not be altogether
forgotten, but they're certainly not a politically significant grievance, not a
festering sore.

Leadership can play an important role in shaping the outcome of conflicts,
and in each of these two cases the winners' cause was personified by a single
charismatic leader whose actions and rhetoric made reconciliation much
more likely. Abraham Lincoln and Martin Luther King both had their share
of rivals and detractors—neither was as secure in his leadership as we like to
think in retrospect—but each had the vision and the political skills that he
needed to keep the possibility of reconciliation alive. Two things they had in
common strike me as particularly important here.

In the first place, both Lincoln and King often spoke of reconciliation—
and not just as the aftermath of victory, but as part of the victory itself. You'll
remember, from Lincoln's Second Inaugural: "With malice toward none, with
charity for all, . . . let us strive on to finish the work we are in, to bind up the

nation's wounds." And this, from Dr. King: "The aftermath of nonviolence is reconciliation and the creation of the beloved community." Whether words like these reassured their enemies is hard to say, but certainly other words could have been spoken that would have made reconciliation much more difficult.

In the second place, both the Union cause and the civil rights movement had well-defined and limited goals. When they won, the settlements imposed on the losers were largely limited to the accomplishment of those aims. Lincoln famously remarked that the North was fighting to preserve the Union—that and that alone. Of course, most Confederates didn't believe him. They thought all along that emancipation was part of the deal (and for some Northern politicians it was), but it became official policy only after a year and a half of successful Confederate resistance, and even then it was presented as a war measure— a means to victory, not an end. And even emancipation was a limited and clear-cut goal. The government in Washington did not seek the perpetual subordination of the white South, much less its extirpation. After Appomattox, full civil rights were restored to ex-Confederates willing to swear allegiance. There were no mass executions or deportations. To my knowledge the only Confederates tried and punished were the civilian conspirators in Lincoln's assassination and the hapless commandant of Andersonville Prison, Captain Henry Wirz. Jefferson Davis was imprisoned, but never brought to trial; after his release he spent the rest of his long life writing vindications of the Lost Cause.

To be sure, abolition meant a significant loss of wealth for the minority of white Southerners who were slaveholders, but economically it was of a piece with the wartime destruction of railroads, factories, housing, and livestock. Beyond that the federal government never intended or delivered any serious redistribution of property—not even to the modest extent of "forty acres and a mule" for freedmen. Nor did Washington effectively intervene after the war to protect the civil rights of the freedmen. The government tried for a while, but gave up in the face of determined white opposition and the need for national unity. (I mention this lest we think that reconciliation is always an unmixed blessing.)

A century later, the civil rights movement returned to some of that unfinished business. Here again we see a cause with significant objectives, but limited and well-defined ones: in this case, voting rights and an end to de jure segregation. Southern blacks' grievances had a clear solution. The Civil Rights Act of 1964 and the Voting Rights Act of 1965 gave the movement its victory, and what was left was largely a mopping-up operation. Attempts to expand the movement's objectives to address larger, more amorphous, and less regionally concentrated problems of economic justice and foreign policy were not notably successful, and once again, as in the 1870s, Southern whites discovered that the new regime was not as bad as they had feared it would be; indeed, that it even had its good points.

In these two examples reconciliation was largely a function of the winners' behavior, during and after the conflict—thus the importance of understanding the victors' leaders. But reconciliation in these cases, and no doubt in general, also depends on a variety of circumstances that aren't under the winners' control. Let me mention three of them that these examples highlight. First, why the losers were fighting—the actual motivations of combatants, which may not be the same thing as the stated political ends of the conflict. Second, how the losers understand their loss—in particular, who or what is blamed for it. And, third, the behavior and rhetoric of the losers' leaders.

Why people fight often seems obvious, because they'll tell us. Confederates were fighting to preserve their slave society and their rights as freeborn Americans. They were less squeamish about that first reason than some of their descendants are today. The opponents of the civil rights movement were fighting to preserve segregation and white supremacy, and again, they weren't embarrassed to say so. But it can be a mistake to take these statements at face value. There may be cultural explanations for conflict at levels that individuals aren't even aware of.

Consider a proposition advanced in 1961 by Leslie Dunbar, who was then the executive director of the Southern Regional Council, the South's oldest biracial civil rights organization. Dunbar predicted that there would be resistance to desegregation—sometimes violent resistance. But, he added, "Once the fight is decisively lost (the verdict has to be decisive) . . . the typical white Southerner will shrug his shoulders, resume his stride, and go on. He has, after all, shared a land with his black neighbors for a long while; he can manage well enough even if the patterns change. There is now one fewer fight which history requires of him. He has done his ancestral duty. He . . . can relax a bit more."

Note that word *duty*. Dunbar knew that many of his fellow white Southerners wouldn't give up segregation without a fight, because they felt a duty to defend their society, their people, and their history. But having fought, and lost ("the verdict has to be decisive"), duty would have been served. I suspect Dunbar was as correct in his analysis as in his prediction. More than that, I suspect that many nonslaveholding whites fought for the Confederacy for the same reason, as do many of those who defend the Confederate flag today. I'm reminded of a remark by a high school principal in East Tennessee, talking about why boys in his school fight, when challenged: "Now [a boy] may lose, and that's no disgrace. But if he will not fight, that is a disgrace." It's a matter of honor. Bertram Wyatt-Brown and Edward Ayers are only two of the several historians who have written recently about how that concept plays out in the South, and Richard Nisbett, a psychologist, has written about it, too.

What does this have to do with reconciliation? Well, if losing is no disgrace, it doesn't have to be avenged. Losing may be painful, but sometimes the pain can be offset by "the satisfaction that proceeds from the consciousness of duty faithfully performed." (Those are the words of Robert E. Lee, in his farewell address to the Army of Northern Virginia after Appomattox.) But, as Dunbar said, the verdict has to be decisive. Under this ethic, the only excuse for not continuing to fight is that you are decisively whipped. And almost a necessary condition for the sort of acceptance I'm discussing here is attributing your loss to your opponents' strength, not your own unmanly weakness—and not traitors, dissident minorities, or stabs in the back, either. As I argued in Ulster, it mattered a great deal that when push came to shove the opponents of desegregation were facing federalized National Guardsmen or the United States Army. Just so, in 1864 Generals Grant and Sherman simply crushed the Confederacy with overwhelming force. Succumbing to overwhelming force, after what can be construed as valiant resistance, is no disgrace.

There's a variation on this sort of explanation for loss that seems to me even more likely to lead to reconciliation. It's rare, but we can see glimmerings of it in these two Southern cases. In the 1870s and again in the 1970s at least some white Southerners concluded that God had been on the other side: not just in Napoleon's sense that He's on the side of the big battalions, but that defeat had been God's will. And here we return to the importance of leadership—in this case, the leaders of the losers—the old leaders, if they're still around, or whatever new ones emerge. (Here, as always, leaders are constrained by circumstances, including what their followers will hear, but let's assume that they usually have at least some latitude.) Leaders formulate and propagate explanations for the loss, they set examples of how to respond to defeat, and sometimes they still have enough power to determine how others respond.

The historian Eugene Genovese, in a book called *A Consuming Fire: The Fall of the Confederacy in the Mind of the White Christian South*, shows that at least some prominent Southerners concluded that the Confederacy's defeat was divine punishment for the South's collective sins. Not that the institution of slavery was wrong (that acknowledgment would take another generation or two), but that *Southern* slavery was wrong—wrong in not legally recognizing slave marriages, wrong in denying slaves the literacy needed to read God's word, and so forth. Most of the people Genovese quotes are clergymen, and many of them had urged these reforms before the war, so their analysis could be paraphrased as: Southerners were wrong not to have done what their clergymen told them to do. But I think there's more to it than that. For a truly devout people, as most Southerners were and many still are, the hand of the Lord can be seen in history, although, to be sure, He often works in mysterious ways.

For most white Southerners, though, I suspect a less theological message from a different sort of leader made a bigger difference. It was very important at the end of the war that Robert E. Lee, the most respected figure in the Confederacy, rejected the call of many prominent Confederates—including Jefferson Davis, his president—to fight on with guerrilla warfare in the Southern mountains and disbanded the Army of Northern Virginia at Appomattox. Lee retired to private life and worked for sectional reconciliation even in the face of what he saw privately as the provocation and bad faith of Congressional Reconstruction. Again and again he reminded his countrymen of, in his words, "the duty of every one to unite in the restoration of the country and the reestablishment of peace and harmony." We can't ignore the violent resistance to black and carpetbag rule in the period before 1878, but it would have been far worse without Lee's stoic example. This is what made him—rightly, I think—an American hero, for a century or more.

Something similar happened on a smaller and cheesier scale after 1965. Some leaders of the white supremacist cause even apologized—notably George Wallace, who won reelection to the Alabama governorship in the 1970s with a third of the black vote. Other old-timers just adjusted, like Strom Thurmond, who quickly appointed African Americans to his staff and started sponsoring bills to establish National Black Colleges Week. More important was the emergence of a new crop of Southern politicians. In 1971, *Time* magazine devoted a cover story to a half-dozen white "New South" governors who took office that year, elected in part by newly enfranchised black voters and speaking a very different language from their predecessors. One of those governors was Jimmy Carter: however much of a dud he proved to be as president, his election and his appeal to black voters were important symbols of regional and racial reconciliation.

Say what you will about white Southerners, as losers go, we seem to be good ones. Of course, we've had a lot of practice.

Let me close with a story about a Confederate soldier that bears on the question of maintaining one's honor by losing to superior force. When this fellow went off to war in 1861, he told his family not to worry: "We can whip them Yankees with cornstalks." After Appomattox he stumbled home, beaten, bedraggled, but head held high. Someone asked, "Thought you said we could beat 'em with cornstalks—What happened?"

He said, "Damn Yankees wouldn't fight with cornstalks."

SIX SOUTHERNERS

These are appreciations of six talented Southerners. Five of them are, or were in their lifetimes, my friends (the other is Shelby Foote), but I'd have said good things about them even if they were strangers.

CLEAR-EYED SOUTHERN BOY

This review for Chronicles *magazine, written in 1985, refers to Ed Yoder as "undeniably some sort of conservative." Ed denies it, but I stand by that characterization, qualified by "some sort." I meant it as a compliment. (You may notice that in this book I'm ignoring my advice to Ed about presenting collected material in chronological order. So sue me.)*

• • •

The Night of the Old South Ball: And Other Essays and Fables is a collection of essays and columns by the estimable journalist Edwin M. Yoder Jr. They cover a wide range of topics, among them Sherlock Holmes, *I'll Take My Stand*, the King James Bible, and Flannery O'Connor. A good many have to do with the South, one way or another, and Yoder confesses that he likes the South, with all its faults, better than the Sunbelt, with whatever its virtue may be. He suspects, deep down, that the South is gone, or going, and certainly the settled, small-town South that he and I grew up with seems to be doomed. In an essay on W. J. Cash, though, Yoder has some smart things to say about the role of intellectuals (most certainly including journalists like Cash—and himself) in keeping ideas like that of the South alive and breathing.

For the most part, Yoder's tastes are utterly sound, and the few I don't share (a devotion to Henry James, for instance) I'm compelled to respect. He is a fair but generous critic; I've been the beneficiary, notably in a foreword to one of my books. And he is a gentle man, like John Stuart Mill, whom he celebrates in one of these essays, always ready to try to see the point of those with whom he disagrees. (If this were all there were to liberalism, how much more attractive that ideology would be.) This style, evident throughout this collection, makes it all the more effective when Yoder rounds on something or someone: it must have been egregiously awful to have provoked him. His dislikes are as well-chosen and well-expressed as his enthusiasms: I'm surprised that Tom Wicker isn't ashamed to show his face in public.

That these essays are not in chronological order is unfortunate on two counts. In the first place, it is disconcerting to read, for instance, why Yoder finds the outgoing Carter administration disappointing and then to read of his high hopes for the incoming Carter administration. More importantly, one reason for a collection like this is to allow a reader to get acquainted with the writer's mind, and no one—certainly not Yoder—has the same "mind" for twenty years. Or, more precisely, the same mind in different contexts can look quite different.

The early pieces here display a mid-sixties Southern liberalism, probably pretty much the outlook that guided Yoder when he wrote for the *Daily Tar Heel* at the University of North Carolina, an outlook well-represented at that institution since the days of Howard Odum and Frank Porter Graham: at worst, naive; at best, large-souled, optimistic, and, withal, very Southern. But America has changed since then, and so have Yoder's circumstances. He's no longer the boy-journalist crusading against bigotry and ignorance. Now he lives just across the Potomac from the Great Wen, and consorts up close on occasion with the mighty. Lately, Yoder seems to be becoming something of an American version of a Tory "wet": skeptical about ideologues, whether of the Right or Left, but undeniably some sort of conservative. He hasn't changed all that much, though: many Southern liberals of the fifties and sixties look equally conservative by latter-day standards. It's almost a question of taste.

A MAN OF LETTERS

I can't recall why I was asked to introduce Shelby Foote when he spoke at Lenoir-Rhyne University in 1999, but I do remember that I jumped at the chance.

. . .

Shelby Foote was born in 1916 in Greenville, Mississippi, in the Delta country south of Memphis that historian James Cobb has called "the most Southern place on earth." Greenville was and may still be the most cosmopolitan part of the Delta—indeed, in Foote's youth, it was cosmopolitan for a town of its size anywhere. The fecund soil of the Delta nurtured not just cotton but writers and observers like Will and Walker Percy, David Cohn, Hodding Carter Jr. . . . and Shelby Foote.

Foote and his friend Walker Percy went to the University of North Carolina in the 1930s. In Chapel Hill the playwright Paul Green was teaching in the English department, Howard Odum and his colleagues in sociology were documenting the South's many problems, Fletcher Green and J. G. de Roulhac Hamilton were renowned historians of the region, and W. T. Couch was creating a major university press. I would like to believe that UNC shaped Mr. Foote in important ways, that it made him a different and better person than Ole Miss or Tulane or Princeton would have. I don't know if this is actually true, but we at Carolina have certainly been proud of the connection, which continues: our Southern Historical Collection now houses his papers.

After leaving Chapel Hill, Mr. Foote pursued three overlapping and reinforcing careers, any one of which would have done credit to an ordinary mortal. He has been a novelist, a historian, and a public figure—what might be called a celebrity-pundit. Throughout he has been a "man of letters" (the old term for it). In 1949, at the age of thirty-three, he published his first novel, *Tournament.* It was followed by four more in the next five years: *Follow Me Down* in 1950, *Love in a Dry Season* in 1951, *Shiloh* in 1952, and (in 1953 he rested) *Jordan County* in 1954. Five fine books would make a pretty good career, but there would be a sixth, *September*—published in 1977, after a second career intervened.

Editors at Random House noticed that this young novelist's portrayal of the Civil War was realistic, accurate, and detailed, that it was good history, but also gripping narrative that showed a novelist's ability to enter into the minds of those on both sides. With 1961 fast approaching, they asked him to write a short history of the war to mark its centennial. Twenty years, three volumes, and three thousand pages later, he finished *The Civil War: A Narrative.*

Walker Percy got it right when he hailed *The Civil War* as "an unparalleled achievement, an American *Iliad.*" It brought as much order as can be brought to the story of a conflict with more than 10,000 separate military actions, including "76 full-scale battles, 310 engagements, 6337 skirmishes, and numerous sieges, raids, expeditions, and the like" (Foote's book provides these numbers), while offering unforgettable details like the fact that one-fifth of Mississippi's state budget in the first year of peace went for artificial limbs. It remains the one history of the Civil War to read if you're only reading one.

Foote's fiction alone or his history alone would be enough to account for the esteem in which he is held by readers and by his peers. Together, they make him virtually unique in our era. It is no wonder that he has been invited to visiting lectureships at several universities, received innumerable awards and honorary degrees, been honored with membership in the Fellowship of Southern Writers, and selected as a Guggenheim Fellow (three times!).

But I haven't mentioned yet his third career, which began about 1991, when Ken Burns's documentary series on the Civil War was shown on PBS. Foote was an obvious choice for a consultant, and he turned out to be a marvelous on-camera commentator. I was in California that year, in Palo Alto, and my friends there complained that the Burns series was pro-Confederate, or at least (as they put it) that "the South got all the good lines." Many of those lines came from the memorable and charismatic chap with a goatee and a wonderful Mississippi drawl, whose charm and wit were such, I'm told, that he received a number of marriage proposals. The Confederacy may have lost the war, but it seems to have won the documentary, and that was largely the doing of Shelby Foote.

Daniel Boorstin said once that a celebrity is someone who is well-known for being well-known, but Mr. Foote's celebrity is not that kind of celebrity. It is gratifying to see someone become famous because he *deserves* to be famous, someone whose fame is based on solid accomplishment over several decades. This is the kind of fame that inspires not envy but humility and admiration and a sense that maybe there is some justice in this world, after all.

By the way, Mr. Foote has not put literature behind him: I note incidentally that he has recently edited three volumes of Chekhov short stories for the Modern Library. If Oprah can sell Charles Dickens, maybe Shelby Foote can sell Chekhov.

TWO ALABAMIANS

This is the foreword to Common Threads, *a collection of Chip Cooper's photographs and Kathryn Tucker Windham's stories. Chip has now moved up from photographer for the Crimson Tide to artist-in-residence in the University of Alabama's honors college (although at Alabama perhaps "moving up" is not exactly the phrase for a transition from the football program to the honors college). Kathryn died, full of years and full of honors, in 2011.*

• • •

Southerners will fool you sometimes. When my wife, Dale, and I visited Alabama a while back, Chip Cooper met us at the Birmingham airport. To look at this big, exuberant, long-haired guy in his shorts and baseball cap, you wouldn't be at all surprised to learn that his day job is taking pictures of athletes and boosters for the University of Alabama Crimson Tide. But you probably wouldn't guess that his evocative photographs of the Deep South's natural and built landscape have been collected in two stunning books and appeared in juried shows from Montgomery to Paris (the one in France), or that he is a student of his art who can talk casually and knowledgeably about painters and other photographers, if you ask him to. As I said, he'll fool you.

Chip loaded us into his monster SUV and we sailed off down the interstate, through a sort of parody of the latest New South, stopping for lunch at a franchise Italian restaurant in a shopping center, past piney woods and rampant kudzu, into Selma, where we pulled up beside Kathryn Tucker Windham's modest one-story house. Mrs. Windham, a cheerful woman in her eighties, greeted us, served us juice and cookies, and did a fine job of being the garden-club lady that, among other things, she is.

She'll fool you, too. This is a woman who, some fifty years ago, straight out of journalism school, became the first female police reporter for the *Alabama Journal*. She wrote many of the books that fill her house—cookbooks, history books, memoirs, ghost stories, a book of her photographs, a score or so altogether—before undertaking yet another career as an award-winning storyteller. Along the way she somehow found time to diversify National Public Radio with her luscious accent and sunny disposition. She has a garden, to be sure, but it includes a couple of trees with blue bottles on their branches to ward off evil spirits. And she shares her house with a ghost named Jeffrey.

Alabama seems to specialize in producing spunky, independent women—Tallulah Bankhead comes to mind, or Virginia Durr, or the reformer Julia Tutwiler (about whom Kathryn has written and performed a one-woman show). After we'd spent some time with Kathryn touring Selma, with special attention to its cemetery and historic buildings, listening to her stories about dying Confederates and silver hidden from the Yankees, it wasn't surprising to find that Selma's splendid new public library has a room named in her honor. What was surprising was that they hadn't named the whole building for her.

Kathryn Tucker Windham and Chip Cooper might seem at first to be unlikely friends. One is a lady from the Black Belt, the other a boy from the hill country. One was a child in the 1920s, the other in the 1950s. And of course one is best known as a writer, the other as a photographer. But these differences are superficial. Where it really counts, these two Alabamians have a lot in common. For starters, both wear their considerable learning and accomplishment lightly, in the Southern manner. And both the writer and the photographer tell great stories, paint great pictures—one with her words, one with his camera. Their stories and pictures reflect a shared attachment to their native land: its people, its buildings, its trees and flowers. You can see some of them in their book.

Most of Kathryn's stories are charming recollections of the small-town South between the world wars, as seen through the eyes of a happy child. They're full of the colorful and eccentric characters that Southerners tend to take for granted, and there's even the dead mule that Professor Jerry Leith Mills says all Southern books must have. Of course this South had great and terrible problems, and many memoirs have established that not all the children were happy, but it's good to be reminded that, day to day, fathers took their daughters swimming, policemen rounded up stray cows, teenagers flirted at the post office, and little girls had tea parties for their dolls.

If Kathryn is remembering an older South, Chip documents its lingering presence. His photographs of spider lilies and flowering trees, of churches and cemeteries and front porches, remind us that once you get off the interstate highways much of the physical South of Kathryn's childhood can still be found. No one I know captures the natural beauty of the South better than Chip, but I like even better his photographs of things that men and women have built—houses, stores, automobiles, machinery. These have a beauty of their own, even though (maybe even because), like Kathryn's dead mule, they have begun to decay.

Not one of Chip's photographs in this book includes people, but scarcely an image is without the ghostly presence of someone's hand. Who drove that car? Drank in that juke joint? Mourned at that grave? Even the nature photographs are haunted by human agency: fields have been plowed, forests have been cut, flowers were once planted. For me, at least, nearly all of his pictures, like Kathryn's vignettes, provoke sweet-sad reflection about the generations who've gone before us.

Neither Kathryn nor Chip falls into cheap nostalgia, but there is an unmistakably elegiac quality to the words and images in this book. And that's something they have in common not just with each other but with many other Southerners. Like most of us these days, Chip and Kathryn live and work in a South of shopping malls, mobile homes, and Mercedes plants, and neither, I presume, really regrets it. But they know another South, one that still flourishes in Kathryn's memories and her stories, and has left its fossils, its souvenirs, lying about for Chip to photograph.

A GOOD THING FROM AUBURN

When Wayne Flynt retired from Auburn's history department in 2005, some of his former students organized a Festschrift, published the next year as History and Hope in the Heart of Dixie. *I was happy to explain in this foreword why Wayne deserved such a tribute.*

• • •

In his book *The Last Intellectuals,* Russell Jacoby lamented what he saw as the disappearance of the sort of old-fashioned intellectuals "who write with vigor and clarity . . . for the general reader." He argued that such folks have become "as scarce as low rents in New York or San Francisco," replaced by "high-tech intellectuals, consultants and professors—anonymous souls, who may be competent, and more than competent, but who do not enrich public life." One certainly sees his point, but one also sees (at least I do) that he wasn't looking very hard.

Jacoby should get out more, to places like Auburn University, where the history department has been home to a distinguished public intellectual who has certainly enriched public life in Alabama. Jacoby's argument, important and provocative as it is, suffers from what might be called Manhattan myopia. For him and for many other New Yorkers, intellectuals write for "little magazines," not the *Mobile Register* and *Alabama Heritage;* they hold forth in Greenwich Village coffeehouses or at the 92nd Street Y, not before the Dothan Rotary Club. These Yankees might well paraphrase Nathanael's question about Nazareth

(John 1:46): "Can any good thing come from Auburn?" To which the answer, of course, is "Sure—and one of them is Wayne Flynt."

Not that Flynt's influence and reputation have been restricted to his home state. He has spoken at innumerable American colleges and universities, addressed learned symposia in places like Cambridge and Prague and Vienna, and even taken his tales of the American South to audiences in India and the Far East. He has been honored by his peers, notably with the presidency of the Southern Historical Association. But few academics of his distinction have been as willing, or able, to engage the citizens of their homeplace on important issues of the day. Not just in his scholarship but in his public life Flynt has followed the advice of another great Alabamian, Booker T. Washington, and cast down his bucket where he is, with remarkable results. He has been tirelessly active, addressing the meetings and sitting on the boards of groups with names like the Campaign for Alabama, the Alabama Poverty Project, Voices for Alabama's Children, the American Cancer Society's Committee for the Socioeconomically Disadvantaged, and Alabama Citizens for Constitutional Reform.

No doubt he is greatly in demand as a speaker in part because he has that "command of the vernacular" that Jacoby believes most American intellectuals have lost. Listen to him tell an interviewer about the pleasures of creek fishing: "The formula is simple: Find a small Appalachian river or creek. Seine your own bait. Walk in the creek if possible. If not, use a canoe. Never fish a lake. Never ride in a boat with a motor." Even someone who prefers high-tech bass fishing with electronic fish-finders, or who doesn't fish at all, can savor those words. The same gift accounts for the fact that apparently every American newspaper you've ever heard of, and a good many you haven't, have called him for comment on various issues. He usually obliges with something pithy and true. (As one newspaperman I know would put it, he "gives good quote.") When Alabama repealed its antimiscegenation law, for instance, he told *USA Today* simply, "A lot of white folks want to turn the page."

But Flynt has a well-deserved reputation not just for plain speech but for hard truths. As an Auburn alumni newsletter put it, "If you want an after-dinner speaker who'll lull you into sweet dreams of the Old South, don't invite Auburn University Historian Wayne Flynt." Flynt plainly loves his state and its citizens, but often with the wry realism of Zora Neale Hurston, who once wrote with exasperation, "My people, my people. . . ." It speaks well for Alabama that the invitations to address civic clubs, public libraries, and community forums keep pouring in.

More than invitations, in fact. Flynt's career seems to contradict what Jesus had to say (Mark 6:4) about prophets' being without honor in their own country. His CV is littered with prizes and awards from his fellow Alabamians: from the Alabama Library Association, the Alabama Historical Association, the University of Alabama Press, the Children's Hospital of Alabama, the Alabama Arthritis Foundation—the list goes on. The *Mobile Register* named him Alabamian of the Year in 1992, and (perhaps the best indicator of the respect he commands) he was chosen by the governor and the presiding judge for the thankless job of official "facilitator" in an interminable lawsuit over equity in the funding of public schools.

Finally, Flynt must be nearly unique among academic advocates of reform in his willingness to put his money where his mouth is. He endowed the Mae Ellis Moore Flynt Teaching Excellence Award of the Alabama Association of Historians, for instance, to reward outstanding K–12 history teachers like his mother. He has also come up with at least one radical, commonsense proposal of the sort that I identify with another maverick Baptist, Will Campbell. When Alabama Baptist churches helped to defeat a state lottery in support of education, Flynt called on them to give up their tax exemptions to support local schools—and his own church, Auburn First Baptist, did just that. "I got tired of all the pious talking and no acting," he said. "Ours is a traditional, mainline Baptist church with money problems like most Baptist churches. I figured if we can do it, anybody can do it."

In 2000, Samford University, his alma mater, gave Flynt an honorary Doctor of Humane Letters degree (along with Wendell Berry, another prophetic voice from the South). The citation described him as "a teacher, scholar and writer whose high-wattage light has beamed into the darkness surrounding issues of poverty, race, education and state government." Certainly he has brightened the corner where he is.

Which raises some interesting questions. How can someone, these days, be such a successful public intellectual in Alabama (I won't say "of all places")? Why does an accomplished historian and professor devote so much time and energy to the unrewarding grind of trying to reform his home state? And— perhaps even more of a puzzle—why do so many Alabamians not just listen to him, but apparently *want* to listen to him?

In part, this may be a regional thing. Jacoby is right that this sort of engagement is rare these days, but it may be less rare in the South than in other parts of the United States. In his classic study of American race relations, *An American Dilemma,* Gunnar Myrdal wrote that the Southern social scientists of his time compared favorably to their Northern colleagues precisely in that "statesmanship enters more naturally into [their] writings" and "the significance for human happiness of the problems under study is always a present thought in the South." Just so, listen to Flynt sixty-odd years later, on what Auburn University should be: "I don't want Auburn to be the Berkeley of the South; I want Auburn to be the Auburn of the South. I want it to find out what it can do to make a difference in the lives of the people of this state; stop worrying about being something we can't be and that most Alabamians don't want us to be; begin to define who we are and what our mission ought to be from the perspective of serving the population of this state." This is not a popular view among faculty members at state universities these days, but it may get more respect in the South than elsewhere.

There's another reason, though, and a more important one, for Flynt's speaking out, and for his receiving a hearing. John Andrew Rice, founder and first rector of North Carolina's Black Mountain College (also, I should note, nephew of both a South Carolina Methodist bishop and Senator Ellison D. "Cotton Ed" Smith, an evangelist of a different stripe) once observed that "If you scratch a Southern teacher, a preacher will wince." In Flynt's case, of course, this is quite literally true. And I think an important component of his visibility and influence is that his social thought comes not from Karl Marx or the *Nation* magazine but straight from the Sermon on the Mount. When he rebuked Alabama politicians for not addressing the state's high child-poverty rate, for example, he reminded them of what Jesus said about "the least of these" (Matthew 25:45). When an interviewer asked him about Alabama's problems, his immediate response was that "Christian love and a sense of justice demand that we remember where we come from and not forget the people we leave behind." (Characteristically, he preached to the unconverted as well, adding, "If we have no sense of Christian charity and no sense of justice, then we sure better do something out of a sense of our own self-interest.")

This sort of rhetoric is not uncommon in Alabama. When Governor Bob Riley—a Republican, but also a longtime Sunday school teacher in Ashland's First Baptist Church—claimed that "it is immoral to charge somebody making

$5,000 an income tax" and argued for tax reform by saying, "We're supposed to love God, love each other and help take care of the poor," the Associated Press, mystified, called Flynt for comment. He explained patiently that Governor Riley was "locating the debate in the Bible and biblical justice to the poor," and stopped just short of saying, "It's a Southern thing; you wouldn't understand."

But Flynt understands, and so do most of his fellow Alabamians. He gets a hearing in Alabama because Alabamians are used to being exhorted by preachers, and usually listen politely. A cynic might say that they're also used to ignoring those exhortations. But at some level maybe they feel a little guilty about that, and recognize that they are the better for it

"SOUTHERN CONSERVATISM"
The View from Brooklyn

In 2011 the James Madison Program at Princeton held a conference on the work of Eugene Genovese, and I got to comment on a few of the many provocative things my Sicilian American friend had said about the American South. Ill-health kept Gene from attending the conference, and he died the next year. (The first part of what I said is adapted from an essay in my book Minding the South.)

• • •

For many years Gene Genovese has been not only the foremost living historian of the Old South's slave society (and maybe the "living" isn't needed) but also an exemplary public intellectual, bringing his formidable intelligence and analytic skills to bear on issues of the day in a variety of forums. What he has to say on almost any subject is worth hearing, not because he has always been right, as he would be the first to acknowledge, but because what he says is in-variably *interesting,* and because he says it so well. That's certainly true of what he has had to say about the species of conservative thought that he called, in his Massey Lectures at Harvard, "the Southern tradition."

Consider Gene's collection of essays and reviews, *The Southern Front,* pub-lished in 1995. Early in the book he presents three biographical reflections on what he calls "Representative Carolinians." (That's an uncharacteristic inaccuracy, by the way. Would that James Johnson Pettigrew and James Henley Thornwell had been "representative.") Two of these pieces began as admiring reviews of books I have read, and they are good books, but I can honestly say that the reviews make even better reading. Taken together, these three essays exemplify a number of features that mark the entire book, and indeed much of Gene's incidental and occasional writing of the last few decades: admiration for what he sees as worthy and unjustly neglected aspects of Southern thought; impatience with cant (especially politically correct cant); generous sympathy with men and women of integrity, intellect, and courage committed to lost (even rightly lost) causes; learning, tough-mindedness, and wit.

If the collection has a central theme, it has to do with Gene's alarm at the excesses of unchecked individualism, and his search for a corrective. He once found that in Marxism, and perhaps still does, with some major, rueful reservations; but he argues that similar themes can be found in a strain of Southern conservative thought that originated in the defense of slavery and flowed into the last century through the Vanderbilt Agrarians and Richard Weaver to Mel Bradford and other, lesser lights. (And incidentally, he pays the authors of *I'll Take My Stand* the courtesy of taking them seriously as doing what they thought they were doing—unlike my otherwise estimable colleague Louis Rubin, who tried to defang them by making their "South" some sort of trope.)

Obviously those of us who share Gene's views at least in some respects will take the most satisfaction from seeing them so well argued. But even those who disagree with his prescription, or who don't see the problem to begin with, would profit from reading these pieces. They will find, in the first place, simply a wealth of little-known *fact*. It's good to learn about Pettigrew and Thornwell and Mel Bradford and Eugene Rivers—all fascinating men, who should be better known than they are. But it's as great a pleasure to learn more about Gene Genovese, who is at least as interesting as the people he writes about. Reading him is like traveling with an amusing and perceptive companion. There's something gallant about his defense of unfashionable scholars he believes have been ignored or treated shabbily by the academy, and he has a remarkable talent for unearthing such folk and celebrating their contributions (thereby, excuse the expression, expanding the canon). There can't be many others who have read the major works of both the Stalinist historian Herbert Aptheker and the (Pat) Buchananite journalist Sam Francis—and Gene is probably unique in admiring both of them.

When I first read his essays on the religion of Southerners I found it ironic that a professed atheist should have a more penetrating understanding of Christian theology and the life of faith than most seminary professors of my acquaintance—but that irony has since been resolved, with Gene's return to the faith of his fathers. Somewhere he has said explicitly that entering into the minds of his antebellum subjects led him to take religion seriously, and he may have picked up his splendid manners the same way. Long before it became fashionable, he was calling for civil discourse, with all points of view freely expressed and evaluated on their intellectual merits. Again and again, he has illustrated how courteous and principled disagreement is expressed, and has disarmingly sought (and often found) common ground with many who would be only too glad to treat him as an adversary. He's not all sweetness and light, though. Did you know that a switchblade knife is also called a *stiletto siciliano*? Gene wields a deft one—and when he smells cowardice or bad faith, he can take up another traditional Italian weapon, the truncheon, as he does in the epilogue to *The Southern Front,* where he assails some of his fellow leftists, less for their complicity in the crimes of Stalinism than for their lack of candor about it.

But to return to his affectionate treatment of "the Southern tradition" (by which he means—I'll only say this once—*a* Southern tradition, and a white one). I recently dug up a letter I wrote to him, after looking at an early draft of his book with that title. It was almost fulsome, but I was younger then. My one criticism was that he didn't give enough attention to what is basically an empirical question, to wit, are his "Southern conservatives" anything other than scattered and ineffectual fossils? It was phrased as a question, but in fact I was pretty sure I knew the answer.

The problem is that Gene wasn't talking about Southern conservatives as most of the world understands that phrase. There are a great many of those, self-defined, but Gene's Southern Conservative (I'll capitalize the C for his variety) is not a generalization from these specimens but an ideal, and one to which only a very few individuals are more or less in approximation. As John Donald Wade's contribution to *I'll Take My Stand* concludes, "Fo' God, I believe Mas' Lucius done dead!" Yes—Mas' Lucius, Richard Weaver, Mel Bradford, and nearly all of their ilk.

I thought Gene didn't say enough about this, but when I looked at the book again the other day, I found that he actually did, so maybe he paid some attention to what I wrote. Anyway, it's there, and it should be, at least in *Gene's* book, because he very much wants this variety of conservative thought to be a political as well as an intellectual force to be reckoned with. He explicitly acknowledges that Southern Conservatives are a tiny minority and can only exercise influence in coalition with others. Writing in the mid-1990s, he mentioned three possibilities.

First, he observed that Pat Buchanan's 1992 presidential campaign had brought together traditionalists and "free-market libertarians." He found this hopeful, but in truth there were probably even fewer Buchananite libertarians than Southern Conservatives. The mainstream of libertarianism (if there is such a thing—anyway, the Cato Institute and readers of *Reason* magazine) had little to no sympathy with Buchanan. Gene was no doubt thinking of the libertarian component of the John Randolph Society—Murray Rothbard and some of his disciples—not an imposing force even at the time. No, forget libertarians; there aren't enough of them to begin with, and there are even fewer who can overlook their many disagreements with traditionalists

Another possibility Gene suggested was an alliance with socially and culturally conservative black quasi-nationalists like his friend the Reverend Eugene Rivers. He pointed out the manifest similarities between the political thought of Lani Guinier and that of John C. Calhoun. But that proposed coalition seems to have excited almost no one other than Gene and (for the record) me. It certainly seemed to be a non-starter with black folks, who are understandably suspicious of conservative white Southerners of any stripe—and all too many of the latter didn't like the sound of it either. That last may not have surprised Gene: he was pretty clear-sighted about the racism that is the perennial serpent in the bosom of Southern nationalism.

Finally, Gene expressed hopes for some sort of cooperation between Southern Conservatives and the Religious Right. But the idea that a handful of intellectuals could steer or even seriously influence that movement strikes me as—I'm sorry—ludicrous. The Religious Right is mighty enough that it doesn't have to listen to anyone who doesn't bring power, votes, or money to the table, and it's precisely the lack of those that is a problem for Southern Conservatives. To be sure, some traditionalist conservatives are influential in the councils of the Christian Right—Albert Mohler, president of the Southern Baptist Theological Seminary, is one, but he is not exactly a Southern Conservative in Gene's sense of that phrase. And in fact, it seems as unlikely to me as it did to Allen Tate in his Southern Agrarian phase that an evangelical Protestant *can* be that sort of conservative. But that's an essay for another day.

So, where do we go from here? Well, to begin with, I think we need to recognize that the South is no longer the repository for "the Southern tradition." Perhaps that tradition was once culturally if not numerically dominant in the South, but it certainly isn't now. The South of Calhoun and Fitzhugh has been stomped flat by—what? Not even Jefferson's South. Maybe Andy Jackson's—or, hell, Davy Crockett's. Anyway, the answer to the question I was asking in the 1990s is even clearer now: Southern Conservatives are only a Remnant in their own country. Maybe even especially there.

But they should not despair. They've never have been the only Americans to articulate these principles. In fact, if you're looking for articulation, forget *I'll Take My Stand* and turn to *Who Owns America?* in which some of the Agrarians hooked up with an assortment of Distributists, neo-Thomists, and capital-*H* Humanists—something like the bar scene in *Star Wars*—to make explicit much that was only implied in the earlier book. And these days something very similar is alive and well in the burned-over district of Upstate New York (of all places), where my buddy Bill Kauffman—like me, a former writer for *Chronicles*—lives and writes splendid books with titles like *Bye Bye, Miss American Empire*. Moreover, oddly, this intensely localistic tradition is also flourishing in the placeless nowhere of the Internet: check out the website of something called the Front Porch Republic, for instance. These ideological compatriots at least give Southern Conservatives someone to talk to.

And even if they are a Remnant, that's not a bad thing to be. In an essay called "Isaiah's Job," Albert Jay Nock (a thinker I admire almost as much as I admire Gene) cites not just Isaiah, but Plato, Marcus Aurelius, and the Lord God of Israel to support his argument that in sorry times being a Remnant is the only course open to honorable men and women. They can take comfort from the realization that they are keeping ideas in the ideological gene pool, where later generations may find them useful. As T. S Eliot, a traditionalist of another stripe, once wrote, "We fight for lost causes . . . rather to keep something alive than in the expectation that it will triumph." At the very least, Southern Conservatives who hold fast to what they believe can take with them what General Lee called "the satisfaction that comes from duty faithfully performed."

MILLENNIUM AMUSEMENT

Back in 1998, with the Millennium at our throats, Mike Burg, president of Edge Marketing in Charlotte, North Carolina, approached me with a challenge: Could I identify the twenty greatest Southerners of the century just ending, for a television package he was thinking of producing?

Well, everybody else was making end-of-the-century lists, so why not? I took on the job and assembled a panel of thirteen distinguished Southerners to help me choose the list. The panel was composed of men and women who had written or thought about the South, chosen to be broadly representative of professional fields and subregions. Here are their names and short biographical sketches, as of 1999:

Raymond Arsenault, John Hope Franklin Professor of Southern History and director of the University Honors Program at the University of South Florida, St. Petersburg, was the author of *The Wild Ass of the Ozarks, St. Petersburg and the Florida Dream, 1888–1950,* "The End of the Long Hot Summer: The Air Conditioner and Southern Culture," and "The Folklore of Southern Demagoguery."

Jim Auchmutey, for twenty years a reporter and editor for the *Atlanta Journal-Constitution,* had written two books on Southern food, *The South: The Beautiful Cookbook* and *The Ultimate Barbecue Sauce Cookbook,* and coedited *True South: Travels through a Land of White Columns, Black-Eyed Peas, and Redneck Bars.* (Jim still thinks Colonel Sanders should be on the list.)

Roy Blount Jr., a contributing editor of the *Atlantic Monthly* and a columnist for the *Oxford American*, was the author of a number of books including *Crackers, First Hubby, Be Sweet: A Conditional Love Story*, and *Roy Blount's Book of Southern Humor*.

John B. Boles, William P. Hobby Professor of History at Rice University and managing editor of the *Journal of Southern History*, had written many books, including *Black Southerners, 1619–1869, The Great Revival: Beginnings of the Bible Belt*, and *The South through Time: A History of an American Region*.

Don Carleton, the Parten Fellow in the Archives of American History and director of the Center for American History at the University of Texas at Austin, had written books including *Red Scare* and *A Breed So Rare*.

Ronald D. Eller, associate professor of history and director of the Appalachian Center at the University of Kentucky, was the author of *Miners, Millhands, and Mountaineers: Industrialization of the Appalachian South*.

Jimmie Lewis Franklin was professor of history at Vanderbilt University and past president of the Southern Historical Association. His books included *Journey toward Hope: A History of Blacks in Oklahoma*.

Lisa Howorth, a freelance writer living in Oxford, Mississippi, had taught art history and Southern studies at the University of Mississippi and edited *The South: A Treasury of Art and Literature* and *Yellow Dogs, Hushpuppies, and Bluetick Hounds: The Official Encyclopedia of Southern Culture Quiz Book*.

Doug Marlette was a Pulitzer Prize–winning editorial cartoonist for *Newsday* and creator of the syndicated comic strip (and musical comedy) *Kudzu*. He lived in Hillsborough, North Carolina.

Deborah Mathis, a national correspondent for Gannett News Service in Washington, D.C., was also a nationally syndicated columnist and television commentator. An Arkansas native, Mathis was the author of *Yet a Stranger: Why Black Americans Still Don't Feel at Home*.

Linton Weeks was a staff writer for the *Washington Post*. He had been the first director of the *Post*'s online newspaper, and founding editor of *Southern Magazine*.

Charles Reagan Wilson, director of the Center for the Study of Southern Culture and professor of history at the University of Mississippi, was coeditor of the *Encyclopedia of Southern Culture* and author of *Baptized in Blood: The Religion of the Lost Cause* and *Judgment and Grace in Dixie: Southern Faiths from Faulkner to Elvis.*

Odessa Woolfolk, a retired administrator from the University of Alabama at Birmingham, was the founding president of the Birmingham Civil Rights Institute and continued to be a civic activist. Her fields of interest were economic development, community organization, social welfare, public education, and the arts.

Although Mike Berg had asked initially for a list of "the twentieth century's greatest Southerners," we settled on the easier task of identifying influential ones. While we were at it, Mike suggested, why not use the panel to identify "defining moments" of the passing century, and we agreed to give it a go.

THE TWENTIETH CENTURY'S MOST
INFLUENTIAL SOUTHERNERS

To identify influential Southerners, I began by compiling a preliminary list of 345 names culled from the indexes of reference books or supplied by some of the 114 friends, colleagues, and anonymous Web surfers who responded to my request for comments and suggestions. (I can almost guarantee that anyone you're likely to think of as a possibility was on that list.) I asked the panelists to indicate which of the individuals on the list *had* to be included among the twenty most influential Southerners of the century, and which others deserved *serious consideration.*

Three names were consensus choices from the beginning:

Martin Luther King
Elvis Presley
William Faulkner

Two were Nobel laureates and the third was—well, *Elvis.* Everyone agreed that they had to be on the list.

Three more quickly became unanimous choices:

Jimmy Carter (another Nobel laureate)
Billy Graham
Louis Armstrong

Another five were *almost* unanimous choices, with just one judge (not always the same) who said only that they should be seriously considered, not that they *had* to be on the list:

Lyndon Johnson
George Wallace
Margaret Mitchell
Muhammad Ali
Woodrow Wilson

Another eight were "must-have" choices of a majority of panelists, and the other panelists said that they should be seriously considered.

Hank Williams
Sam Walton
Bill Clinton
Tennessee Williams
Ted Turner
Huey Long
Booker T. Washington
Rosa Parks

Which left us needing only one more name. There was no one else that a majority of panelists thought *must* be on a list like this, but five of the thirteen panelists thought Michael Jordan had to be there, and another three thought he deserved "serious consideration." So number 20 on our list was old #23:

Michael Jordan

For the record, the next-highest ratings went to Oprah Winfrey, with four "must-haves" and two "serious considerations." Other figures with significant support from a minority of panelists were George Washington Carver, C. Vann Woodward, Bear Bryant, Jesse Jackson, Eudora Welty, D. W. Griffith, Richard Wright, Bill Monroe, and W. J. Cash.

Surely every name on this list will be known to almost every sentient American, and that's partly the point. We had to deal with a number of problems of definition, starting with the meaning of "influence"—obviously, it's not the same as greatness, much less goodness. Martin Luther King and George Wallace were both influential, for instance, but surely few admirers of one would argue that the other was a great man. By all accounts, even Governor Wallace suspected toward the end of his life that his influence hadn't been a good one. Just so, Sam Walton was influential: Walmart has certainly changed small-town American life. But for the better? I think the jury's still out on that one.

It works the other way around, too. Someone can be saintly—"great" in the sense that really matters—without being influential. In my opinion, James McBride Dabbs was great, as were some other white Southerners who took an early and unpopular stand against racial injustice. Thank God for whatever influence their witness had, but for the most part they were voices crying in the wilderness, not candidates for the century's most influential.

Ella Baker, an unsung heroine of the civil rights movement, didn't make the list either. Never heard of her? That's my point: she's *unsung.* Obviously, and unavoidably, influence—at least as we measured it—has something to do with fame. That's almost certainly why our final list ignores some very influential scientists. The ideas of E. O. Wilson of Alabama, father of sociobiology; Eugene Odum, from Chapel Hill, who made "ecosystem" a household word; and James Buchanan, Tennessean and Nobel laureate in economics for his development of "public choice" theory are enormously influential. Thinkers like them may be the "unacknowledged legislators of the world" (as Shelley called poets), but the problem is that they are *unacknowledged,* by the public and by the humanities majors on our panel. Similarly, Ray Wilson Scott has been even more important for competitive bass fishing than Michael Jordan has been for basketball and endorsements, but Scott is famous only in a fairly limited circle: he didn't even come close to making the list.

Just so, presidents of the United States, even mediocre and ineffectual ones, are influential more or less by definition. Notice that all the Southern presidents—even that ambiguous Southerner, Woodrow Wilson—make the list ex officio, so to speak. So does Huey Long, a serious contender who influenced national politics by his presence and threat.

While we're at it, who's a Southerner? Louisville's Muhammad Ali is on the list, but Joe Louis, who was born in Alabama but moved to Detroit when he was twelve, is not. Colonel Harland Sanders didn't make the short list, but he finished strong: I don't think anyone held it against him that he came from

Indiana. Thurgood Marshall was influential, no doubt about it, but the panel eventually concluded that someone born in Baltimore and educated in Pennsylvania and D.C. and who spent his working life in New York and Washington wasn't a Southerner.

Even the "twentieth century" turned out to be a problem. Our panel eventually decided that Mark Twain, who lived until 1910, was really a nineteenth-century figure, while Booker T. Washington, who lived only five years longer, was twentieth-century.

Martin Luther King Jr. and Rosa Parks are here, as major and well-known figures in the central drama of the twentieth-century South. (Mrs. Parks is unique in that her influence stems from just one significant action—but what an action!) And Booker T. Washington makes the list as the South's most influential black leader before King. The world of literature is well represented by William Faulkner, his fellow Mississippian Tennessee Williams, and Margaret Mitchell, all of whom shaped how the world thinks about the South, and how Southerners think about themselves. Southern music is a presence, as it should be, represented by Elvis, Satchmo, and Hank. Muhammad Ali and Michael Jordan are Southerners known around the world for their athletic accomplishments. Billy Graham is known around the world, too, and I for one think it's grand that we have a preacher on the list. Finally, Sam Walton—as mentioned above—and Ted Turner are here, reflecting the South's recent emergence as an economic powerhouse and seedbed of entrepreneurial innovation.

You don't have to agree with every choice. (Don't get me started.) But this is a pretty good list, if I do say so myself. All of these men and women changed the South, one way or another, and many of them changed the world.

FORTY DEFINING MOMENTS OF THE TWENTIETH-CENTURY SOUTH

When asked to identify "defining moments" of the twentieth-century South—events that symbolized, set in motion, or represented the culmination of important changes for the region—the panel settled on forty: twenty before midcentury and twenty after. There was less consensus on defining moments than on influential Southerners, and there was some unavoidable arbitrariness in defining what a "moment" is, but it will surprise no one to see that the two big stories of the twentieth-century South are the transition from an agricultural to an urban society and the transformation effected by the civil rights movement. Events listed in *italics* were chosen by ten or more of the thirteen panelists.

1901–1950

1901 The Spindletop oil strike, which marked the beginning of the Texas/Oklahoma/Louisiana oil industry.

1903 The Wright brothers' flight at Kitty Hawk.

1906 The Atlanta race riot, one of the bloodiest episodes of the Jim Crow era, and arguably the low point of race relations in the South.

1915 Leo Frank's lynching.

1915 The premiere of *Birth of a Nation,* the movie whose success inspired the second KKK.

1917   *The beginning of the Great Migration, spurred by World War I.*

1919   The start of the Florida land boom.

1925   *The Scopes Trial pit William Jennings Bryan against Clarence Darrow in a struggle over the teaching of evolution.*

1927   Ralph Peer recorded the Carter Family and Jimmie Rodgers in Bristol, the beginning of commercial country music.

1927   The Mississippi flood of 1927, one of the great natural disasters of the century, that destroyed thousands of homes.

1931   The trial of the "Scottsboro Boys," nine black teenagers in Alabama falsely accused to raping two white women.

1933   *Creation of the Tennessee Valley Authority (TVA), which laid the foundations for rural electrification and industrialization in the Tennessee River Valley.*

1934   The great textile strike of 1934, one of the most bitter episodes in the troubled history of Southern labor relations.

1935   Creation of the Rural Electric Administration.

1935   Assassination of Huey Long, populist Louisiana governor and senator.

1936   *The invention of the Rust mechanical cotton picker, which completed the work of the boll weevil in displacing Southern agricultural workers.*

1939   The premiere in Atlanta of *Gone with the Wind*, a film that shaped the way the world thought of the South.

1939   *Willis Carrier's perfection of the air conditioner, which laid the basis for modern industrialization and for migration to the South.*

1948   *Strom Thurmond's presidential campaign on the Dixiecrat ticket.*

1950   William Faulkner's Nobel Prize.

1951–2000

1954   Brown v. Board of Education, *which declared school segregation to be unconstitutional, the beginning of the end for Jim Crow.*

1954 *Elvis at Sun Studios in Memphis married rhythm and blues and country music, laying the foundations for rock and roll.*

1956 *The Montgomery bus boycott, the opening of the civil rights movement, brought to national attention a young minister named Martin Luther King.*

1957 The integration of Little Rock Central High School.

1960 The Greensboro sit-ins, when black college students sat at a segregated Woolworth's lunch counter, a trial run of the method of nonviolent resistance.

1962 James Meredith's enrollment at Ole Miss.

1962 *Baker v. Carr*, in which the Supreme Court decided that federal courts could rule on challenges to electoral apportionment, ending rural domination of state legislatures.

1963 John F. Kennedy's assassination in Dallas.

1963 The March on Washington.

1964 *"Freedom Summer" and the Civil Rights Act of 1964, when hundreds of college students went to Mississippi to help blacks register to vote and when federal legislation outlawed segregation in public accommodations.*

1965 *The Selma-to-Montgomery voting rights march, which led Congress to pass the Voting Rights Act, transforming Southern politics.*

1968 Martin Luther King's assassination in Memphis.

1969 "Houston, the Eagle has landed"—the moon landing.

1971 The opening of Disney World.

1972 The election of African Americans Barbara Jordan and Andrew Young to Congress.

1974 Hank Aaron's 715th home run broke Babe Ruth's record.

1976 *The election of Jimmy Carter, which showed that a Southerner could be elected president again.*

1980 *The debut of the Cable News Network (CNN), the first step in turning Atlanta into a telecommunications center of global significance.*

1994 The congressional elections that saw a Republican Party dominated by white Southerners take control of Congress.

1996 The Atlanta Olympics presented the South and its de facto capital to the world.

THE SOUTHERN FOCUS POLL

In 1991, as director of the University of North Carolina's Institute for Research in Social Science (IRSS, now the Howard Odum Institute), I struck a deal with Pamma Mitchell, who was in charge of data-gathering operations for the *Atlanta Journal-Constitution* (*AJC*). The IRSS would conduct a twice-yearly public opinion poll, using a national sample of telephone numbers but "over-sampling" numbers from the South, to allow a more fine-grained description of the Southern population than the typical national survey provides. We would use our office telephones (out-of-hours), cast-off computers, software (a one-time purchase), and trained undergraduate interviewers. The *AJC* would pay the bills, but they would get a high-quality survey for roughly half what it would cost otherwise.

Thus was born the Southern Focus Poll, conducted more or less regularly until 2001, when the *AJC* had to economize.

We agreed to ask questions that the newspaper could use for feature articles—stuff like your favorite baseball team, plans for the Fourth of July, whether Elvis is still alive—and could also ask questions of interest to us (or, more precisely, to me), like ones about Southern identity and the legacy of the Civil War.

Beverly Wiggins, associate director of the IRSS, oversaw interviewer training and the poll's operations, and she and I worked together with Pamma to construct the questionnaires. After the *AJC* had its pick of the data, Beverly and I wrote press releases about some of the other questions, which were picked up by a great many small-town newspapers and sometimes circulated nationally by the Associated Press—good, cheap publicity for IRSS, UNC, and the *AJC*.

When the journal *Southern Cultures* was first established, we were starved for material, so I started a regular back-of-the-book department called "South Polls," presenting simple cross-tabulations of data from the Southern Focus Poll, with a minimum of commentary.

What follows is a selection of "South Polls" articles dealing with an assortment of topics: food, speech, ancestry, recreation, manners, etc. They are preceded by a piece I wrote to introduce the *Journal-Constitution*'s readers to our project.

These "South Polls" articles have been somewhat condensed: in particular, I haven't shown breaks that made little difference (e.g., if roughly the same percentage of men and women gave a response, I have not included the data showing that). One break that often did make a considerable difference was that between the "Deep South" and the "Peripheral South"; note that for our purposes, the Deep South comprised South Carolina, Georgia, Alabama, Mississippi, and Louisiana.

WHY A SOUTHERN POLL?

Why should we survey Southern public opinion? The South, some will observe, is not a political unit like the United States, or Georgia. It had a brief and ambiguous political existence, true, but it no longer legislates, collects taxes, or makes war. It has no constitution, no president or legislature, no foreign policy. It has no Border Patrol, and it's not clear where its borders are, anyway. Most of the questions that the Gallup and Harris polls ask about national issues, or that state polls ask about state issues, don't translate into questions that can be asked of Southerners about the South. Moreover, some skeptics say, the South is not even very different, anymore, from the rest of the United States. We're all pretty much alike these days, aren't we? (True, at the same time other skeptics are likely to say that parts of the South are so different from each other that there's no point in putting them together.)

But even if these objections were correct—which I don't grant for an instant—there would still be reasons to isolate the South for study. One is the same reason we might want to study New England, the Pacific Northwest, or any other major American region. Whatever else it may be, the South is a substantial market and an important component of the American and, increasingly, of the world economy. Indeed, the South is now the most populous American region, with a landmass the size of Europe, 80 million people, and an economy that would rank among the largest in the world if it were a separate country.

In fact, in this respect, it makes more sense to study the South than ever before. When the Southern states seceded in 1861, Karl Marx commented from England that the Confederacy wasn't a nation at all, just a battle cry. He meant that the new country had few truly national institutions to tie it together. He could also have observed that the Confederacy had no obvious capital city, no metropolitan hub from which commerce and communications radiated. (Richmond was more a political choice than a strategic one.)

Now, however, huge regional corporations span state lines. Interstate compacts address a variety of regional problems. The annual meetings of innumerable trade and professional associations bring Southerners together from all over the region. *Southern Living* is only the best known and most successful of scores of regional magazines whose very titles attest to the South's existence and vitality. And, like it or not, Atlanta has emerged as the de facto capital of this newest South (although, to be sure, it's a South that seems to have irrevocably lost Texas). Ironically, in Marx's sense the South is now more of a nation than it has ever been before—more, even, than when it was politically independent. So why *not* study it?

And of course the South is more than an economic entity. It is also a place that enlists the loyalty and affection of many of its inhabitants, who retain and are continually reinventing a distinctive culture. There is a case to be made for studying, not the South exactly, but Southerners, defined as people who somehow identify with the region and with each other, and who are set apart from other Americans by both real and imagined cultural differences. We can study their opinions, values, and beliefs in the same way that we study those of African Americans, American Jews, Italian Americans, or any other cultural or ethnic group. And hundreds of scholars around the world do study and teach Southern history, literature, and folklore.

Although the correlation between "Southerners" and "residents of the Southern states" is less than perfect, it is good enough for most practical purposes. Migration to the South from other parts of the country does mean that fewer white residents of the Southern states now identify themselves as Southerners. On the other hand, Southern blacks are much more likely to do so now than a generation ago.

Questions like these—who identify themselves as Southerners and what they mean by it—are ideally suited for a Southern regional survey. So are questions about favorite-son presidential candidates, about migration to the South, about images of Southerners in the mass media, and a host of other interesting topics. Such questions tend to slip through the cracks between national and state polls. Often they don't make sense to non-Southerners; even when they do, national survey organizations seldom ask them. On the other hand, every Southern state except Oklahoma and West Virginia (if you count them) has one or more state polls, and they sometimes do ask questions about the South. But generalizing from a single state to the region as a whole is a risky business. It's far better to look at thirteen states than to assume that any one of them looks like all of them together.

Another reason to focus on the region is that it lets you say something about variation within the South. The Southern subsamples of national polls are usually big enough to examine differences between the South and the rest of the country. A national poll of 800 respondents, for instance, would include about 240 from Southern states, which would give percentages for Southerners accurate to within about six points. But if you want to look at different kinds of Southerners, the numbers get pretty small, pretty fast. If you're interested in differences or similarities between black and white Southerners, for instance, you would be generalizing from a sample of about 50 blacks—too small for any real confidence. If you're interested in Southern Hispanics, forget it.

So there are a great many reasons, substantive and methodological, to supplement national and state polls with regional surveys. But the real reason to look at the South is that it has been and remains an interesting place. Fifty years ago, in his classic *The Mind of the South*, W. J. Cash wrote that "there have arisen people, usually journalists or professors, to tell us that it is all a figment of the imagination, that the South really exists only as a geographical division of the United States and is distinguishable from New England or the Middle West only by such matters as the greater heat and the presence of a larger body of Negroes. Nobody, however, has ever taken them seriously. And rightly."

Most of us still don't take them seriously.

WHERE IS THE SOUTH?

The South has been defined by a great many characteristics, but one of the most interesting definitions is *where people believe that they are in the South.* Answers to that question would define the South as what geographers call a vernacular region—that is, the area people have in mind when they speak of the South.

Until recently we did not have the data to answer the question of where that might be. In the 1990s, however, fourteen Southern Focus Polls asked respondents from the eleven former Confederate states, Kentucky, and Oklahoma, "Just for the record, would you say that your community is in the South, or not?" The last twelve surveys asked the same question of respondents from West Virginia, Maryland, Delaware, the District of Columbia, and Missouri (all except Missouri included in the Bureau of the Census's "South"). The pooled data from these surveys provide big enough samples to characterize each state.

The data in the table below show that if we define the South as "where most people believe they're in the South," the Southern Focus Poll's definition of the South—i.e., "the 11 former Confederate states, Kentucky, and Oklahoma"—makes sense, while the Bureau of the Census definition does not. In those thirteen states, and only in those states, a majority of respondents tell us that they're in the South. The states are ranked in a gradient that makes sense to anyone familiar with American cultural geography. Large portions of Texas, Virginia, Kentucky, and Oklahoma are *not* in the South by many measures.

Percentage who say their community is in the South (% base in parentheses)

Alabama	98	(717)	Virginia	82	(1,014)
South Carolina	98	(553)	Kentucky	79	(582)
Louisiana	97	(606)	Oklahoma	69	(411)
Mississippi	97	(431)			
Georgia	97	(1,017)	West Virginia	45	(82)
Tennessee	97	(838)	Maryland	40	(173)
North Carolina	93	(1,292)	Missouri	23	(177)
Arkansas	92	(400)	Delaware	14	(21)
Florida	90	(1,792)	D.C.	7	(15)
Texas	84	(2,050)			

Note: Question not asked in other states.

A related definition of the South might be *where the residents consider themselves to be Southerners*. Although this is obviously affected by the presence of non-Southern migrants, it is the definition to use if one wants to isolate self-defined Southerners for study.

The same Southern Focus Polls asked respondents from the thirteen Southern states, "Do you consider yourself a Southerner, or not?," and starting with the second survey those from other states were asked, "Do you consider yourself or anyone in your family a Southerner?," and if so, whether they considered themselves to be Southerners. The next table shows the results.

Percentage who say they are Southerners (% base in parentheses)

Mississippi	90	(432)	West Virginia	25	(84)
Louisiana	89	(606)	Maryland	19	(192)
Alabama	88	(716)	Missouri	15	(197)
Tennessee	84	(838)	New Mexico	13	(68)
South Carolina	82	(553)	Delaware	12	(25)
Arkansas	81	(399)	D.C.	12	(16)
Georgia	81	(1,017)	Utah	11	(70)
North Carolina	80	(1,290)	Indiana	10	(208)
Kentucky	68	(584)	Illinois	9	(362)
Texas	68	(2,053)	Ohio	8	(396)
Virginia	60	(1,012)	Arizona	7	(117)
Oklahoma	53	(410)	Michigan	6	(336)
Florida	51	(1,791)			

Note: All others less than 6 percent.

In thirteen states, majorities of respondents told us they are Southerners. As it happens, they were the same thirteen states where most told us they were in the South. It doesn't have to be that way—there could easily be a Southern state where most inhabitants say they're not Southerners—but even in Florida, where most residents were not born in the South, a (bare) majority define themselves as Southern. At least for now.

LAZY NO MORE

Thomas Jefferson was one of the first to pontificate about what makes Southerners Southern. In 1785 he wrote to a French friend outlining "the characters of the several states." "In the South," he said, "they are fiery, voluptuary, indolent, unsteady," but also "generous" and "candid," while in the North they were— pretty much the opposite. More than two hundred years later, results from a Southern Focus Poll conducted at the University of North Carolina show that most Americans still see Southerners as different. But how we're seen as different may be changing, in at least one important respect.

The table below shows how Southerners and non-Southerners responded to a series of questions about whether Southerners are more or less courteous than other Americans, more or less religious, and so forth.

"In general, do you think Southerners are more _____ or less _____ than people in other areas of the country?"

How Southerners see themselves:	More (%)	Less (%)
Courteous	80	6
Religious	72	7
Conservative	70	15
Loyal to family	67	5
Contented with life	67	9
Patriotic	61	8
Hardworking	46	16

**"In general, do you think Southerners are more _____ or less _____
than people in other areas of the country?"** [continued]

How Southerners see themselves:	More [%]	Less [%]
Concerned about the environment	43	26
Intelligent	29	19
Violent	17	48
Pushy	14	67

**"In general, do you think Southerners are more _____ or less _____
than people in other areas of the country?"**

How non-Southerners see Southerners:	More [%]	Less [%]
Courteous	71	2
Religious	68	2
Conservative	59	12
Loyal to family	55	3
Contented with life	54	6
Patriotic	44	6
Hardworking	23	22
Concerned about the environment	24	21
Intelligent	7	14
Violent	12	36
Pushy	13	49

Some ancient regional images persist. More courteous, more religious, more conservative, more loyal to family, more contented with life, less "pushy"—all of these generalizations about Southerners were established well before the Civil War. You can find them full-blown, for instance, in the writings of Alexis de Tocqueville, the Frenchman who toured the United States in the 1830s, and you can still find them today. Are these images accurate? Sometimes it's hard to say. It's difficult, for instance, to measure courtesy and pushiness (or, anyway, we don't often do it), so opinions are about all we have to go by. But in many respects it appears that the common perceptions are correct. By most measures Southerners really are more likely to be religious, for instance. We also tend to be more conservative, more contented with life, and more patriotic, at least in the conventional sense.

If we're more "loyal to family," however, you wouldn't know it from our divorce rate. Even if people thought the question was about loyalty to blood relatives, most evidence suggests that regional differences in this respect are pretty small, as group differences in the United States go. Similarly, it's hard to reconcile the belief that Southerners are less violent than other Americans with our homicide rate, which has always been the highest of any major region in the nation. That older people and black Southerners are less likely to share this belief may suggest that the well-publicized violence of the civil rights era has not been forgotten in all quarters.

To a longtime South-watcher, however, the most striking of these results has to be that many people now see Southerners as more hardworking than other Americans, or at least no lazier than average. This represents a major change, because Jefferson was by no means the last to say that we in the South are "indolent." Tocqueville, for instance, remarked that the Southerner "scorns not only labour, but all the undertakings which labour promotes"; "his tastes," the Frenchman said, "are those of an idle man." There never was much solid evidence to support this belief, and in a region where most people worked on farms it seems unlikely on the face of it, but it's a fact that until recently the paramount Southern trait in both the Southern and non-Southern mind has been some variation on this theme. If you liked Southerners, you probably said something like "Southerners take life easy." But apparently this is changing. Older non-Southerners are still likely to see us as less industrious than other Americans, but Southerners of all ages and young people everywhere now have the opposite impression. Why is this?

One possibility lies in the use to which the old stereotype was put. In the past, taking it easy was often used to explain the region's economic backwardness (which meant that nobody had to think about matters like absentee ownership and the effects of tariffs). The South may be poor, folks said, but Southerners know that there are more important things in life than making money; our critics put it more bluntly: the South is poor, they said, because its people are lazy. But the dramatic economic development since World War II may have undermined that theory by removing what it was meant to explain. Regional images are also shaped by popular culture, and in this respect mass media images of the South may well have changed. The old image was often that represented by Junior Samples of *Hee Haw,* lying out in the front yard with his dog. The new one is—what? Julia Sugarbaker of *Designing Women?*

Country music's new popularity may be contributing as well. Much country music is essentially white workingman's (and, now, workingwoman's) blues, and it presents a different picture of Southern life than the popular music of the past. Just compare "Nine to Five," for example, to "When It's Sleepy Time Down South."

In any case, for whatever reason, it looks as if a belief that has been around since the birth of the American Republic will soon be gone with the wind. "The lazy South" may always have been just a stereotype. Now it's not even that.

EMBATTLED EMBLEM

The rebel flag (properly, the battle flag of the Army of Northern Virginia) has become very much an "embattled emblem," as a 1995 exhibit and symposium with that title at Richmond's Museum of the Confederacy recognized and illustrated. Southern Focus Polls in 1992 and 1993 included some questions on the subject, as well as a related one asking what the Civil War was about. The questions were:

"[Do you own] a Confederate flag?"

"Some people say the Confederate flag reminds them of white supremacy and racial conflict. Other people say the Confederate flag is a symbol of Southern heritage and pride. Do you think the flag is more a symbol of racial conflict or of Southern pride?"

"People get into the same argument about the song 'Dixie.' Do you think 'Dixie' is more a symbol of racial conflict or of Southern pride?"

"Do you think the American Civil War was fought mostly about slavery, or was it fought mostly about something else?"

It appears that favorable attitudes toward the flag are more widespread than the flag itself. Only about one Southerner in ten actually owns one, a figure not appreciably higher than that for non-Southerners.

"Do you own a Confederate flag?"

	Yes	No	(N)
South (%)	11	88	(859)
Non-South (%)	9	91	(446)

But substantial majorities of Southern respondents—better than three to one—see the flag as a symbol of regional heritage and pride; and, perhaps surprisingly, majorities almost as large of non-Southerners agree.

"Do you think the flag is more a symbol of racial conflict or of Southern pride?"

	South [%]	Non-South [%]
Racial conflict	19	15
Southern pride	70	72
No opinion	11	13
[N]	[892]	[447]

The problem is that the flag has come to mean many different things, and neither the Sons of Confederate Veterans nor the NAACP has a monopoly on interpretation. Although the question about the meaning of the flag doesn't exhaust the possible interpretations, it picks up two of the principal ones, and it does reveal substantial disagreement, especially between white Southerners and black ones, with the latter substantially more likely to see the flag as a symbol of white supremacy and racial conflict. Southerners of all sorts are less likely to feel that way about the song "Dixie," but the correlates of the two questions are similar: blacks, young people, the better educated, and migrants to the South are more likely than others to see Confederate symbols as signifying racism.

Percentage responding

	Flag symbol of race conflict	"Dixie" symbol of race conflict	Civil War about slavery	Own a flag
Southern Total	19	8	48	11
Lived in South				
10 years or less	29	10	62	4
More than 10 years	19	5	50	9
All my life	17	8	44	13
Race				
White	14	5	49	13
Black	49	32	37	2

Percentage responding [*continued*]

	Flag symbol of race conflict	"Dixie" symbol of race conflict	Civil War about slavery	Own a flag
Age				
18–24	25	21	52	18
25–44	21	9	52	11
45–64	15	4	43	12
65 or older	13	4	41	5
Education				
11th grade or less	12	6	36	7
High school graduate	14	8	53	15
Some college	22	10	51	11
College graduate	24	8	45	10

Oddly, believing that the Civil War was about slavery and actually owning a flag of one's own do not "behave" the same: blacks are *less* likely to believe the war was about slavery, for instance, and young people are *more* likely to own Confederate flags.

The question about the meaning of the flag was asked often enough that data from several surveys can be pooled to examine variation in opinion within the black and white Souths. In the table below, a number *greater* than one indicates that a majority believe it stands for Southern pride; a number *less* than one, that it stands for racial conflict.

Among blacks, only the old, those with less than a high school education, regular churchgoers, Republicans, and those in a very few other categories are likely to think the flag signifies Southern pride. Among whites, there is no identifiable subpopulation where a majority do *not* believe that, although the ratio is relatively low among political liberals, college graduates, and recent migrants to the South.

"Do you think the flag is more a symbol of racial conflict or of Southern pride?"
Ratio: Southern pride/racial conflict

	White	Black
Total sample	5.5	0.8

"Do you think the flag is more a symbol of racial conflict or of Southern pride?"
Ratio: Southern pride/racial conflict (*continued*)

	White	Black
Lived in South		
10 years or less	2.3	0.9 (7)
More than 10 years	4.2	0.7
All my life	8.4	0.8
Southern accent		
Strong	8.4	0.9
Noticeable	5.7	0.6
None	3.6	0.6
Age		
18–24	4.4	0.6
25–44	4.4	0.7
45–64	7.5	0.9
65 or older	7.4	2.0 (52)
Residence		
City	4.0	0.7
Suburb	4.4	0.5
Town	6.5	0.9
Rural	8.7	0.9
Education		
0–8 years	24.5 (23)	1.8 (53)
9–11 years	11.0 (17)	2.0
High school grad	9.9	0.9
Some college	5.9	0.6
College grad	3.2	0.3
Church attendance		
Never	3.5	0.3
Several times/year	5.3	0.5
2–3 times/month	5.4	0.7
Once/week	6.2	0.8
More than once/week	7.5	1.9 (41)
Income		
Less than $10,000	4.2	1.2 (40)
$10–20,000	6.3	0.9

"Do you think the flag is more a symbol of racial conflict or of Southern pride?"
Ratio: Southern pride/racial conflict *(continued)*

	White	Black
$20–30,000	5.3	0.8
$30–40,000	6.0	0.7
$40–60,000	6.7	0.4
Over $60,000	4.3	0.4 [5]
Political views		
Strong liberal	1.8	0.6 [3]
Liberal	4.8	0.6 [13]
Moderate	4.6	0.9
Conservative	7.9	0.7
Strong conservative	8.9	0.6
Don't know	19.7 [23]	2.7 [39]

Source: Pooled data from Spring 1992, Spring 1993, and Fall 1993 Southern Focus Polls.

Note: Percent "don't know" is between 5 and 15 for whites, and between 15 and 35 for blacks, unless otherwise noted in parentheses.

LAY MY BURDEN OF
SOUTHERN HISTORY DOWN

The Confederate heritage appears to be of waning importance in the South, or—perhaps more accurately put—it appears to be of importance to a dwindling number of Southerners. In 1994 the Southern Focus Poll asked residents of the South and other Americans, "Did you have any ancestors living in the United States in 1860?" If the answer was yes, respondents were asked, "Did any of your family fight in the Civil War?" If the answer to that question was yes, they were asked, "Which side did they fight for—for the Confederacy, for the Union, or did members of your family fight on both sides?"

Twenty-nine percent of Southerners indicate that their ancestors did not fight in the war (18 percent because they weren't in the country at the time), and 43 percent don't know whether they did or not. Only a quarter of Southern respondents believe that they had ancestors in the war—and nearly a third of those have ancestors on both sides or only on the Union side. Non-Southerners are even less likely to have ancestors in the war, primarily because more of them are descended from postwar immigrants.

"Did any of your family fight in the Civil War?" (If yes) "Which side did they fight for?"

	CSA	Union	Both	Didn't fight	Not in U.S.	Don't know
Southern	18	4	4	11	18	43
Non-Southern	4	8	3	13	29	42

Overall, 22 percent of Southern respondents report ancestors who fought for the Confederacy. That figure rises to 26 percent among respondents who consider themselves Southerners and to 28 percent in the five Deep South states and among lifelong residents of the region. It is also higher (27%) in non-metropolitan areas than in cities, and among those over forty-five years old (30% vs. 19% of those under that age). Among the standard demographic categories, only among college graduates does the percentage who believe they have Confederate ancestors exceed one-third (34%), a relatively high level that reflects a decrease in "don't know" responses as education increases. Not surprisingly, almost no black respondents (only 3%) report Confederate ancestors.

When asked, "Can you name any Civil War battles, right offhand?" Southern and non-Southern respondents display equal (high) levels of ignorance, although Southerners are more likely to mention some battle other than the Union victory at Gettysburg.

"Can you name any Civil War battles, right offhand?"

	Gettysburg	Other	Can't name any
Southern	24	33	44
Non-Southern	34	25	41

When asked what the conflict was about, small majorities of both Southern and non-Southern respondents agree that it was "more about slavery than it was about states' rights or any other issue," although Southern respondents are slightly more likely to disagree strongly.

"The Civil War was more about slavery than it was about states' rights or any other issue."

	Strongly agree	Somewhat agree	Somewhat disagree	Strongly disagree	Don't know
Southern	28	24	17	20	11
Non-Southern	28	26	22	16	8

In the South, the percentage of disagreement with the statement is 37 percent for the entire sample. It is higher for lifelong residents of the region

(40%), whites (37% vs. 22% for blacks), men (45% vs. 30% for women), those over forty-five (41%), and those with incomes of $60,000 a year or more (46%). Only among college graduates do more respondents disagree (50%) than agree (45%) that the war was primarily about slavery.

The poll also included two "mirror-image" questions, each asked of half the sample, which tapped respondents' attitudes toward a hypothetical Confederate ancestor: (1) "If I had an ancestor who fought in the Confederate army, I would be proud that he fought for what he thought was right"; and (2) "If I had an ancestor who fought in the Confederate army, I would be ashamed, knowing what I know about the reasons for the war."

"If I had an ancestor who fought in the Confederate army–"

	Strongly agree	Somewhat agree	Somewhat disagree	Strongly disagree	Don't know
"I would be proud that he fought for what he thought was right."					
Southern	58	28	4	4	6
Non-Southern	53	27	4	4	12
"I would be ashamed, knowing what I know about the reasons for the war."					
Southern	7	16	29	36	12
Non-Southern	7	15	25	37	16

Regional differences are surprisingly small for the first question and non-existent for the second. Note that over 80 percent of both Southern and non-Southern respondents agree with the first statement and over 20 percent agree with the second, suggesting that some (minuscule) fraction may agree with both, which is not impossible but seems unlikely. This is almost certainly an example of what survey researchers call "acquiescence" bias, a tendency to agree rather than to disagree when asked a question that one really hasn't thought about.

Even keeping that in mind, however, responses to the following question may be surprising. Southerners are quite likely to agree that the Civil War doesn't mean much to them personally—at least as likely to agree as to disagree—and the war doesn't seem to mean much more to Southerners than to non-Southerners.

"It's important to remember our history, but the Civil War doesn't mean much to me personally."

	Strongly agree	Somewhat agree	Somewhat disagree	Strongly disagree	Don't know
Southern	21	28	17	28	6
Non-Southern	20	28	20	29	3

Within the South, agreeing that the Civil War doesn't mean much personally is more common among women (55% vs. 41% for men), those with an eleventh-grade education or less (59% vs. 43% for college graduates), and oddly, among older people (53% of those over sixty-five, 46% of those eighteen to twenty-four).

If anything, Southerners are more likely than non-Southerners to agree that we should let bygones be bygones.

"We would be better off if we paid less attention to history and put the past behind us."

	Strongly agree	Somewhat agree	Somewhat disagree	Strongly disagree	Don't know
Southern	25	14	19	38	3
Non-Southern	16	12	20	50	3

Evidently the "burden of Southern history" isn't what it used to be.

WHITHER THE CENTRAL THEME?

Writing in 1928, the historian Ulrich B. Phillips asserted that the "central theme of Southern history" and "the cardinal test of a Southerner" was a commitment to white supremacy. (It went without saying that by "Southerner" he meant *white* Southerner.) But the Spring 1999 Southern Focus Poll was only one of many polls at the turn of the century to show that Southern racial attitudes had changed dramatically since Phillips wrote. Differences between Southern attitudes and those of other Americans were by then the smallest recorded since public opinion polling began in the 1930s. Moreover, the remaining differences were usually smaller among younger people than among older ones, which suggests that they will be even smaller in another generation.

To be sure, many different "Souths" are combined to produce the figures below. These figures will vary from the Deep South to the mountains, in the Southwest and in Florida, from rural communities to metropolitan areas—not to mention from black to white Southerners. And the "non-South" is an even more unwieldy agglomeration of different communities. But the point remains that, overall, differences between Southern and non-Southern racial attitudes are now only a matter of degree, and usually of pretty small degree at that.

Percentage who agree that:	South	Non-South
Effects of integration on South have been		
positive	48	46
negative	12	11

Percentage who agree that: [*continued*]	South	Non-South
Opportunities for minorities are		
better in South	15	9
worse in South	18	30
Race relations are		
better in South	14	4
worse in South	24	34

Asked of those who have lived in community more than 5 years

	South	Non-South
In past 10 years, community has become "somewhat"		
or "much more" ethnically and racially diverse	38	39
In past 10 years, local _____ population has increased "quite a lot."		
African American	14	12
Hispanic	30	19
Asian	11	13

Asked of those who have lived in community more than 5 years and
who said community has become somewhat or much more diverse

	South	Non-South
Increasing community diversity is a		
good thing	45	56
bad thing	11	10
Having children learn about diversity is a		
good way to help eliminate racism	85	91

Asked of those employed, but not self-employed

	South	Non-South
Employer efforts to hire minority employees have been		
too much	7	7
too little	10	12
Affirmative action often discriminates against white men	47	44
More than half of people in neighborhood		
are same race as respondent	63	71

Percentage who agree that: (continued)	South	Non-South
Asked of churchgoers		
No people of different race attend respondent's church	27	21
Parents would not have objected to respondent dating someone of a different race	29	37
Would not disapprove of family member dating someone of a different race	70	80
Would not disapprove of family member marrying someone of a different race	68	80
Family member has dated someone of a different race	50	59
Family member has married someone of a different race	31	34
Would not disapprove if family member adopted a child of another race	88	94
Family member has adopted child of another race	8	12
Feel "very comfortable" interacting with people of a different race	47	54
Own racial views have become _____ with age		
more conservative	11	7
more liberal	31	32
Asked of those with children		
Children's racial views are _____ than one's own		
more conservative	7	4
more liberal	24	25

The racial attitudes reported by our respondents may seem unrealistically positive (frankly, they seem that way to me), but the numbers do summarize what they said. It may be that their responses were partly shaped by what survey researchers call "social desirability bias"—a tendency to give the response thought to be most culturally acceptable. Even so, however, it is an interesting fact that apparently it is no longer acceptable to express racially bigoted views to a stranger on the telephone.

"SOUTHERN WOMEN ARE . . ."

Studies of regional stereotypes usually ask people to describe "Southerners" in general, but Southern women in particular may have carried a heavy burden of image. Some of it has been laid on them by others; some has been self-inflicted. In the fall of 1992, the Southern Focus Poll interviewed 583 residents of Southern states and 350 residents of non-Southern states about a variety of public issues, but also about perceived differences between Southern women and other American women.

The "steel magnolia" image is widespread. Men and women, Southern and non-Southern, tend to see Southern women as more strong-willed, yet more friendly, less assertive, less independent, less self-centered, less feminist, and less career-oriented than American women in general.

Southerners of both sexes are more likely than non-Southerners to see Southern women as independent and strong-willed, while Southern men are especially likely to say that Southern women are less career-oriented and less feminist. Non-Southern women are least likely to give the conventional, stereotypical responses.

Southern respondents were less likely to have had any particular Southern women in mind when answering these questions. Not surprisingly, if they did, they were more likely to mention relatives.

The importance of the media in sustaining regional imagery is evident. Many respondents were thinking of Southern women they did not know personally: public figures, entertainers, and fictional characters. Ann Richards, Coretta Scott King, Rosalynn Carter, and Barbara Jordan were frequently mentioned public figures, while Dolly Parton was the entertainer most often mentioned, followed by several other country music singers.

Among characters from fiction, Scarlett O'Hara seems to be an especially potent figure for non-Southerners, named by a quarter of those who had a particular Southern woman in mind. Eight percent of both Southerners and non-Southerners who named other fictional characters chose from the cast of the television program *Designing Women*.

"Would you say that Southern women are more _____ or less _____ than American women in general?"
(other responses are "no difference" and "don't know")

	SOUTH		NON-SOUTH	
	Men	Women	Men	Women
Strong-willed				
Southern women more	52	49	39	38
Southern women less	21	21	17	25
Friendly				
Southern women more	81	76	69	60
Southern women less	7	7	6	8
Assertive				
Southern women more	31	30	25	28
Southern women less	46	44	34	34
Independent				
Southern women more	30	30	21	15
Southern women less	48	41	42	40
Self-centered				
Southern women more	22	22	18	21
Southern women less	56	48	39	29
Feminist ("that is, sympathetic to the women's movement")				
Southern women more	18	28	14	20
Southern women less	64	43	48	41
Career-oriented				
Southern women more	15	16	9	10
Southern women less	61	52	48	48

"When you think of Southern women, are there any
particular women you think about?"

	Southern	Non-Southern
Don't know/no answer	58	47
Self	1	–
Relatives	9	6
Friends	4	7
Scarlett O'Hara or Vivian Leigh	6	13
Other fictional characters	2	2
Public figures or their wives	13	12
Entertainers	3	5
Other and unknown	5	9

WE SAY GRACE AND WE SAY "MA'AM"

For as long as some people have thought of themselves as Southerners, they have believed that their manners were better than (or at least different from) those of other Americans, who have, by and large, been willing to grant them that. Lately, however, some have seen and lamented a deterioration of distinctively Southern manners.

In 1993 the Southern Focus Poll asked 859 residents of Southern states and 446 residents of non-Southern states about the manners they were taught when they were growing up and about what parents are teaching their own children these days.

Perhaps surprisingly, the results reveal only small intergenerational changes. Moreover, when it comes to obeying adults and writing thank-you notes, differences between the South and the rest of the country are quite small.

What are significant are persisting differences between the South and the rest of the country in respectful forms of address to adults—calling them "Mr." and "Mrs.," and especially "sir" and "ma'am." These differences are as large now as a generation ago. (As Hank Williams Jr. sings, "We say grace and we say 'ma'am' / If you ain't into that, we don't give a damn.")

Sirring and ma'aming are especially common among native Southerners (even those who now live outside the South), among residents of the five Deep South states, and among rural and less well educated respondents. Although the practice is decreasing among black Southerners, it is still substantially more common among them than among whites. Outside the South, it is more common among men and older respondents than among women and the young, but the relation to age and sex is not significant in the South.

Then: "When you were growing up, did your parents teach you to _____?"
Now: "How about when raising your own children? Do you (did you/will you) teach your children to _____?"

	SOUTH		NON-SOUTH	
	Then	Now	Then	Now
Do as told by adults	98	93	95	89
Write thank-you notes	77	80	72	79
Call adults "Mr." and "Mrs.," not first names	91	85	80	72
Call adults "sir" and "ma'am"	82	80	52	46

Note: Asked only of respondents with children

Percentage who were taught/teach their children to call adults "sir" and "ma'am"

	SOUTH		NON-SOUTH	
	Then	Now	Then	Now
Region				
Deep South	90	90		
Outer South	78	76		
New England			46	31
Middle Atlantic			60	58
East Central			55	45
West Central			45	45
Mountain States			45	36
Pacific Coast			42	39
Residence at age 16				
South	89	86	88	83
Border States	74	76	72	75
Non-South	56	62	45	38
County of residence				
Non-metropolitan	87	86	53	44
Metropolitan	79	76	51	46

Percentage who were taught/teach their children to call adults "sir" and "ma'am" [*continued*]

	SOUTH		NON-SOUTH	
	Then	Now	Then	Now
Race				
White	79	79	49	43
Black	98	89	73	76
Sex				
Male	86	82	60	58
Female	78	79	45	38
Age				
18–24	83	*	42	*
25–44	80	78	46	40
45–64	83	82	60	50
65 or older	83	83	58	57
Education				
11th grade or less	94	86	57	55
High school graduate	86	86	53	45
Some college	81	81	47	42
College graduate	72	71	52	48

*Too few cases for stable percentage

Y'ALL SPOKEN HERE

Y'all (or *you-all*) is probably the best-known Southernism. Certainly it's what Yankees invariably turn to when they want to imitate Southern speech. And with good reason: over two-thirds of Southerners, compared to only one non-Southerner in six, told the Southern Focus Poll in 1994 that they hear this expression "very often." Almost half of Southerners said they use the expression "very often" themselves, compared to only 11 percent of non-Southerners.

In the South, both hearing *y'all* and saying it oneself are pretty much un-affected by education and income, and both are almost as common among urban Southerners as among rural ones. Oddly, although *y'all* is employed at least occasionally by solid majorities of both black and white Southerners, blacks are only half as likely as whites to say it "very often" and nearly twice as likely to claim they never say it at all (30% vs. 16%). Outside the South, the pattern is reversed: there, blacks are far more likely than whites to use *y'all*.

Some Southern ways are threatened by the influx of non-Southerners, but this one more than holding its own. Younger Southerners are even more likely than older ones to say *y'all*. It also seems that many non-Southerners who move to the South add this useful expression to their vocabulary. Migrants to the South say *y'all* more than stay-at-home non-Southerners do, and the longer people have lived in the South, the more they use the word.

The poll also shows that *y'all* may be catching on among younger non-Southerners. Non-Southerners under twenty-five are more than twice as likely as those between twenty-five and sixty-four to use the expression "very often," and six times as likely as those sixty-five or older.

"There's a Southern expression, *y'all*—how often do you hear people say that? Very often, sometimes, only occasionally, or never?"

Percentage who say "very often":	Southern	Non-Southern
Total sample	69	17
Race		
White	71	15
Black	60	38
Other race	58	21
Age		
18–24	81	28
25–44	74	16
45–64	64	17
65 or older	54	10

"How often do you use that expression yourself—very often, sometimes, only occasionally or never?"

Percentage who say "very often":	Southern	Non-Southern
Total sample	47	11
Residence at age 16		
South	55	18
Border States	40	23
Non-South	20	10
County of residence		
Metropolitan	46	12
Non-metropolitan	49	9
Race		
White	52	10
Black	25	19
Age		
18–24	52	22
25–44	52	11
45–64	46	9
65 or older	30	4

"How often do you use that expression yourself—very often, sometimes, only occasionally or never?" [*continued*]

Percentage who say "very often":	Southern	Non-Southern
Education		
11 years or less	48	5
High school grad	45	10
Some college	46	15
College graduate	48	10
[N]	[934]	[461]

THE CHEROKEE PRINCESS IN
THE FAMILY TREE

One form of "race-mixing" that both black and white Southerners have long viewed with unconcern or even with pride has been intermarriage (preferably in the remote past) with the South's Native American population. Southerners from the First Families of Virginia to the Presley family of Tupelo, Mississippi, have believed themselves descended from Indian ancestors, and often boasted of it. Although fewer than 2 percent of Southern residents responding to the Spring 1996 Southern Focus Poll replied "Native American" or "Indian" when asked, "What race do you consider yourself?" 40 percent said they had Indian ancestors (45 percent said they did not, and 14 percent didn't know). Southerners are more likely to claim Indian ancestry than are non-Southerners, only 25 percent of whom did so (66 percent said they had none, and 9 percent didn't know).

Residents of the South are now more likely to claim descent from American Indians than from Confederate soldiers (the Fall 1994 Southern Focus Poll found that only 22 percent did the latter).

Forty-four percent of native Southerners believe that they have Indian ancestors, compared to 25 percent of native non-Southerners; interregional migrants are intermediate. Both in the South and elsewhere, younger respondents are more likely than older ones—and women slightly more likely than men—to claim Indian ancestry, but there is no consistent relation to education or income. Believing that one has Indian ancestry is especially common among black respondents: majorities both in the South and elsewhere do so.

"Do you happen to know whether any of your ancestors were American Indians?"

	South (% yes)	Non-South (% yes)
Total sample	40	25
Residence at age 16		
South	44	36
Border States	43	32
Non-South	27	25
Race		
White	36	22
Black	53	62
Sex		
Male	39	21
Female	41	28
Age		
18–24	41	31
25–44	45	26
45–64	37	24
65 or older	27	17

MOMMA'NEM

Although the Southern mother doesn't have the national fame of her Jewish counterpart, she has been celebrated locally in novels, verse, folklore, and song. And when we're referring specifically to a Southern mother, the word that comes to mind is "Momma" (or "Mama"). With the possible exceptions of "Maw," stereotypically linked to the mountain South, and "Mammy," which is another story altogether, no label for one's maternal parent is more Southern. When we speak of Elvis's devotion to his momma, when Merle Haggard sings "Mama Tried," when Jeff Foxworthy jokes about the Southern word "momma'nem" (as in, "How's your momma'nem?")—in none of these contexts would "Mom," "Mommy," or, God knows, "Mater" be quite appropriate.

In 1995 the Southern Focus Poll asked 801 respondents from Southern states and 481 from non-Southern states, "When you were a young child, what did you call your mother?" and asked of those with living mothers, "What do you call her now?"

"When you were a young child, what did you call your mother?"
"What do you call her now?"

	AS YOUNG CHILD		NOW	
	South	Non-South	South	Non-South
Momma/Mama	28	9	19	3
Mother	13	8	21	12
Mom	43	60	52	70
Mommy	9	14	2	4

"When you were a young child, what did you call your mother?"
"What do you call her now?" [*continued*]

	AS YOUNG CHILD		NOW	
	South	Non-South	South	Non-South
Ma	3	5	2	7
Maw	1	1	1	1
[Given name]	1	—	2	1
Other	1	2	2	2

The results reveal that in the South, as elsewhere, the all-American "Mom" is now the most popular form of address, but "Momma" and its variants are still serious contenders. (Outside the South, this is so only in the Mountain States.) Three-quarters of non-Southern Americans report calling their mothers "Mom" or "Mommy" as children; in the South only half did so, and in the Deep South states (South Carolina, Georgia, Alabama, Mississippi, and Louisiana) barely a third did. "Mother" is also relatively strong in the South, particularly in adulthood.

Regional variation among non-Southern respondents

As young child, called mother*	North-east	Middle Atlantic	East Central	West Central	Mountain States	Pacific Coast
Momma/Mama	10	5	5	10	24	9
Mother	8	5	9	5	16	12
Mom	51	62	66	74	46	52
Mommy	13	20	11	7	11	18
Ma	13	4	8	3	—	4

*Five most common only

This particular Southernism may be threatened. Migrants to the region are far less likely than natives to have been raised in this usage. Moreover, younger Southerners are a good deal more likely than older ones to have called their mothers "Mom" or even "Mommy." But for the time being, it's a good bet that someone who calls his mother "Momma" is Southern.

Like many indicators of cultural Southernness, this one is more common among black and rural Southerners, and among those with lower levels of formal education. It is also more common among Democrats and women.

Variation among Southern respondents

As young child, called mother:	Momma/ Mama	Mother	Mom	Mommy
Subregion				
Deep South	41	17	33	2
Outer South	24	12	47	11
Lived in South				
10 years or less	9	8	60	11
More than 10 years	20	9	54	10
All my life	36	15	36	7
County of residence				
Metropolitan	23	14	46	10
Non-metropolitan	38	12	36	7
Race				
White	26	14	44	6
Black	43	8	31	9
Sex				
Male	23	13	49	6
Female	32	13	39	11
Age				
18–24	19	5	49	19
25–44	27	7	51	9
45–64	29	23	36	5
65 or older	42	21	27	6
Education				
11th grade or less	31	11	38	7
High school grad	32	13	39	10
Some college	28	12	43	9
College graduate	23	15	51	7
Party preference				
Democrat	38	13	32	11
Republican	23	12	50	8
Independent	23	13	49	6

A DOUBLE-WIDE WHAT?

For her novel *Devil's Dream*, Lee Smith wrote the great country-music lyric,

> On a double bed in a double-wide
> With a double shot of gin,
> I'm a single gal in a one-horse town,
> Sleeping alone again.

When she sent her manuscript to her New York publisher, Smith reports, it came back with the copy-editor's marginal query, "A double-wide what?"

It's a safe bet that a Southerner wouldn't have to ask. More than half of the South's new housing stock is now made up of mobile homes, single- and, yes, double-wide, and most Southerners have at least a secondhand acquaintance with this unpretentious if image-challenged form of shelter. In fact, according to a 1995 Southern Focus Poll of 801 residents of Southern states and 481 residents of the non-South, two out of every five residents of the South have lived in a trailer-house at one time or another. Other Americans are only about half as likely to have done so; only in the Mountain States does the frequency approach Southern levels.

In the South, having lived in a mobile home is less common among migrants to the region, city folk, blacks, those with high levels of education and income, those sixty-five or older, and regular churchgoers. Native Southerners, residents of rural areas and small towns, whites, those under sixty-five, those with low levels of education and income, and infrequent churchgoers are more likely to have done so—in fact, most non-metropolitan Southerners and most of those with less than a high-school education have.

Outside the South the correlates of mobile-home living are roughly similar, although the relationship to income and education is less strong, and non-Southern women are particularly likely to deny ever having lived in a trailer.

Percentage of respondents who said they had ever lived in a mobile home (or trailer)

	South (% yes)	Non-South (% yes)
Total sample	39	23
Region		
Deep South	43	
Outer South	38	
New England		14
Middle Atlantic		18
East Central		22
West Central		27
Mountain States		41
Pacific Coast		23
Lived in South		
Less than 10 years	32	
More than 10 years	40	
"All my life"	42	
County of residence		
Metropolitan	32	20
Non-metropolitan	52	42
Race		
White	41	24
Black	33	14
Sex		
Male	38	29
Female	40	19

Percentage of respondents who said they had ever lived in a mobile home (or trailer) [*continued*]

	South [% yes]	Non-South [% yes]
Age		
18–24	34	11
25–44	43	31
45–64	43	24
65+	20	8
Education		
11th grade or less	51	23
High school grad	45	29
Some college	40	23
College grad	24	19
Income		
Less than $20,000	44	20
20,000–39,999	47	30
40,000–59,999	37	31
60,000 +	23	13
Church attendance		
Never	48	26
Less than weekly	44	27
Once a week	34	17
More than once a week	34	21

PASS THE GRITS

Grits. The national dish of the South, celebrated in a Roy Blount poem and a Stan Woodward film. But who eats it? (Or is it "them"?) A 1991 Southern Focus Poll of 1,171 Southerners found that more Southerners never eat grits than eat them frequently.

Percentage who eat grits —

Frequently 22	Sometimes 23	Seldom 20	Never 34

The Fall 1992 Southern Focus Poll followed up on this serious matter, with a slightly more specific set of answers. It also asked a sample of non-Southerners the same question. Not surprisingly, Southerners are more likely to eat grits than non-Southerners. Even so, roughly a third of Southern respondents say they never eat the stuff.

"Do you ever eat grits?" (If yes) "How often do you eat them?"

	Southerners (%)	Non-Southerners (%)
Almost every day	4	–
More than once a week	10	3
A few times a month	12	3
Just occasionally	40	33
No, never	34	61
(N)	(744)	(476)

Obviously, some Southerners aren't doing their share. Urban and well-educated Southerners, younger folks, and migrants to the region (even those who've been here a while) are letting down the side. On the other hand, black Southerners, folks in the Deep South, and regular churchgoers (obviously not mutually exclusive categories) have nothing to apologize for.

Among Southern respondents, percentage who eat grits

	More than once/week	Never
Subregion		
Deep South	28	17
Outer South	9	40
Lived in South		
"All my life"	19	29
More than ten years	4	42
Ten years or less	8	48
Residence		
Metropolitan	11	37
Non-metropolitan	21	28
Race		
White	13	34
Black	23	19
Age		
18–24	8	43
25–44	15	37
45–64	16	29
65 and older	13	24
Education		
11th grade or less	21	25
High school grad	14	40
Some college	17	30
College grad	7	35
Church attendance		
Never	11	41
Less than once/week	16	34
Once/week	12	34
More than once/week	13	28

While we're at it, who are these grits-eating non-Southerners? Mostly, they're black and/or migrants from the South. Notice that Southern-born non-Southerners are unlikely to eat grits "never"—no more likely, in fact, than resident Southerners. But even more than in the South the age gradient bodes ill for the future.

Among non-Southern respondents, percentage who eat grits–

	More than once/week	Never
Race*		
White	1	62
Black	28	32
Ever lived in South		
Yes	5	41
No	1	69
Residence at age 16		
South	9	32
Border States	–	70
Non-South	2	63
Age		
18–24	2	86
25–44	2	63
45–64	2	50
65 and older	3	56

*Education, income, and metro/non-metro differences reflect this racial difference.

SOUL FOOD

Lisa Howorth has observed that Southerners can be distinguished by what goes into their mouths and what comes out of them. Many of the questions on the Southern Focus Poll have dealt with one or another of these things. In 1995, 907 residents of the Southern states and 506 other Americans were asked whether they had ever consumed a number of distinctively "Southern" foods, a few non-Southern specialties for comparison, and such nonfood comestibles as moonshine, chewing tobacco, and snuff. A 1992 poll had already asked about grits (see above).

The data below document some expected differences, as well as revealing some surprising nondifferences.

"Now I'm going to list some unusual foods. For each one, tell me whether you eat it often, sometimes, seldom, or never. If you've never heard of it, tell me that, too."

	OFTEN		NEVER OR DON'T KNOW	
	South %	Non-South %	South %	Non-South %
Grits*	26	5	34	61
Okra	40	11	22	48
Boiled peanuts	15	5	46	75
Moon Pie	15	4	37	66
Catfish	36	14	20	37
Sweet potato pie	22	14	24	41
Pork rind	15	9	38	49

"Now I'm going to list some unusual foods. For each one, tell me whether you eat it often, sometimes, seldom, or never. If you've never heard of it, tell me that, too." [*continued*]

	OFTEN		NEVER OR DON'T KNOW	
	South %	Non-South %	South %	Non-South %
Fried tomatoes	16	12	39	47
Chitlins	4	2	81	81
Moonshine	1	–	76	80
Chewing tobacco	†	†	77	80
Snuff	†	†	85	87
Venison	16	15	39	37
Caviar	2	2	71	68
Arugula	2	2	90	86
Lox	2	3	82	74
Kielbasa	10	17	60	40

* From an earlier survey. "Often" is "a few times a month" or more.
† Question was, "Have you ever [chewed tobacco/dipped snuff]?"

The table below shows patterns within the South for some of the items that show the greatest regional differences.

Percentage of respondents who have *ever* eaten—

	Okra	Catfish	Moon Pie	Sweet potato pie	Boiled peanuts	Kielbasa
Southern total	78	80	63	76	54	40
Subregion						
Deep South	86	80	71	88	72	28
Outer South	76	80	60	71	47	45
Residence at age 16						
South	82	80	68	78	55	34
Border States	66	82	63	74	45	42
Non-South	66	79	45	67	46	69
Race						
White	80	82	64	73	53	43
Black	71	70	63	97	51	24

Percentage of respondents who have *ever* eaten— [*continued*]

	Okra	Catfish	Moon Pie	Sweet potato pie	Boiled peanuts	Kielbasa
Age						
18–24	55	80	67	66	50	22
25–44	77	80	66	73	53	46
45–64	90	82	67	82	57	44
65 or older	79	76	42	79	52	31

Urban-rural differences and differences by education and income (not shown) are negligible, except that rural, less well educated, and lower-income respondents are less likely to have eaten kielbasa. Residents of the Deep South states and native Southerners are less likely, too, and more likely to have eaten most of the "Southern" foods. Young people are less likely to have eaten okra, sweet potato pie, *and* kielbasa.

Black-white differences are large, but inconsistent. Black respondents are more likely to have eaten sweet potato pie (nearly all had), but less likely to have eaten catfish—and kielbasa.

LIVING AND DYING IN DIXIE

Is there a distinctive "Southern way of death"? If so, how many Southerners adhere to it? Is it dying?

In 1997 the Southern Focus Poll asked 815 residents of Southern states and 407 residents of non-Southern states to answer "a few questions about funerals and some of the practices and rituals we have about death and dying." The results are displayed below, along with responses to a question about pulling over for funerals, asked on an earlier survey.

Southerners are somewhat more likely than other Americans to have been to services or wakes in private homes, to have been to open-casket services and services involving conspicuous displays of emotion, to have visited a cemetery recently, to think about their own death often, and to pull over for funerals. That they are more likely to report the recent death of "a close friend or family member" may suggest a more inclusive definition of those categories. Cremation may be becoming more frequent in the South, but it appears that it will remain less common there than elsewhere for some time to come.

	South	Non-South
"Have you ever been to a wake, viewing, or funeral service in someone's private home?"		
(% yes)	39	28
"Was the body of the deceased present?"		
(% yes)	32	24

	South	Non-South
"Was there an open casket?"		
[% yes]	30	22
"Have you ever been to a wake, viewing or funeral service where people were so upset that they were wailing and moaning?"		
[% yes]	60	54
"Have any of your close relatives ever been cremated?"		
[% yes]	18	34
"How likely do you think it is that you will ask your survivors to have your body cremated?"		
[% somewhat or very likely]	38	47
"Within the past twelve months, about how many times did you visit a cemetery?		
[% more than once]	50	46
"Within the past twelve months, has anyone you considered a close friend or family member died?"		
[% yes]	63	54
"On a scale of 1 to 10, with 1 being never and 10 being all the time, how often would you say you think about your own death?"		
[mean]	4.1	3.9
[% all the time]	6	2
Asked only of those with vehicles **"Do you pull over for funerals?"**		
[% yes]	88	79

Within the South, these "Southern" ways are more common in the Deep South, among lifelong residents of the region, and in rural areas. They are also more common among frequent churchgoers, usually among women, and among African Americans. They are also more common among older respondents, except that the young are more likely to think about their own death often. Differences by education, income, and party preference (not shown) are largely due to racial differences.

	Pull over for funerals	Been to viewing	Think of own death	Cremation unlikely
Southern total	88	39	6	62
Subregion				
Deep South	90	45	8	75
Outer South	88	37	5	58
Lived in South				
10 years or less	84	31	4	43
More than 10 years	89	41	2	49
"All my life"	90	41	6	71
County of residence				
Metropolitan	86	39	4	59
Non-metropolitan	92	41	8	70
Race				
White	88	41	3	62
Black	91	32	23	74
Sex				
Male	85	42	4	60
Female	91	37	7	65
Age				
18–24	86	20	10	63
25–44	87	32	6	60
45–64	89	52	4	64
65 and older	92	53	4	64
Church attendance				
Never	82	38	5	50
Less than once/week	88	38	6	60
Once/week	89	39	5	66
More than once/week	93	44	7	76

THE "SOUTHERN ACCENT"

Linguists insist that the speech of different parts of the South and different kinds of Southerners differs from generic Midwestern speech in different ways—that there are, in other words, many different Southern accents—and most Southerners are attuned at least to the differences between up-country and low-country, and between black and white. But outsiders like the folks who make television programs tend to ignore these distinctions, as do many Southerners, perhaps especially when they're outside the South. And it is possible to classify people as having strong or weak regional accents, even if their accents are different.

Relying on that fact, we asked interviewers for the Fall 1998 and Spring 1999 Southern Focus Polls to rate the "Southern accents" of 1,645 respondents, residents of the thirteen-state South, as strong, detectable, or none. Although these student interviewers are not trained linguists, their crude ratings have turned out to be excellent predictors of a great many things. People rated as having strong accents are reliably more "Southern" in everything from their religious beliefs to their dietary preferences.

This should not be surprising; the same circumstances that instill regional speechways should be more likely to produce typically regional attitudes, values, and behaviors as well. What are those circumstances? Among residents of the South, that is, what sorts of people have identifiably Southern accents?

The table below indicates that roughly a third of our respondents fall in each of the three categories. But strong accents are more common in the Deep

South states (South Carolina, Georgia, Alabama, Mississippi, and Louisiana) than in the peripheral South. They are also more common among natives than among migrants, although migrants who have been in the South more than ten years are likely to have picked up at least a detectable accent, and one out of five has acquired a strong one.

There are no appreciable differences by race or gender, but there is a discernable age gradient: although most younger respondents have at least a detectable accent, they are somewhat less likely to have one than are older respondents. Democrats and regular churchgoers are slightly more likely to speak with an accent than Republicans and the unchurched.

There is plainly a social-class dimension to this. Respondents with low incomes and/or little education are more likely to have regional accents, as are those from non-metropolitan areas. This almost certainly reflects in part the fact that migrants tend to be of higher income and education than natives and are concentrated in Southern cities, but the differences persist when looking only at natives.

Percentage with "strong" accent vs. "none" (balance rated "detectable")

	Strong	None
Southern total	30	36
Subregion		
Deep South	40	22
Peripheral South	26	42
Lived in South		
10 years or less	6	78
More than 10 years	18	47
"All my life"	44	20
Considers self Southerner		
Does	41	20
Does not	6	70
County of residence		
Non-metropolitan	42	22
Metropolitan	23	44

Percentage with "strong" accent vs. "none" (balance rated "detectable")
(*continued*)

	Strong	None
Age		
18–24 years old	22	42
25–44	27	41
45–64	34	31
65 or older	37	27
Education		
11th grade or less	53	20
High school grad	37	27
Some college	29	37
College grad	19	48
Income		
Less than $20,000	36	32
$20,000–$39,999	32	34
$40,000–$59,999	30	36
$60,000 or more	21	43
Political Party		
Republican	27	37
Democrat	34	32
Independent	24	40
Other	29	39
Attend church		
Never	26	45
Less than once/week	30	36
Once a week	30	36
More than once/week	33	31

SOUTHERN FOODWAYS
(MOSTLY BARBECUE)

You might say that I have a (ahem) consuming interest in food these days. I've always been good at eating the stuff, and in retirement I have more time for the pleasures of the table. I've also been *writing* more about food. I got book-length serious when I wrote a book called *Holy Smoke: The Big Book of North Carolina Barbecue* (2008) with my wife, Dale, and William McKinney, and when you've written a book about something, people ask you to talk about it and write more. So lately much—possibly most—of my writing has to do with barbecue. Observe that eight of these twelve pieces do.

In my dotage, I've also gone back to honing my cooking skills—which could use some honing. As someone who's now a cookbook writer, I probably shouldn't admit it, but when I was a Boy Scout I failed the cooking test to advance to First Class. Twice.

BARBECULTURE IN THE
TWENTY-FIRST CENTURY

This is extracted from a talk I gave at Centre College when I was teaching there not long ago. It draws in part on previously published material, including a presentation to the Southern Foodways Alliance that was included in Cornbread Nation 2: The United States of Barbecue *(2004). The situation in Atlanta has improved.*

• • •

I don't think you can really understand the South if you don't understand barbecue—as food, process, and event. Look at a map of restaurants affiliated with the National Barbecue Association. Of course, many of the best barbecue joints aren't the kind of establishments that would join or even know about something called the National Barbecue Association. Nevertheless, if you look at that map, it shows plainly that (for the time being, at least) barbecue is Southern. But it has started to metastasize, popping up wherever large numbers of expatriate Southerners are found—no surprise, because that's usually who has cooked it: Southerners who took their tastes and their techniques and even their clientele with them during the Great Migration out of the South in the first half of the last century.

Like those migrants, barbecue followed well-established migration paths. In Oakland and Los Angeles and East Palo Alto you'll find pork ribs, to be sure, but also beef brisket and hot links and baloney—naturally, since most Southerners on the West Coast came from Texas and Oklahoma. Mississippians and West Tennesseans who went to Chicago and Detroit took Memphis-style barbecue along. And in the Northeast you'll find the distinctive barbecues of the Carolinas and Georgia, cooked and seasoned with techniques that came north on the Chickenbone Special. One of my favorite northeastern joints, mostly because of its location, was the late Jake and Earl's in Cambridge, Massachusetts, run by Chris Schlesinger from Norfolk, Chris wrote *The Thrill of the Grill,* a pretty good cookbook (although the title contributes to Yankees' endemic confusion about the difference between grilling and barbecuing).

To be sure, barbecue, like jazz, has sometimes changed when it left its Southern birthplace. And, in my opinion, (like jazz) not always for the better. A few years ago I read about a New York restaurant called "Carolina," that served mesquite-grilled pork on a bed of lettuce with Dijon mustard. And just last year Dale and I ate at the Arkansas Barbecue in East London's old Spitalfields Market. Although the proprietor has changed his name to "Bubba" and actually comes from Maryland, he cooks pretty good pulled pork and brisket. But he caters to British taste by serving them with mushy peas.

Anyway, barbecue may someday lose its Southern accent and become an all-American institution, as Coca-Cola did a century ago, and as NASCAR and country music and the Southern Baptist Convention may be doing today. But it hasn't happened yet. Even in the East End of London barbecue still retains its identification with the South. It's still not just Southern food, but almost *the* Southern food.

Which makes it odd that some conspicuous parts of the South are not especially good places to find it. South Louisiana, of course, but that's not what I'm talking about. I mean towns and cities that have got above their raisin'—or, anyway, want to get above it. My friend Clyde Egerton has written a country song that goes "I'm a Quiche Lady in a Barbecue Town." Well, in some Southern towns there are a lot of quiche ladies of both sexes, domestic and imported, so many in some places that they call the shots. What you get then is a quiche town.

Atlanta is one of them. You can still find good barbecue in Atlanta, but most of the joints are hidden away—off the beaten track, in obscure and sometimes unsavory neighborhoods. Harold's, near the prison, was one of the best, but it has closed. The Auburn Rib Shack, just down from the Ebenezer Baptist Church, also went out of business a while back. It's almost as if downtown Atlanta is ashamed of barbecue—finds it too country, too low-rent.

Actually, I was being polite when I said "almost as if they're ashamed." Damn it, they *are* ashamed. When the Olympics came to town, a friend of mine from North Carolina was put in charge of arranging to feed the crowds. He lined up a local African American concessionaire to welcome the world to Georgia with a wonderful array of Southern food—most definitely including barbecue. But the Atlanta Olympic Organizing Committee was desperately eager that visitors understand that Atlanta is a cosmopolitan place (a "world-class, major-league city," as a welcome sign at the airport once proclaimed), so when the committee saw the proposed menu, they vetoed it, and hired a food-service firm from Buffalo to sell hotdogs and hamburgers. It seems that the most-quoted sentence I've ever written (you can learn these things from Google) is, "Every time I look at Atlanta, I see what a quarter of a million Confederate soldiers died to prevent."

One of the reasons I like Texans is their attitude toward barbecue. Go to Dallas: There's Sonny Bryant's smack downtown, not far from Neiman-Marcus. Go to Houston: Goode Company's right out in public where people can find it. These places say: Welcome to Texas. Have some Texas food. We like it and you will, too.

Yes, there are Southern cities with barbecue pride. But the real home of real barbecue is in the small-town South. Not Charlotte, North Carolina, say, but Shelby, an hour west, where Dale and I go for supper when we're in Charlotte: barbecue as good as we've ever had at Bridge's Barbecue Lodge. Seriously, start listing great barbecue towns: The only barbecue Mecca with over one hundred thousand population—the only one over fifty thousand—is Memphis. (I will not speak here of Kansas City, where in fact you can get some pretty good smoked meat cooked by expatriate Southerners and their descendants. I will not speak of it because it is a Johnny-come-lately that presumes to call itself "the Barbecue Capital of the World," and it should be punished for that effrontery.)

No, the real barbecue capitals—and there's more than one—the real barbecue capitals of the world are small towns like Goldsboro, North Carolina; or Lexington, where Vince Staten found sixteen barbecue restaurants for sixteen thousand people. They're places like Lockhart or Luling or Llano, Texas. They're towns like Owensboro, Kentucky (although I was distressed to read that there are now only three barbecue joints in Owensboro; there were eleven in 1960.) The South's big cities may have barbecue, sometimes good barbecue, but it's not a religion. And, in many of them, the best on offer these days is at branches of barbecue chains. Let me say a word about that development.

I don't approve of chain restaurants in general, and I dislike barbecue chains more than most. It was Rousseau who memorably observed the paradox that man is born free and is everywhere in chains. Expansion is not good for barbecue joints. That's a rule almost as reliable as Vince Staten's maxim that a place without flies is no good. (You should ask what the flies know that you don't.) I'm sorry, but Dreamland in Birmingham just isn't as good as Dreamland in Tuscaloosa. If the owner's not around to keep an eye on things, it's a pretty safe bet that both the food and the, ah, ambience will suffer. And it's especially sad when a chain imports somebody else's traditions to a place that ought to celebrate its own. I think about this every time I eat Memphis dry ribs at Corky's in Jackson, or Red, Hot and Blue in Chapel Hill. (Which is actually pretty often, because when it comes to barbecue it's almost true that the worst I ever had was good, as Dave Gardner once observed on another subject. At least I think he was talking about another subject. Sometimes it's hard to tell with Brother Dave.)

Nevertheless, places with local barbecue traditions should shun synthetic tradition, or at least label it as an alien import, even if it comes from Memphis and tastes pretty good. When I have a choice I prefer the local product, ideally served up in a cinder-block building with a dancing pig sign out front.

One reason I prefer it has nothing to do with the food. Go into one of these places in or near a small Southern town and you're quite likely to find that it has brought all sorts of unlikely people together, just about everyone except quiche ladies: businessmen and construction workers, farmers and lawyers, cowboys and hippies, black and white and everything in-between and sideways, Protestants and Catholics, even Jews. (I love it that the owner/operator of the Old Smokehouse Barbecue, in Anniston, Alabama, was Gershon Weinberg.) I once suggested half-seriously that if the South needs a new flag—as it surely does—we could do worse than to use a dancing pig with a knife and fork. You want to talk about heritage, not hate? That represents a heritage we all share and can take pride in. Barbecue both symbolizes and contributes to community. And that's without mentioning its noncommercial manifestations—for instance, in matters like fund-raising for volunteer fire departments, or political rallies.

I'll close by pointing out that there's another side to this coin. It's often the case, and it is in this one, too, that community is reinforced by emphasizing differences from outsiders. There's no denying that barbecue can be divisive. The only constant is slow cooking with smoke (and, yes, I know some places cook with gas only and call their product "barbecue," but I don't). Suppose we ignore Texas beef and Owensboro mutton and go with the pork favored by the Southeastern majority. Do we cook shoulder, ribs, or whole hog? What kind of sauce—mostly vinegar? tomato? mustard? How hot? How sweet? Will we baste or not? Or forget the sauce and go with a dry rub? OK. The meat is done. What are the divinely ordained side dishes? Carolina hushpuppies? Alabama white bread? Arkansas tamales? (Check out McClard's in Hot Springs.) Cole slaw is almost universal, but I've only seen boiled white potatoes in eastern North Carolina; rice only in South Carolina; jalapeños only in Texas and Oklahoma.

Questions of what to cook, how to cook it, and what to serve with it are not resolved by the individual whim or creativity of the cook. Old-school barbecue cooks differ in technique and in skill, but they are working in traditions that pretty much tell them what to produce. And those traditions reflect and reinforce the fierce localism that has always been a Southern characteristic, the "sense of place" that literary folk claim to find in Southern fiction, the devotion to states' rights and local autonomy that was an established characteristic of Southern politics long before it became a major headache for the Confederate States of America. This delightful variety has come under challenge, but what barbecue you're served can still usually tell you where you are.

It seems that the second most quoted sentence I've ever written is this one, from a 1988 review of Greg Johnson and Vince Staten's *Real Barbecue*: "Southern barbecue is the closest thing we have in the U.S. to Europe's wines or cheeses; drive a hundred miles and the barbecue changes." I hope for my grandchildren's sake that it stays that way.

THERE'S A WORD FOR IT
The Origins of "Barbecue"

This contains some material drawn from Holy Smoke: The Big Book of North Carolina Barbecue, *and it was published in* Southern Cultures *as a teaser for the book. It also let me expand on a subject that deserves more attention than we'd given it.*

• • •

What could be more Southern than barbecue? Even when entrepreneurs have taken the dish to other parts of the world, the names of their establishments pay tribute to the origins of their product, either explicitly (Memphis Championship Barbecue in Las Vegas, Memphis Minnie's in San Francisco, the Carolina Country Kitchen in Brooklyn, the Arkansas Café in London) or at least by implication (Jake and Earl's in Cambridge, Massachusetts, Daisy May's in Manhattan, Dixie's in Bellevue, Washington). Rivaled only by grits as the national dish of the South, barbecue would appear to be as Southern, as indigenous, as it comes.

But, for all that Southerners have made barbecue our own, the fact remains that this symbol of the South, like kudzu, is an import. The technique of cooking over hardwood coals or a low fire, or with smoke and indirect heat from hardwood, at a low temperature (about the boiling point of water) exists in a great many different cultures, and has from time immemorial: Europeans and Africans were both familiar with it before they arrived in the New World and found the native Indians doing it. The hogs and cattle that are the usual subjects of the enterprise were brought from Europe, as was the vinegar that goes into most sauces. The peppers that usually go in as well are a West Indian contribution. And tomatoes—well, that's a long story, but let's just say that they weren't grown and eaten in colonial North America.

Even the word *barbecue* seems to have been imported (although it underwent some changes after it was naturalized in Great Britain's southern colonies). The word came into English only some five hundred years ago. In the first decades of the 1500s Spanish explorers in the Caribbean found the locals using frameworks of sticks to support meat over fires. They did this either to slow-cook it or to cure and preserve it (as we do with country hams and jerky today)—which one depends on the heat of the fire and the height of the framework. Both on the island of Hispaniola (modern-day Haiti and the Dominican Republic) and on the northern coast of South America this apparatus was called something that the Spanish heard as *barbacòa*, which soon became a Spanish word (one that is making its way into the South these days, via Mexico). A French expedition to Florida in the 1560s included an artist, Jacques Le Moyne, one of whose sketches of Timucua Indian life shows a mixed grill of alligators, snakes, and some kind of wildcat on just such a frame. The Native Floridians also had a word like *barbacòa* for this rig, and indeed for all sorts of wooden structures, including watchtowers and raised sleeping platforms.

Some twenty years later, in 1585, Sir Walter Raleigh sent some folks to look things over on the coast of what would later be North Carolina. One member of that party was John White, "Gentleman of London," who later became governor of the ill-fated Roanoke Island colony (and grandfather of Virginia Dare who was, as every North Carolina schoolchild once knew, the first English child born in North America). White made sketches of what he saw, including Croatan Indians "broyling their fishe over the flame—they took great heed that they bee not burntt." Unfortunately, he didn't say what the indigenous Tar Heels called their cooker, but whatever they called it, it's obviously a *barbacòa*, too.

William Dampier, naturalist and sometime pirate, wrote in 1697 about a visit to some West Indians when he and his companions "lay there all night, upon our Borbecu's, or frames of Sticks, raised about 3 foot from the Ground." Yankees and Australians who talk about putting meat "on the barbecue" can appeal to Dampier for precedent, but in colonial North America and England, as in the South today, the word usually referred to a process of cooking or to what was cooked, rather than to the frame on which it was done.

The earliest use of the English word that I've encountered comes from 1661, when Edmund Hickeringill's *Jamaica Viewed* reported that animals "are slain, And their flesh forthwith Barbacu'd and eat," but by 1688 in a play called *THE Widdow Ranter OR, The HISTORY of Bacon in Virginia*, "the rabble" fixing to lynch one Colonel Wellman cry, "Let's barbicu this fat rogue." That the word could be used casually on the stage shows that by then it must have been familiar to London audiences. (The play was written by the remarkable Aphra Behn, the first Englishwoman to be a professional writer, and "Bacon" in the title refers to the leader of Bacon's Rebellion of 1676, not to side meat.) About the same time the Boston Puritan Cotton Mather used the word in the same gruesome sense, when he reported that several hundred Narragansetts slaughtered by New England troops in 1675 (among them women, children, and elders burned in their lodges) had been "terribly Barbikew'd."

A few years later John Lawson, surveyor-general of North Carolina, also used the word without explanation. In his *New Voyage to Carolina* (1709). Lawson encountered "barbakued"—that is, smoked and dried—venison, fish, and even peaches. Some Santee Indians served him "fat barbacu'd Venison" that sounds like a sort of jerky: "the Woman of the Cabin took [it] and tore in Pieces with her Teeth"—pulled, not sliced—"so put it into a Mortar, beating it into Rags," then boiled it. But he was also served "roasted or barbakued Turkey, eaten with Bears Fat." Not long after that, the physician and naturalist John Brickell gave a very similar account (so similar in fact that it may have been plagiarized) in his *Natural History of North Carolina* (1737).

The one suggestion I've found that the English word was not taken from the Spanish version of a Caribbean Indian word comes from Robert Beverly's *History of the Present State of Virginia* (1705). Beverly reported that the Indians of the Carolinas and Virginia had "two ways of Broyling viz. one by laying the Meat itself upon the Coals, the other by laying it upon Sticks rais'd upon Forks at some distance above the live Coals, which heats more gently, and drys up the Gravy," and added, "this [latter] they, and we also from them, call Barbac-ueing." (Whether they had the same word as their Caribbean cousins or not, they plainly got the grilling versus barbecuing thing.)

The English may have copied the Indians' vocabulary, but they didn't feel constrained to copy their stone-age gear. Anglo-Saxons and Celts had been roasting meat for a few thousand years themselves, and had made a few improvements in the matter of cooking frames. In 1732 Richard Bradley, in *The Country House-wife,* gave directions for "an Hog barbecued": "Take a large Grid-iron, with two or three Ribs in it, and set it upon a stand of iron, about three Foot and a half high, and upon that, lay your Hog, . . . Belly-side downwards." And a 1744 advertisement in the *Boston News-Letter* offered for sale "A Lusty Negro Man, works well at the Smith's Trade; likewise a Grate for to burn Coal; a large Gridiron, fit for a large Kitchen, or a Barbeque." (It also offers the earliest example I've found of the *-que* spelling, although spelling was so random at the time that it hardly signifies.)

Still, the process of cooking or smoking meat on some sort of frame remained identified with the Indians. When Colonel George Washington, trying to get provisions for his troops during the French and Indian War, wrote his superior officer in 1758, "We have not an ounce of salt provision of any kind here; and it is impossible to preserve the fresh (especially as we have no Salt) by any other means than barbacuing it in the indian manner," he was evidently writing about smoking meat to cure it, not to cook it. Later, however, the future Father of His Country often wrote about going to "barbecues" where cooking was the object: for example, "Went in to Alexandria to a Barbecue and stayed all Night" (1769), "Went to a Barbicue of my own giving at Accotinck" (1773), "Went to the Barbacue at Accatinck" (1774). (Notice that his spelling was as independent as his subsequent politics.)

Washington's use of *barbecue* to refer to a social event was not unusual: That use of the word dates from at least 1733, although it was apparently an Americanism. When a young Virginian wrote to a London friend in 1784 that he was "continually at Balls & Barbecues," he added, "the latter I don't suppose you know what I mean" and went on to explain:

> it's a shoat & sometimes a Lamb or Mutton & indeed sometimes a Beef splitt into & stuck on spitts, & then they have a large Hole dugg in the ground where they have a number of Coals made of the Bark [?] of Trees, put in this Hole. & then they lay the Meat over that within about six inches of the Coals, & then they Keep basting it with Butter & Salt & Water & turning it every now and then, until it is done, we then dine under a large shady tree or an harbour made of green bushes, under which we have benches & seats to sit on when we dine sumptuously.

This was the kind of thing the itinerant Anglican parson Charles Wood-
mason probably smelled, roaming the South Carolina backcountry in 1768,
when he wrote in his journal: "I had last Week Experience of the Velocity and
force of the Air—By smelling a Barbicu dressing in the Woods upwards of six
Miles," and it sounds pretty nice, if you get to sit under the "harbour." Less so,
of course, if you're a slave on the digging and basting crew.

Even though the word had been naturalized in the thirteen colonies, the
British continued to see it as West Indian. Also, most references at this time
were to whole hogs (or whole other animals) being cooked—the practice in
the Caribbean and, now as then, in eastern North Carolina. When the poet
Alexander Pope wrote in 1733 that a man named Oldfield, who was famous
for his appetite, "Cries, 'Send me, Gods! a whole Hog barbecu'd!'" he added
a note for his English readers explaining that "a whole hog barbecu'd" was
"A West-Indian Term of Gluttony, a Hog roasted whole, stu'd with Spice, and
basted with Madera Wine." Just so, Samuel Johnson's famous *Dictionary* (1755)
defined the verb *to barbecue* as "a term used in the West-Indies for dressing a
hog whole; which, being split to the backbone, is laid flat upon a large grid-
iron, raised about two feet above a charcoal fire, with which it is surrounded"
and *barbecue*, the noun, as "a hog drest whole in the West Indian manner."
Virtually identical definitions, probably cribbed from Johnson, can be found
in many, many subsequent dictionaries. In 1828 Noah Webster's *Dictionary
of the American Language* also defined the word as, "in the West Indies, a hog
roasted whole," but expanded the definition: "It is, with us [i.e., Americans],
used for an ox or perhaps any other animal dressed in like manner."

Webster was from Connecticut, but an 1816 *Vocabulary, or, Collection of
words and phrases, which have been supposed to be peculiar to the United States
of America* [etc.], had given the first indication that barbecue was becoming
a Southern thing. Quoting an English source from 1798, it said that barbecue
was "a porket . . . stuffed with spices and other rich ingredients, and basted
with Madeira wine," then added, "Used in the Southern states" (although "not
peculiar to the United States; it is used in the West Indies also").

Notice that these dictionaries show the emergence of yet another use of
this versatile word: a barbecue could mean the critter being barbecued. And
not just a hog; in 1796 Hugue Henry Brackenridge wrote a humorous reply
to a challenge to duel, which read in part, "I do not see any good it would do
me to put a bullet through any part of your body. . . . You might make a good

barbecue, it is true, being of the nature of a raccoon or an opossum; but people are not in the habit of barbecuing anything human now."

So by the mid-1700s we had barbecue as a kind of equipment for a style of cooking called barbecuing, and we had barbecue as an event of the sort that George Washington and his contemporaries went to, and we had barbecue as a word for the subject of the undertaking—pig, ox, shad, whatever (although this last use seems to have disappeared). But we apparently did not yet have barbecue as the point of all this: the dish prepared on a barbecue-device and served at a barbecue-event, what a barbecue-creature becomes after it is bar-becue-processed. When did barbecued pork become pork barbecue?

Someone may come up with an earlier example, but the earliest I've found comes from 1808. Oddly enough, it comes from a Yankee—although he was disparaging Southern folkways at the time. In a speech on the floor of Con-gress, Representative Josiah Quincy of Boston denounced the kind of partisan stump speech commonly delivered "in this quarter of the country . . . while the gin circulated, while barbecue was roasting." (It was a Southern thing. He didn't understand.) By the middle of the nineteenth century this use of the word was increasingly common in print, especially in Southern newspapers, usually in the context of political rallies. In 1859, for instance, the *Weekly Stan-dard* of Raleigh wrote that one politician's "constituents had been bought up by whiskey and barbecue." The next year, the same paper wrote of a gathering in Shelby, "The barbecue was excellent. Not a Douglas man was found upon the ground." In 1868 the *Petersburg Index* reported that the three thousand Democrats at a rally in Nash County, North Carolina, "marched to the grove, near by, where a bountiful supply of barbecue, vegetables, etc., etc., refreshed the 'inner man,' and to which ample justice was done."

True, as late as 1894, when the *Statesville (N.C.) Landmark* wrote of an occasion where "several hundred ladies were present, and the contents of their baskets, supplemented by 'barbecue' from the committee, composed the repast," the paper put the noun in quotation marks, suggesting that the usage remained colloquial. Still, by then everyone seems to have known that it meant something you could put on a plate or a sandwich.

Once that was understood, Southerners could begin the eternal argument about what barbecue *is*.

BARBECUE AND THE SOUTHERN PSYCHE

There aren't many books I wish I'd written, but Searching for the Dixie Barbecue *is one of them. This review, published in* Southern Cultures, *says why.*

• • •

Wilber "Pete" Caldwell, who lives in Gilmer County, Georgia, has written on subjects as diverse as public architecture and cynicism. Now, in *Searching for the Dixie Barbecue: Journeys into the Southern Psyche,* he turns his attention to barbecue, and he obviously had a really good time writing this book.

He begins with a brief essay on the history of pit-cooked meat from Prometheus onward, but concludes that barbecue is an American—specifically, a Southern—invention, if only because most Southerners believe that barbecue isn't barbecue if it's not *called* barbecue. Bringing in Prometheus (and the *Iliad,* and Brillat-Savarin) reveals his learning—worn lightly, thank goodness, since nothing could be more dreary than a pedantic treatment of this subject except maybe a postmodern one. (In one instance, alas, the learning is deployed carelessly: "Harleian" is not the writer of a medieval cookbook but the name of the British Library collection that includes it.) (I'm just showing off.)

Caldwell moves on to a series of loosely connected chapters that answer a great many fascinating questions that it hadn't occurred to me to ask. For instance:

- how barbecue manners differ from regular table manners, and when each is appropriate.

- how three places in the same county can all have "the best barbecue in [the county/the state/the South/the nation/the world]," and what "world-famous" might mean in that context.
- why some Southerners don't like Brunswick stew (because it reminds them of school cafeteria food).
- why side dishes are generally boring (because they are "designed not to distract from the main event").
- what Southerners usually tell the truth about (e.g., war records, athletic achievements) and what they feel free to lie about because everyone knows they're lying (e.g., fishing, barbecue).
- why everyone, black and white, knows that black barbecue and white barbecue are different, despite the fact that they're apparently not.
- how "never" and "generally not" are used (as in the rule that one never serves cornbread with barbecue, except when one is serving greens with the barbecue, but one does not generally serve greens with barbecue), and what that tells us about Southern thought.

In this last example I have paraphrased to avoid Caldwell's phonetic rendition of Southern speech, an uncharacteristic misstep which sometimes lends an unfortunate Simon Suggs flavor to the proceedings. In general, however, he has a good ear; it lets him have fun, for example, with the names people give to barbecue sauces. He offers some of his own, like "Piney Woods Wilber's 'Let the Big Dog Eat' Georgia BBQ Sauce," and even gives the recipe for one with a name not family-friendly that starts with a gallon each of catsup and vinegar and winds up with a quart of 10W-30 motor oil and "Clorox Brand Bleach as needed."

Caldwell savors places like the Red Pig Barbecue in Concord, North Carolina, which used to sport its "C" health rating as a badge of honor, and he offers a useful index for calculating an establishment's "funk factor," with a base score for architectural features (e.g., +10 for no windows), adjusted for various add-ons and deductions (e.g., minus ½ point for designated handicapped parking; plus ½ point for plastic flowers, displays of firearms, or pictures of Jesus; minus one full point if the place has a website). This doesn't just work for barbecue joints, by the way. Before my all-time favorite oyster shack in South Carolina was rebuilt after a fire, it had a damn near perfect score.

This is not all fun and games, however. Caldwell has actually done some serious (well, sort of serious) research. He reports, for example, on a survey of the side dishes served by fifty establishments. (He doesn't consider Brunswick stew a side dish: It gets its own chapter.) Nearly all serve the "holy trinity" of coleslaw, baked beans, and potato salad. Potato chips, french fries, and hush-puppies follow at a considerable distance, with corn on the cob far behind, and nothing else served by more than a handful of the places.

If there seems to be a consensus on what should be served with barbecue, let me add, in the same empirical spirit, that Caldwell's photographs reveal an encouraging independence when it comes to spelling. Only four of the sixty-six signs displayed spell the word "barbecue" that way: fully half prefer "Bar-B-Q," another quarter go with "BBQ," and "Bar-B-Que" is also popular.

By the way, there are ninety-some of those photographs, and they would make a good coffee-table book in their own right. Most show places in the top quartile of funkiness, and a few are off the scale. I'm happy to report that three-quarters are from Georgia, which means there's still a lot of "research" left for those of us from other states

BBQ & A

An Interview for *BBQJew.com*

In 2009, Dan Levine (aka Porky LeSwine) interviewed my wife and coauthor Dale and me for his blog, BBQJew.com. Dan and I subsequently founded the Campaign for Real Barbecue, which he serves as Chief Smoke Detector and I as Éminence Grease. (Check us out at TrueCue.org.) The revised, paperback edition of Holy Smoke *includes Dan as a Chevalier du Tasty Swine.*

• • •

Husband and wife writing team John and Dale Reed have written an instant classic, *Holy Smoke: The Big Book of North Carolina Barbecue*. And considering that they have a Jewish son-in-law and have lived in Israel, we welcome them into the fold as honorary BBQ Jews. (We're an inclusive people.) The 'cue-loving couple were kind enough to share some swine with us and to put up with our questions.

BBQ JEW: How many plates of barbecue would you estimate you have eaten?

DALE: We've each probably eaten something between five hundred and a thousand plates, starting at Turnage's in Durham in 1961 or so. That works out to—what?—only two or three hundred pounds.

JOHN: Not all that much, compared to some folks we know.

BBQ JEW: John, when you taught at Hebrew University in Jerusalem, did you find any good barbecue in the Promised Land (perhaps basted with milk and honey)?

JOHN: No barbecue, although we occasionally bought pork chops from a Christian Arab butcher who mostly sold to the embassies.

DALE: Very occasionally, because they were very expensive.

BBQ JEW: What brought you to write *Holy Smoke*?

JOHN: We were eating barbecue one evening with David Perry, the editor in chief at UNC Press, and we discovered that he and I both cooked out of a book called *Legends of Texas Barbecue,* by a friend of ours named Robb Walsh. Someone at the table—we really don't remember who—said, "You know, somebody ought to do something like this for North Carolina."

DALE: John and I sort of looked at each other and said, "We will!"

JOHN: So we sent David a proposal, and the press bought it.

DALE: We knew William McKinney when he was a UNC undergraduate and the founder and moving spirit of the Carolina Barbecue Society, and we knew he'd videotaped interviews with some of the great names in North Carolina barbecue, so we got him on board as soon as we could.

JOHN: William's also our whole-hog cooker. The instructions for doing that and for building a pit are his. Me, I cook shoulders, but I'm happy to leave whole-hog cooking to the professionals.

BBQ JEW: In researching the book, did you come across any fellow Jews involved in NC BBQ in any way?

JOHN: Well, none of the pitmasters or restaurant owners. Actually, though, I think two of the eight guys we listed as Chevaliers du Tasty Swine—champions of the cause—are Jewish. Barry Farber's a UNC grad who has made a career as a radio talk-show host in New York and who experimented back in the seventies with a North Carolina barbecue joint in New York.

DALE: He got the real stuff flown in flash-frozen from Fuzzy's in Madison, but he gave up when he went in one day and found the Greek guys who were running the place serving the barbecue on bagels.

JOHN: Alexander Julian's the other. He's the big-time New York fashion designer from Chapel Hill who took payment in barbecue for designing the Charlotte Hornets' uniforms. He gets frozen barbecue shipped to him regularly.

DALE: We know a good many Jews in other states who are in the barbecue business, starting with Gershon Weinberg, who used to run the Old Smokehouse Barbecue in Anniston, Alabama, and going on to our buddy Bob Kantor, a Brooklyn guy who runs Memphis Minnie's, a terrific wood-cooking place on Haight Street in San Francisco.

JOHN: You know a piece by Marcie Cohen Ferris in *Cornbread Nation 2* called "We Didn't Know from Fatback"? It's got to be the last word on the subject of Jews and barbecue.

BBQ JEW: We prefer to think of it as the first word. We hope to have the next.

OK, let's say Yom Kippur is ending and it's time to break the fast. BBQ Jews of all stripes are depending on you to recommend the restaurant that serves the most divine swine in the nation. Where do you send them?

JOHN: Look, there are a couple of dozen places in North Carolina that we wouldn't hesitate to recommend. Shoot, there are a half dozen in Davidson County. On a given day, any one of them might have the best barbecue in the state (which means, of course, the best in the nation).

DALE: On a particular day, our advice might be terrible, because any wood-cooking place is going to have good days and bad days. You want one that doesn't have many bad days and that doesn't need a good day to cook great barbecue.

JOHN: Yeah, if you want uniformity, go to a place that cooks with gas or electricity. You'll get uniformly mediocre barbecue. At best, uniformly OK.

BBQ JEW: An artful dodge. You guys are good.

At gunpoint: Eastern or Lexington style?

JOHN: This answer's not going to make anybody happy, but whichever is nearer. You sometimes get the sense that partisans would rather have a second-rate plate of their own style than a first-rate plate of the other. Not us.

DALE: If I had to choose between excellent examples of both, I'd probably go with Piedmont-style, because I really, really like "outside brown," and you get more of it with shoulders—especially if you know to ask for it.

JOHN: She just says that because her people are German.

DALE: We make a big deal in our book about the Teutonic origins of Lexington-style.

JOHN: I'd be hard-pressed to say. I would have agreed with Dale once. But the more I've learned about this, the more I like Eastern-style. In part, that's because I'm a traditionalist, and Eastern-style is pretty much what barbecue was everywhere for most of the nineteenth century. It carries the weight of all that great history. But there's more to it than that. A guy named Steve Stephens called North Carolina barbecue "the crack cocaine of pork"—he meant you can't put it down—and Lexington-style is like the gateway drug for folks who didn't grow up with it. The sauce is sweeter, as a rule, it has that tomato tang, and the meat has fewer surprises in it. It may be easier for the uneducated palate to like. But once you've come to like the vinegar-based sauces of the Piedmont, you find yourself wanting something more. . . .

BBQ JEW: We're petitioning the Orthodox Union to create a law pronouncing wood-cooked barbecue to be kosher. Would you back that rule change and are there any other general barbecue laws you would like to see?

DALE: We'd like to see a ruling that anything rubbed with kosher salt isn't treyf.

BBQ Jew: What's the most important thing you look for in a barbecue restaurant?

JOHN: Barbecue. I'm not being facetious; the meat's what matters, at least as far as I'm concerned. I don't give a damn about the décor or the "ambience." As our buddy Vince Staten says, "My taste is mostly in my mouth."

DALE: Me, too. We also don't care (much) about the side dishes or the desserts or the wine list, or even the service. If the barbecue's mediocre, nothing else matters. If the barbecue's great, nothing else matters.

BBQ JEW: Do you have a barbecue joint pet peeve?

DALE: We've become fundamentalist about wood-cooking. Good barbecue can be cooked with hardwood charcoal out of the bag, but out of the burn barrel is better. And fossil fuels should be banned.

JOHN: We don't bother with gassers, which has saved us a good deal of time and money over the years.

BBQ JEW: John, we've seen a photo of you in your military uniform from your teaching days at The Citadel. Might there be a photo from Hebrew University of you sporting a yarmulke?

JOHN: Yeah, when in Rome. . . . As a matter of fact, there's a photo Dale took of me and our kids at the Seder we went to in Jerusalem in 1974. I'll send it to you and you can post it, if you want.

BBQ JEW: Consider it done. . . .

[*It was. The photo can be found at* BBQJew.com.]

CONTRA LOS HEREJES

In 2013 Texas Monthly *asked me to speak for North Carolina barbecue in a "debate" with their barbecue editor, Daniel Vaughn. Daniel and I already knew each other and don't actually disagree about much, but we did our best to pick a fight for the magazine's readers. This is a longer version, posted on Daniel's blog, of the exchange published in the magazine. Daniel got the last word in his blog, but this is my book, so I get it here.*

• • •

Daniel,

So, we are to debate the relative merits of North Carolina and Texas barbecue. Let me begin by saluting a worthy opponent, defending a worthy, if mistaken, cause. This is a dispute worth having. I wouldn't waste my ammunition on Memphis or Kansas City.

I know you've eaten our barbecue, and I have eaten yours. Our Texan son-in-law has escorted my wife and me to number of towns near Austin that start with *L* and a few that don't. We've eaten wood-cooked meat in Austin itself, and in Houston and Dallas and Brownwood and elsewhere.

And y'all are right about many things. I admire your loyalty to tradition, no matter how misguided the loyalty or recent the tradition; in particular, I applaud your devotion to cooking with wood. (I prefer your barbecue to "North Carolina barbecue" cooked with gas or electricity, but, hell, I prefer Sloppy Joes to that.) Most Texans also understand that sauce, if used at all, should season the meat, not smother it; in both of our states, barbecue's not about sauce. So I want it understood up front that I recognize Texans as barbecue brethren—erring brethren, but brethren nevertheless—and when I criticize, it is more with sadness than with indignation.

Let's stipulate at the outset that we'll be discussing the traditional cooking styles of our respective states, not what's served at the pick-your-meat, pick-your-sauce, mix-and-match, International House of Barbecue places that are increasingly common in our cities. True, they're *in* North Carolina or Texas, and they're serving what they call barbecue, but it's not North Carolina barbecue or Texas barbecue; it's food from nowhere, for people from nowhere, who deserve nothing better. But we both know that there are different barbecue traditions within North Carolina and Texas, so we each need to specify what it is that we're championing.

I have the easier job of it. It's true that there are two varieties of North Carolina barbecue, an eastern and a western (more properly, "piedmont") style. But any outsider will recognize immediately that the two styles are much more like each other than either is like what passes for barbecue anywhere else. Jim Auchmutey, who knows a thing or two about the subject, said once that North Carolina should put "The Vinegar State" on its license plates. He's a Georgian and exaggerates, but in both regions of North Carolina mops and sauces do consist mostly of vinegar, salt, and cayenne pepper, with perhaps some sugar, just a touch of ketchup in the piedmont, and not much else. My fellow Tar Heels enjoy arguing endlessly about that tincture of ketchup, but North Carolina sauces are vinegar with stuff in it, not (as in Kansas City and on grocery-store shelves) ketchup with stuff in it.

Similarly, whether one should cook whole hogs (eastern) or pork shoulders (piedmont) is a matter of great moment within North Carolina, but for even the most fervent partisan the differences pale into insignificance when beef or mutton—not to mention sausage—enters the picture. Many Tar Heels will allow that those other meats can be tasty, but we don't actually believe that they are barbecue, and we wish y'all would call them something else to prevent confusion.

So when I say "North Carolina barbecue"—in fact, when I say "barbecue"—I mean pork, cooked for a long time at a low temperature with heat and smoke from burning coals, and served with a peppery vinegar-based sauce.

What are you talking about?

Awaiting your reply
John

P.S. I won't mention Dickey's if you don't bring up Smithfield's Chicken 'N
Bar-B-Q.

Vaughn replied, as follows:

John,

If Smithfield's Chicken 'N Bar-B-Q, with locations covering the state of
North Carolina, is allowed to use the word *barbecue* to describe the 100%
gas-cooked pork that they routinely sling through drive-thru windows,
then I'm confused at your confusion about applying the term to beautifully
smoked beef (or lamb or goat). That argument just doesn't hold vinegar.

Your definition of barbecue (pork, cooked for a long time at a low temperature with heat and smoke from burning coals, and served with a peppery
vinegar-based sauce) provides for some common ground, but the self-serving
limitation to a single protein seems to exist only because your fair state has
failed to master the art of applying wood smoke to another animal. I know
this firsthand since I've been witness to meager attempts at smoked brisket
in Lexington, revered as a sort of barbecue capital in your parts, I believe.
Here in the Lone Star State we know a thing or three about large hunks of
animals that moo and those that oink too.

You have shared your familiarity with brisket, so I can only assume your
cantankerousness rises from an uncomfortable longing for that finest of
barbecue cuts that still requires some considerable R&D from your North
Carolina brethren. In the real capital of barbecue—Lockhart, Texas—their
knowledge of beef is a given, but there is porcine artistry to discover as well.
Instead of using that most forgiving of barbecue meats, the self-basting pork
shoulder that my four-year-old daughter could probably overcook to the
point that a North Carolinian could enjoy, they smoke large racks of pork
ribs and whole racks of bone-in loin. When those cuts, seasoned only with
salt, pepper, and smoke, are taken from the pits, they are cut and served
with the only liquid appropriate to go alongside barbecue—Big Red. If the
outcome were a more inferior product, then the cook or the patron might

consider enlivening or even covering the flavor of the poorly handled meat with a sauce. I've witnessed this as a common practice in the Carolinas where arguments over sauce seem to trump those about the actual hog. Trying to weasel sauce into the very definition of barbecue is a disservice to those pitmasters who don't require it to make their meat palatable, and furthermore is an insult to the hog. Expect the business end of bull's horn if you utter that definition in Texas.

Daniel

P.S. I too have left Memphis and Kansas City out of this discussion. If their barbecue was better it might migrate beyond their respective city limits, but until that time they can only fight for the bronze medal in the barbecue Olympics. The respectable tradition in North Carolina has unquestionably secured your fine state the silver.

My turn:

Daniel,

I'm sorry that our correspondence is facing some sort of deadline. I'd be happy to explain things for as long as it takes you to understand. Still, I'll do what I can in one letter. It will necessarily be a long one. A few minor points to address before turning to, ah, the meat of the matter:

First, despite my P.S., you just had to mention Smithfield's Chicken 'N Bar-B-Q, didn't you? Look, don't expect me to defend Smithfield's. You're right that they're "allowed to use the word *barbecue*." So is Tony Roma's (headquarters: Dallas, Texas). Who's going to stop them? That doesn't mean that either outfit actually serves barbecue. Let's talk about places that do. As for Dickey's, I'll concede that their product is a better imitation of genuine Texas barbecue than Smithfield's is of the authentic North Carolina stuff. This could be either a point in favor of Dickey's or a strike against Texas barbecue. Your call.

Second, you say you encountered some sorry attempts by North Carolinians to cook beef brisket. I have, too, and yes, if I'm going to eat brisket I'll eat yours. What you ran into isn't a conscious reversion to the time when we did barbecue beef in these parts (see below); it's just an attempt to make money from newly arrived out-of-staters with fixed misconceptions about barbecue. You know what I'm talking about: I see that Red Hot & Blue has come to the Metroplex.

Third, you observe that brisket is harder to cook than pork shoulder. That's true, but so what? Since when does degree-of-difficulty enter into the judging? This ain't gymnastics. For the amateur, part of the appeal of cooking shoulder is that you can sit with it for a long time and think deep thoughts about other things. Hell, if it's difficulty you want, barbecue chicken. Anyway, if we were going to discuss skill I'd argue that whole-hog barbecue is the epitome of the pitmaster's art.

Finally, you didn't answer my question about what Texas barbecue is, and maybe you can't. Texas has regional styles so diverse that you can't defend them all without defending *everything*. But I infer that what you're promoting is the Central Texas version—i.e., a variety of meats and meat products cooked with indirect heat and lots of wood smoke and served with sauce on the side, if at all. What you get in Lockhart and Luling and Elgin and Taylor. If I'm wrong, let's scrub this whole exchange and start over some other time.

Since we apparently agree on the need for wood-cooking (with some differences in technique that aren't worth fighting about) there are really only two points at issue: (1) our consensus versus your indecision on the proper meat to cook, and (2) our commitment to an appropriate use of sauce versus your laissez-faire attitude on the subject. Excuse the pedantic tone of what follows, but I can't help it. I've been a college professor for too long.

Let's start with the meat. It's true that, as a verb, "barbecue" refers to a technique that even in North Carolina has been used to cook many meats. As recently as the 1930s we routinely barbecued not just hogs but sheep, possums, shad, sides of beef—all sorts of stuff. We still barbecue chickens. But as a noun referring to something to eat, it was once understood everywhere that "barbecue" comes from hogs. In 1755, for example, Samuel Johnson's famous dictionary defined it as "a hog drest whole in the West Indian manner" (more about that West Indian manner in a minute). There are many more examples, some even earlier.

There are more hogs than people in North Carolina, but if we are "porcivorous" (in 1728 William Byrd II said we were) it's not just for convenience. Our barbeculture is something like the dogma of the Orthodox Church— settled, unchanging, secure in the truth, threatened only by modernity, not by rival faiths. Meanwhile, y'all west of the Mississippi seem to have erred and strayed into the barbecue equivalent of speaking in tongues and taking up serpents. In fact, for all I know, you may take up serpents and barbecue them. Wouldn't surprise me.

Look, surely it's not my responsibility to defend what has been an understanding universal in Christendom. It's for Texans and Kansas Citians and Owensboroites to justify their departure from it. Martin Luther nailed some theses to the Wittenberg church door: he didn't just go do his own damn thing.

Y'all's restless pursuit of unnecessary innovation is equally evident when it comes to sauce. More history from the professor (sorry):

We first encounter something that is undeniably real barbecue in the 1600s, in the Caribbean, where Indians had been cooking fish and birds and reptiles low-and-slow with wood from time immemorial. When Europeans showed up with hogs (note: *hogs*) the locals realized that this is what the Lord meant to be barbecued, and soon they were into pig-pickings in a big way. And they didn't just cook a hog. At a 1698 feast described by a Dominican missionary, the meat was mopped with a mixture of lime juice and chile peppers, and served with a similar table sauce in two strengths, hot or mild.

In time, this sauce came to the Carolinas (where the lime juice was replaced by more easily obtained vinegar) and it spread inland. Barbecue historian Robert Moss shows that by the time of the Civil War this sauce was employed everywhere in the United States (yes, even Texas). This is the ur-sauce, the one from which all others descend, the perfection from which others have devolved.

Most heretics have gone to thick, sweet, sticky, Kansas City–style sauces, doctored ketchup that lies on the surface of the meat and can disguise poor cooking. Yours is the more forgivable sin of making sauce optional, or even doing without it altogether. At least you showcase the meat, which is a good thing. But you miss the opportunity to season it, as people always have, with a sparing application of a penetrating, salty, peppery sauce.

This classic, time-honored sauce survives essentially unchanged in eastern North Carolina and (as I explained in my first letter) with only trivial alterations in the North Carolina piedmont. Here again, I think it's up to someone who wants to mess with it to explain why. If it ain't broke, don't fix it.

In short (and it really is "in short"—I could go on), North Carolina barbecue stands in a tradition of four hundred years. The history of our barbecue is the history of barbecue itself. That history is interwoven with the history of political campaigns, church homecomings, drive-in restaurants, harvest celebrations, and the Fourth of July. It's what America is all about. You shouldn't disrespect it because it's your heritage, too.

Return to the fold, Daniel. It is not too late to repent.

Thanks for the opportunity to spar with you.

John

THE PIG PICKER
A Barbecue Cocktail

When I wrote a barbecue cookbook (called Barbecue*), the University of North Carolina Press wanted something to put on their website by way of promotion, so I gave them a recipe that wasn't in the book. The nicely ambiguous toast I mention was the favorite of my late pal Leonard "Slats" Cottrell, proud Virginian and fortieth president of the American Sociological Society.*

• • •

We North Carolinians love our vinegar-based barbecue sauces. In fact, we love them so much we don't just splash them on barbecue: East of Raleigh we boil potatoes in sauce-spiked water; west of Raleigh sauce goes in the slaw dressing. So why not a cocktail with sauce in it?

Well, you got it. Amanda Fisher and Paul Bright, compilers of "The Great NC BBQ Map," have devised what they call the Southern Islander Shrub. A shrub, if you didn't know (I didn't), is a drink made with vinegar, sugar, and fruit; this drink mixes a vinegar-based North Carolina barbecue sauce, honey, and pineapple juice (that's the "Islander" part), and adds bourbon. Vinegar? Well, vinegar was introduced to barbecue as a substitute for harder-to-get lime or lemon juice. So think of this as a sort of whiskey sour, with some heat. Continuing the barbecue theme, Amanda and Paul serve their drink in a glass rimmed with smoked sea salt.

This recipe is really good, but my wife doesn't much like pineapple juice, so I started fooling around with alternatives and came up with one that substitutes peach nectar. I also used cane sugar syrup instead of honey. Peaches and cane sugar make this drink even more Southern, don't you think? Here's how to make what I call a Pig Picker.

For the cocktail:

1½ ounces bourbon	1 teaspoon Eastern North Carolina–
1 teaspoon 2:1 cane sugar syrup	style barbecue sauce
1 teaspoon peach nectar	

For the rim:

2:1 cane sugar syrup	Hickory-smoked sea salt

Drizzle the syrup onto one-half of a plate and pile some salt on the other half. Rotate the rim of an old-fashioned glass in the syrup, then in the salt.

Add the four cocktail ingredients to the glass and stir.

Add a large cube of ice and drink "To the liberation of our country."

Some notes on the ingredients:

2:1 cane sugar syrup

Cane sugar is widely available, but if you can't find it, use light-brown sugar instead.

2 parts cane sugar	1 part water

Bring the water to a boil. Add the sugar and return to the boil, stirring. When the sugar has dissolved completely, remove from heat and let cool.

Peach nectar

You can buy peach nectar, often in grocery stores' Mexican food section, but homemade is better.

4 cups peeled, sliced peaches (fresh or frozen)	½ cup sugar (or to taste)
4 cups water	1 tablespoon lemon juice

Bring the peaches and the water to a boil, and boil for 5 minutes. Remove from heat and let cool. Blend in batches, then add sugar and lemon juice and stir well. This freezes well for future use.

Barbecue sauce

I'm not taking sides in North Carolina's Eastern-Piedmont sauce wars, but for this purpose Eastern-style is better. It has more of a cayenne punch and you don't need the additional sweetness that Piedmont-style brings to the table.

1 pint cider vinegar	1 teaspoon cayenne pepper
5 teaspoons crushed red pepper	2 tablespoons brown sugar
1½ teaspoons kosher salt	

Mix the ingredients and let stand at least 4 hours.

Hickory-smoked sea salt

You can buy this or smoke your own or, for this purpose (don't tell anyone I told you this), you can add a couple of drops of "liquid smoke" to a half cup or so of sea salt in a sealed container, shake it, and let it stand for a while. And it doesn't really have to be sea salt, either.

THE THIRD RAIL OF
NORTH CAROLINA POLITICS

The New York Times requested this piece and ran it the day before the 2016 North Carolina presidential primary. Full marks to them for realizing that their readers might not understand how things work in our parts. (Yes, I didn't mention the two candidates who eventually ran against each other. I've never claimed to be a prophet.) By the way, the "snarky commentator" was me.

• • •

Herbert O'Keefe, editor of the *Raleigh Times*, once said that "no man has ever been elected governor of North Carolina without eating more barbecue than was good for him." In our state the linkage between politics and barbecued meat dates back at least to 1766, when Royal Governor Tryon tried unsuccessfully to win the goodwill of citizens annoyed by the Stamp Act by laying on a barbecue in Wilmington. (It didn't work: The local Sons of Liberty poured out the beer and threw the barbecued ox in the river. Note that this was a full seven years before the Boston Tea Party, which gets all the publicity.)

In more recent times, barbecue has even figured as a campaign issue. When North Carolina's secretary of state Rufus Edmisten ran for governor in 1984, for instance, he got in trouble with an offhand remark. "I'd be eating barbecue three times a day for a solid year," he recalled, "and I got up one night and, in a very, very lax moment—the devil made me do it—I made a horrible statement. I said, 'I'm through with barbecue.' Well, you would have thought I had made a speech against my mother, against apple pie, cherry pie, the whole mess."

He lost the election to a Republican (only the second one to be elected since Reconstruction).

In 2012 Michelle Obama also got burned by an ill-advised comment. When she announced that the Democratic National Convention would meet in Charlotte, she spoke of that city's charm, hospitality, diversity, "and, of course, great barbecue." Many Charlotteans were puzzled. A headline in the *Charlotte Observer* read, "Charlotte = great barbecue? Who knew?" Mayor Anthony Foxx said that his city has good barbecue, but not *great* barbecue: "I have had great barbecue in Charlotte that's been brought in on a truck." And one snarky commentator said, "Complete the sentence: As a barbecue town, Charlotte is, one, not what it used to be; two, like Minneapolis for gumbo; three, good enough for Yankees; four, not far from Shelby [home of Bridges Barbecue Lodge]."

But at least the First Lady meant well. You can't say that for Rick Perry. Shortly after the Texas governor announced in 2011 that he was running for president, the *Raleigh News and Observer* turned up an injudicious remark he'd made nearly twenty years earlier. In 1992 the same paper had reported that Perry, then Texas commissioner of agriculture, had eaten some eastern North Carolina barbecue and said he'd had roadkill that tasted better. At the time, some of us wondered why he'd been eating roadkill, but we let it go. When a man wants to be president, however, it's a different matter. A typical response came from Jeffrey Weeks, in the *Charlotte Examiner:* "Rick Perry is not fit to be president of the United States. In fact he is apparently not fit to be a guest in my house." The furor got national attention, and Perry withdrew from the race three months later. Surely not a coincidence.

North Carolina's primary is tomorrow and so far the subject hasn't come up, but it still could. If it does, my advice for aspiring politicians who aren't from around here is, watch what you say. If the subject is unavoidable, you'll get more respect if you're forthright in defense of your heritage. When Elizabeth Dole and Erskine Bowles were contending for the Senate in 2002, they were asked if they preferred the barbecue of eastern North Carolina or that of the Piedmont. Dole spoke for the style of her native Piedmont, but Bowles (who had criticized Dole for ducking tough issues) wouldn't say which he preferred—and he lost.

If obliged to say something about barbecue, you should, like Elizabeth Dole, stand by your place. When President Obama comes to North Carolina he eats ribs with a sweet, sticky, red sauce, and I don't think anyone holds that against him. Even though ribs barely count as barbecue in these parts, he's from Chicago, so that's what he *should* like. "I'm from Chicago and I'm a rib man" may be a sadly mistaken position, but it is not a contemptible one. Generally speaking, honesty is the best policy. So Bernie Sanders should say, "I'm from Vermont and don't know anything about it," and Ted Cruz, "I'm from Texas, so let's not discuss it."

If possible, though, try not to say anything. You're very likely to offend some North Carolina voters, and it's possible that you will offend them all. Just shut up and eat.

HOW HILLARY GOT SMOKED
IN NORTH CAROLINA

In the 2016 presidential election North Carolina was supposed to be a "battleground state," but it wasn't even close. This op-ed for the Raleigh News and Observer *suggests one reason why.*

• • •

Apparently national Democrats have heard that barbecue is a big deal in North Carolina, because when they come to our state they always make a point of eating it. But they usually get it wrong.

In 2000, for example, Al Gore knew enough to stop by a big political barbecue. But a friend of mine who was on the campaign bus says that when Gore got off the bus, he put his suit jacket *on.*

Just so, when Michelle Obama announced that the 2012 Democratic convention would be in Charlotte, she listed "great barbecue" as one of that city's attractions. But actually, Charlotte is an exception to the North Carolina rule. The *Charlotte Observer,* not usually averse to boosterism, published an editorial headlined, "Charlotte = great barbecue? Who knew?"

In 2016 Mrs. Clinton continued this tradition of barbecultural cluelessness.

It would have been so easy for her to visit, say, Wilber's Barbecue in Goldsboro. The owner, Wilber Shirley, is one of the last yellow-dog Democrats, a man who has a picture of FDR on the wall of his restaurant. There's a photograph on the Web of him holding a Barack Obama bobblehead, "show[ing] the President around the smoke house."

Wilber had to settle for the bobblehead because the real Obama has never actually come to his place. The president prefers a place in Asheville that serves ribs (with blueberry-chipotle sauce). He probably does like ribs—he's from Chicago, after all—but trying to score barbecue points with North Carolina voters by eating ribs is like John Kerry's asking for Swiss cheese on his Philly cheesesteak, or Sargent Shriver's going to a tavern in an Ohio mill town and saying, "Make mine a Courvoisier!"

Mrs. Clinton didn't go to Wilber's either. She ate her barbecue at a place in Charlotte called the Midwood Smoke House.

Now, it's true that the food at Midwood is tasty, and its barbecued meats are cooked 100 percent with wood, which is commendable. But eating there is not the way to show voters that you're in touch with what one could call "Deep" North Carolina.

First of all, it's in Charlotte, and to many North Carolinians "Charlotte" brings to mind not just barbecue that's less than great, but also big business, "gentlemen's clubs," and traffic jams. Charlotteans don't help when they suggest that the rest of us are—well, deplorables. (One *Observer* reader wrote, for instance, that "Charlotte has always suffered from an image problem, and it will only change when people separate 'North Carolina' and 'Charlotte' in their minds.") When Mayor Eddie Knox lost the 1984 Democratic gubernatorial primary, he may have been right to blame "the Mecklenburg [County] thing."

So, for starters, Hillary ate her barbecue in the wrong town. Moreover, she ate it at a trendy place in a trendy neighborhood, a place with an "executive chef," a bar that gets equal billing with its barbecue, and a menu offering not just pork barbecue, but also barbecued ribs, brisket, burnt ends, prime rib, ground chuck, sausage, chicken, and salmon, served with your choice of four different sauces.

You often find this pick-your-meat, pick-your-sauce, International House of Barbecue approach in places like Charlotte that are full of newcomers from many different barbecue traditions, or none, but it's not the Tar Heel Way. The one-true-faith North Carolina approach is exemplified by the Skylight Inn in Ayden, where Sam Jones says, "When you come here, it's not what you want, it's how much of it."

To many of us, barbecue from everywhere feels like barbecue from nowhere, and for all the political good it did her, Mrs. Clinton could have skipped the smoked meat altogether and gone to a tapas bar.

I'm sure that Donald Trump knows as little about North Carolina barbecue as Hillary does, but he got better advice. Somebody sent him to Stamey's in Greensboro, a venerable place that advertises its "Old Fashioned Barbecue." Somebody even told him to order chopped barbecue, sweet tea, hushpuppies, slaw, and cherry cobbler. He came away with a photograph, widely circulated, that showed him posing with the restaurant's staff, a fine, smiling cross-section of North Carolina working people, pretty much the kind of folks who turned out on election day to put him over the top.

I'm not saying that Hillary could have won by eating at Stamey's, but would it have hurt?

A TALE OF THREE RESTAURANTS

New Orleans isn't a big barbecue town, but it hardly matters, does it? When you live there (as we did when I was working on a book about the place) you have a lot of visitors, and we were happy to see them—as long as they took us to Galatoire's for lunch. This originally appeared in Front Porch Republic.

• • •

My favorite New Orleans restaurant is Galatoire's, serving French-Creole food on Bourbon Street since 1905. In fact, Galatoire's may be my favorite restaurant, period. I'd want them to cater my last meal. I'd begin with a Sazerac and move on to—well, I'm not going to start listing dishes because I couldn't stop. (OK, just some appetizers: fried eggplant and soufflé potatoes bearnaise, shrimp rémoulade, crabmeat maison, oysters en brochette or Rockefeller. . . .)

But I also like Galatoire's for the comforting fact that if the chef dropped dead tomorrow I might never know it. Nothing important would change. New Orleans has a lot of places like that—not just historic French Quarter restaurants like Galatoire's, but neighborhood Sicilian-Creole places, funky oyster bars, and cramped little corner po-boy shops. Katrina closed many of them for good, alas, but the ones that remain are pretty much the way they were the first time I ate there. Just a little cleaner, maybe, with the new paint. Like Orthodox icon painters, their cooks come and go, some are more skilled than others, but the difference is largely in execution. The subjects are pretty much provided by tradition, revered, and slow to change.

Inevitably, change takes place, but, as in Darwinian evolution, it's usually only incremental. Spinach in Oysters Rockefeller, for example, is a mutation that seems to have survived; otherwise the dish is identical to the original 1899 recipe. For a completely new dish—the equivalent of a new species—to survive, it must overcome the innate conservatism that sees no reason to try something new when the old is just fine. Sure, if that obstacle can be overcome, your creativity will be acknowledged and honored—forever. Oysters Rockefeller will always be identified with Antoine's, even if everyone serves them now (and some do them better than Antoine's). Just so, Oysters Bienville will always be Arnaud's, and blackened anything, K-Paul's. Everyone knows that Pascale's Manale still serves the ancestral "barbecued" shrimp from which other versions have evolved, and when "chargrilled" oysters turned up on Felix's menu, I asked the waitress, "Drago's?" ("Yeah," she said, "but better.") But in a food culture like this, most experiments fail, and leave no trace. Many are never tried in the first place.

Obviously, this way of doing things makes it harder to become a celebrity chef. New Orleans has a few—Emeril Lagasse and Paul Prudhomme, for starters—but a different kind of city would have a lot more. "Celebrity chef" is not a contradiction in terms exactly, but, like "student-athlete," it's an unnatural combination in which one half usually suffers. So it's not at all a bad sign that it takes two clicks on Galatoire's website to find a very small headshot of the chef (or, for that matter, one of the boss, who's not the same person). Compare this to what goes on at a place less than a mile away, where the cult of personality amounts almost to parody. On the opening page of its website, the image of the owner/chef appears to rise slowly into view against the backdrop of a star-spangled sky, to the accompaniment of Chopin's *Fantasie-Impromptu*. When we went there, our waiter opened with a spiel about what the chef had been thinking and doing lately.

You know what? I don't care. I prefer the waiter at Galatoire's who told us to avoid the trout because it wasn't very good that day. That's useful information. But it's simply impossible to imagine a waiter at this other place telling you to avoid the Tasmanian King Salmon.

Think about that, by the way. Tasmanian King Salmon. That ought to drive you nuts if you're a "locovore." Me, I'm not, if that means limiting myself to local produce. What I treasure is local cuisines, and if they call for exotic, expensively imported ingredients, so be it (although let's work on getting them produced locally). But that's not what's going on here. No, we're told that here the chef is "leading the local dining scene into a bold new era of dining with exciting Global-Modern cuisine." That calls, I guess, for global salmon, and if this Aussie fish really is something special, of course there should be a place for it on a menu in Louisiana, and to hell with its carbon footprint. But since "Tasmanian King Salmon" is just a marketing term for "farm-raised Atlantic salmon imported from Down Under at considerable expense" (look it up), it's probably one of those things that should stay in Vegas. It's on that menu just to impress—like the way our food came in a coup de theatre that had a team of waiters popping up in unison, like weird plate-bearing Rockettes.

Look, going to New Orleans and eating "Global-Modern cuisine" is like going to Bologna and ordering sushi. Sure, you can do it, but why would you want to? I feel about the cuisine of New Orleans the way I feel about wood-cooked North Carolina barbecue or the old Book of Common Prayer. This trendy globaloney makes me curmudgeonly—it makes me want to say that natural selection has done its work, so leave it the hell alone.

But I only say that because I'm cross. In truth, I welcome some innovations. I'm not saying you can't tinker with these things, play around. Nothing's perfect. You can honor a tradition by refreshing it, as Chef Donald Link and his colleagues do at their restaurants. For example, the spanking new Cochon Butcher now serves the best muffuletta in town—a completely traditional sandwich, but made from meats prepared right there—and Link once honored his Cajun heritage by serving us an astonishing dinner of crawfish five ways, at his flagship restaurant, Herbsaint.

Let's hope celebrity doesn't spoil the boy; for now, he's perfect. When he couldn't find a reliable supplier of Louisiana frog legs, for instance, he could have served "*cuisse de grenouille des marais du Bangladesh*," but he didn't. Instead he took one of his most popular dishes off the menu and now serves it only when he and his staff have had a chance to spend a night on the bayou gigging the critters. That his cookbook, *Real Cajun,* won a James Beard Award proves that even a blind hog finds an acorn now and then. (The Beard Foundation, usually pretty good on restaurants, can be really fallible about cookbooks and food writing. Witness the fact that Sara Roahen's great *Gumbo Tales* wasn't even a finalist—nor was *Holy Smoke,* the best barbecue book of all time. But I digress.)

Gertrude Stein famously said of her native Oakland that there was "no there there." All she meant was that nothing she remembered from her childhood remained, but her expression was fated to acquire the meaning that has made it a cliché. The world needed a way to say that a place has nothing to let you know where you are, nothing local, nothing for anyone with a sense of place to latch on to, and that was far too good a way to say it. For all too many cities and towns these days,—in general, and certainly when it comes to cuisine—there's no there there. It's ironic that Oakland isn't one of them. Neither is New Orleans. Despite the inroads of national chains, on the one hand, and "Global-Modern cuisine," on the other, it never will be. And thank God for that.

WE SHALL OVEREAT

Brightleaf: A Southern Review of Books was a short-lived (1997–2000) literary bimonthly published in Raleigh. I had a deal with the editor, David Perkins: I wrote a column for him; he didn't pay me; I wrote about whatever I wanted. This is one of those columns.

• • •

Southern food transcends the racial divisions that have provided so much of the subject matter of Southern history. Sharing, swapping, borrowing, and imitating across racial lines have produced a flavorsome (lowercase) creole cuisine. As Reynolds Price has observed, in the South "hardly a dish is less than a product of the joint skills, over three hundred years, of red, black, and white cooks and eaters."

You don't have to know this to enjoy Southern food, but speaking as both a longtime eater and sometime jackleg cook, I can attest that knowing something about the cultural baggage of what you're eating can enhance the experience. Lately a dozen excellent books have begun to give both haute and down-home Southern cuisine the quasi-anthropological attention it deserves, and although reading about it is easier on the waistline (and, in some uptown cases, on the pocketbook) than eating it, some of these books go on to tell the curious where to find particularly flavorsome examples. I've recently come across two guides that will take a place on my shelf next to John Egerton's *Southern Food* and Greg Johnson and Vince Staten's *Real Barbecue.*

In *Backroad Buffets & Country Cafés,* Don O'Briant has given us just what his subtitle promises: "A Southern Guide to Meat-and-Threes & Downhome Dining," an annotated catalogue of more than two hundred places in eleven Southern states "where conscientious cooks still peel and mash potatoes, simmer fresh greens, and pan-fry chicken, where food is prepared from scratch and there are no heat lamps for precooked hamburgers." O'Briant, who writes for the *Atlanta Journal-Constitution,* has pretty close to perfect pitch when it comes to those I know—about a quarter of them, I reckon—so I'm inclined to trust him on the others. ("Full disclosure," as they say: I introduced O'Briant to Mama Dip's Kitchen when he came to Chapel Hill, and his photograph of Mrs. Mildred "Mama Dip" Council has me in it.)

A typical entry is that for Garner, North Carolina's Toot-N-Tell (the name reflects its drive-in origins in the 1940s), which offered O'Briant "one of the most amazing buffets I've seen." He sampled the fried chicken, fried shrimp, barbecued ribs, fried fish, chicken and dumplings, rutabagas, field peas, scalloped tomatoes, cabbage, mashed potatoes, lima beans, banana pudding, and peach cobbler, but what made the Toot-N-Tell unusual was "some chopped meat that was chewy and slightly vinegary [and] tasted a little like clams"—chitterlings, O'Briant learned, somewhat to his dismay, when he asked—and the truly outstanding fried salt pork, or streak-o-lean, of which the restaurant serves five hundred pounds a week (O'Briant had three helpings). These low-on-the-hog cuts are Southern staples, to be sure, but they're getting hard to find these days.

O'Briant supplements his restaurant reviews with little essays by a couple of dozen writers on their favorite places. If this subject can make even ordinary folks lyrical, you can imagine what it does to the likes of Lee Smith, Larry Brown, and Tina McElroy Ansa. My favorite testimonial comes from Josephine Humphreys, who drives the three-hundred-mile round trip from Charleston to Fuller's, a Lumbee Indian establishment in Lumberton, North Carolina, for "the best chicken gizzards I've ever eaten—the only chicken gizzards I've ever eaten."

If your travels take you to New York City for a few days, it would be downright silly to hunt up a Southern restaurant. You really shouldn't pass up the latest exotica. (I've always agreed with *Reason* magazine's Michael Lynch that the best thing about multiculturalism is the food. The slogan of "conservative inclusion," Lynch suggests, should be "Celebrate Diverse Foods.") But if you're stuck in the Big Apple for a long time and get to yearning for a taste of home, or if you just need to impress some skeptical Yankees with the glories of Southern food, you need a copy of *New York's 50 Best Places to Eat Southern,* by South Carolinian Bruce Lane and Arkansas-Texas-Louisiana native Scott Wyatt. (More disclosure: I wrote a blurb for this one—but I meant every word.)

Lane and Wyatt's selections are a varied lot. I've only had firsthand experience with one of them (Virgil's—see below), but on paper my favorites tend to be the funkier and less self-conscious ones that could have made it into O'Briant's book, had he extended his territory northward. At the Carolina Country Kitchen in Bedford-Stuyvesant, for example, Ms. Patricia Lee offers chopped barbecue trucked in from eastern North Carolina, along with collard greens, black-eyed peas, and sweet potato pie. (Across the street, Carolina Country Products stocks hard-to-find Southern groceries.)

It's no accident that most of these places are found in black neighborhoods: That's where you go in New York to find the necessary concentration of discriminating expatriate Southerners, folks for whom this food is not a special-occasion alternative to Szechuan or North Italian but just the ordinary food of their childhoods. But for those who are seeking what one might call a "Southern-theme" restaurant, there are plenty to choose from. Many are Cajun/Creole places, naturally, while others offer "new Southern cuisine," more or less inviting. Some restaurants, however, are the culinary equivalent of television's Hazzard County. You remember, that mythical place where Bo and Luke Duke wrestled gators in the swamps one week and drove at high speeds through the mountains the next—ignoring the fact that no actual Southern county has both swamps and mountains. They offer dishes that are from the South, sure enough, but would never be found on the same menu there. At Brother Jimmy's, for example, on the Upper East Side (otherwise pretty much a wasteland when it comes to Southern food), some Duke grads have constructed a simulacrum of a Southern barbecue joint, with Lynyrd Skynyrd on the stereo and a discount for Southern customers on White Trash Wednesdays. The menu offers pulled pork with a choice of sauces from a half-dozen different parts of the South, Memphis dry ribs, and a variety of Tex-Mex items. Similarly, a Kentucky-born editor once took me to lunch at Virgil's, a sort of all-South place on 44th Street, with everything from Owensboro mutton barbecue to Texas smoked sausage po' boys, Memphis baked beans to key lime pie. I guess Chinese Americans and Italian Americans are used to this sort of conflation but I find it a little unnerving.

Still, that's the kind of incongruous juxtaposition that gave us Southern food in the first place. And the process continues. The fried green tomatoes with shrimp remoulade that I've eaten at Upperline in New Orleans could be deconstructed at length, but I prefer a homelier example. The buffet at Country Junction in Carrboro, North Carolina, where I often eat lunch, offers fine black-eyed peas, turnip greens, fried chicken—utterly typical, except that the cook is Chinese, and many of the construction-worker customers these days are Mexican. Stay tuned to see what those cultures contribute to our stew.

KITCHEN WINDOWS ON THE SOUTH

Anthony Stanonis, the editor of Dixie Emporium: Tourism, Foodways, and Consumer Culture in the American South *(2009), asked me to write this introduction to the "Foodways" section.*

• • •

Some anthropologists and the odd historian aside, it's only recently that the academy has begun to take the study of foodways seriously. In the late 1980s, a couple of accomplished food scholars proposed to my university that they teach an undergraduate honors course on the subject, which they were willing to do without pay. The general response was along the lines of "You can't be serious" (about offering such a course, not about teaching it for nothing). But they were very serious indeed, and they eventually got the course offered on a trial basis. It was immediately oversubscribed, with some of our very best students eager to write the sort of research papers that university teachers dream about their students writing. Now it's taught every year, still oversubscribed, and my university is congratulating itself for having been on the cutting edge.

That course caught a wave that has now washed up all sorts of interesting flotsam. Scholars have begun to see the usefulness of the fact that you are what you eat, as everyone is fond of saying, and it's equally true (and perhaps more interesting, though less often remarked) that you eat what you are—or at any rate what you think you are, or what you want to be. The study of the acquisition, preparation, and consumption of food opens windows into many larger psychological and societal questions. Three essays in *Dixie Emporium:*

Tourism, Foodways, and Consumer Culture in the American South open some of
these windows on the South.

In one, Anthony Stanonis provides a penetrating historical look at how
Southern foodways have reflected and reinforced the patriarchal and racist
assumptions of the dominant class of white Southerners. He persuades me
that they certainly have done that, but there are some subtleties to that story
that I think need emphasizing. In the South, as W. J. Cash wrote, "Negro entered into white man as profoundly as white man entered into Negro, subtly
influencing every gesture, every word, every emotion and idea, every attitude."
Perhaps today that can go without saying, but when he wrote it in 1940 it
was far from the conventional wisdom. Only in our music is this blending as
evident as it is in what Southerners eat. The banjo, for instance, an African
instrument that hardly any African Americans play these days, is at the core
of bluegrass—maybe the "whitest" music there is—while the European guitar
accompanies America's "blackest" music, the blues. But notice that we can still
speak of "black" and "white" music—in fact, we have to.

There is no similar consensus on whether one can speak of black and white
food. I for one don't think we can. The table is one place—maybe *the* one
place—where the cliché "it's not about race, it's about class" actually holds
true. I have yet to encounter convincing evidence of any significant differences
between the cuisines of blacks and whites of similar incomes and education.
"Soul food," for instance, celebrated in the 1970s as the essence of *négritude*,
looks suspiciously like the food of Southern poor whites, who have also generally eaten low on the hog. Things don't get more soulful than South Side
Chicago or Mississippi "gut parties" to eat chitlins and hog maw, but *Southern Cultures* has published a white North Carolinian's account of a "chitlin
function" apparently attended entirely by white boys of the species *good old*.

When this subject was discussed once at a meeting of the Southern Foodways Alliance someone brought up chicken country captain as an example of
a "white" Southern dish that has absolutely no African American roots or constituency, and it's true that this curried chicken concoction seems to have gone
directly from Bengal to the upper-class tables of eighteenth-century Charleston (or Savannah: there's a dispute here). Today it is still eaten mostly by the
country-club set, but I'll bet some members of the South's rapidly growing
black business and professional class have given it a try. Last time I inquired
something like one *Southern Living* reader in eight was African American. And

you could even argue that it is, in a way, part of their heritage. After all, who cooked it in eighteenth-century Charleston?

No, in the South blacks and whites have historically eaten at separate tables, but insofar as their means allowed they ate the same things, a splendid blend of African, European, and Native American. And these days, when blacks and whites come together in fellowship, as they do (albeit all too rarely), it seems to me that there is usually food involved.

In another essay, Carolyn de la Peña provides a fascinating history of Krispy Kreme which, for starters, makes me hungry. (As Roy Blount Jr. observed, hot Krispy Kremes "are to other doughnuts what angels are to people.") It also provokes me to reflection on the many Southern things that have ceased to be Southern not because Southerners gave them up, but because we exported them so successfully. Coca-Cola was an early example, going from a regional thirst-quencher to a symbol of American civilization, then, as the opponents of "coca-colonization" feared, teaching the world to sing in over a hundred languages. Holiday Inn and Walmart have followed the same path. NASCAR, country music, and the Southern Baptist Convention may be doing the same, and until its recent financial troubles (eclipsed, to be sure, by those of Enron, WorldCom, and the Hospital Corporation of America—all Southern enterprises) Krispy Kreme looked set to become not just America's doughnut, but the world's: They were for sale at Harrod's in London in 2002. This is not the model of a disappearing South that most people who have used that phrase had in mind.

Finally, Mary Rizzo has written an essay on Baltimore's "Hon Fest," an annual celebration of spandex, leopard-skin prints, beehive hairdos, and waitresses who call you "hon." Frankly, it looks like fun to me, though a guilty pleasure, now that I have read Rizzo's observations about its erasure of black folks. Moreover, what are we to make of its mocking of working-class whites, however kindly intentioned? As a white Southerner who, far too late in the day, was no stranger to burnt cork, I do not ask this self-righteously.

There is much (excuse the expression) food for thought in all three of these chapters. Each is a fine example of the sort of unexpected insight that an oblique angle on everyday life can provide.

I'll close with a food-related story of my own. Not long ago when I went to a low-rent grocery in Mississippi to pick up some flour tortillas, I found some with a label that I read as "Ole Mexican Foods." I come from East Tennessee where lots of things are "ole"—ole boys, Ole Blue, ole-time religion—so it took a minute before I realized that the word was, of course, *Olé*. The fine print revealed that Olé is headquartered in suburban Atlanta, with branches in Texas, Florida, Kentucky, and both Carolinas.

You want to talk about New Southern Cuisine? Keep your eye on Olé.

A DELICIOUS WAY OF DEATH

When the American Enterprise *asked me in 2005 to review a lighthearted and unobtrusively sociological examination of Southern funeral food by two Mississippi ladies, this is what I wrote. (The magazine ran a much shorter version.)*

• • •

At least since 1976, when Jimmy Carter came out of nowhere (or Georgia, which at the time amounted to much the same thing) to win the Democratic presidential nomination, many Southerners have labored in a minor industry producing guides to the kooky South, often to be found for sale at Stuckey's on the interstate. Some of these books are explicitly written for non-Southerners, others are ostensibly for Southerners but with a sideways glance at a Yankee audience, but in either case they tend to be at best what the British call "twee"—relentlessly cute. At worst they would be downright offensive if the group being described were one less easygoing than Southern whites, who seem resigned to being the object of caricature.

So I wasn't optimistic about one entitled *Being Dead Is No Excuse: The Official Southern Ladies Guide to Hosting the Perfect Funeral.* To my surprise, however, it turns out to be one extended, wry in-joke. Southerners can read it without cringing; non-Southerners should at least find some recipes they can use, even if (as usual) they have trouble figuring out what's serious and what's not. Gayden Metcalfe and Charlotte Hays, the authors, point out that proper funerals are something that the dead have been waiting for all their lives. It is only right that they should have them, and this book tells you how to do it correctly, by the non-negotiable standards of Southern ladyhood.

"There is a time and a place for everything," I remember hearing when I was a child, but I learned the hard way that the elders who said that didn't really mean *everything*. What they indubitably did mean was that everything—in particular, whatever I was doing—has times and places when it is uncalled-for. The gist of this book's message is that a genteel Southern funeral is not the time or place for innovation. This is true even when it comes to comes to talking about death. The authors observe that "nice people do not pass away. They die." For Southerners to call dead people "dead" is "one of the rare instances when we refuse to sugar-coat," but "our ancestors have been dying for hundreds of years, and we plan to continue this tradition."

Of course the South, especially the Deep South, has a reputation for resisting innovation in general. (A Mississippi friend once claimed—in fact, boasted—that the last time his state was on the cutting edge of change was when it pioneered the use of literacy tests to disfranchise black voters.) This reputation is, in fact, a gross misrepresentation of a region that has given us Walmart, CNN, Federal Express, and floating casinos, but there is no denying that the Southern way of death is on the conservative side. Whether you're talking about flower arrangements, hymns, liturgy, or funeral food there's a right way and a wrong way to do things, and the right way is usually pretty much the way it has always been done.

This is not to say that things aren't often done the wrong way. Floral telephones that say "Jesus Called" and floral clocks with the hands stopped at the time of death are at least as common in the South as elsewhere. This only means that not all Southerners are ladies and gentlemen, which is not exactly news, and even Southerners who don't know better than to do that sort of thing can be conservative where it counts. Cremation, for example, is a newfangled way to treat the dead, and the last time I looked fewer than 3 percent of Mississippi funerals involved "cremains." (The figure for Nevada was over two-thirds.)

To be sure, some spontaneous innovations can be acceptable. The authors observe that it was all right—more than all right—when Buddy Gilliam, "Mr. Buddy," refused to die until his daughter agreed to pin a note to his lapel that said, "Hell, no, I don't look nachell." And it was touching when a young woman's friends each took a rose from her coffin, although it would have been entirely different had they been told to. One wants to avoid anything "that has 'funeral director' written all over it."

The authors' aesthetic judgments are unerring. When it comes to flowers, for example, roses are acceptable, flowers from the yard ideal. Carnations are tacky, carnations with glitter are unspeakable, and it goes without saying that the authors share, in a suitably ladylike way, the sentiments of the great Memphis rocker Don Nix, composer of the classic "Don't Put No Plastic Flowers on My Grave" ("I don't care how much money you can save").

As for funeral hymns, the well-bred dead prefer classics like "Mighty Fortress" or Episcopalian standards like "For All the Saints," but the authors observe that some songs that the genteel usually hear only over funeral home sound systems also have their charms. "Sweet Beulah Land," for instance, is "the musical equivalent of Methodist cooking." With lyrics like "I'm kind of homesick for that country / To which I've never been before" it's like pineapple casserole, "a little hokey, but it grows on you." "On Eagle's Wings," though, is "pure kitsch": "The only time it's ever worked was when it was played on a violin in the cemetery, and nobody sang its silly words."

A good rule of thumb for the perfect Southern funeral is "No hymns composed after 1940." (The authors don't point out, but I will, that 1940 is the date of the last reliable Episcopalian hymnal.)

Most of this book turns out to be about food. That figures, since it is a truth universally acknowledged that "nobody in the world eats better than the bereaved Southerner." Even the bereaved recognize this: "When Nellia Bostwick's husband Andrew died in California, she said that the worst thing about it was missing all the good cooking—and missing Andy, too, of course." Obviously a guide to the perfect funeral should provide recipes, and this one does—nearly a hundred, in fact. Six are for pimento cheese alone, three for deviled or (as many God-fearing Southerners prefer) stuffed eggs, many so mouthwatering they make you want to go murder someone, just for the funeral. (Just kidding.)

Being dead is no excuse for, among other things, store-bought mayonnaise. A recipe for homemade comes right after the one for the tomato aspic God meant for it to go with, and the text recaps the long-standing argument over whether it should be thick or runny, which as Southern arguments go is right up there with whether to put tomato in your barbecue sauce. Scaredy-cats who worry about eating raw eggs need to be reminded that the most common last words in the South are said to be, "Hey, y'all, watch this!" (Oddly, the two recipes that do allow commercial mayonnaise call for Hellman's rather than Duke's, the semi-official mayonnaise of the South. Most Southern cooks I know achieve something like the Hellman's effect, if they want it, by using Duke's and adding sugar.)

Like nearly everything else in the South, funeral food is linked in complicated ways to religion, and thus to social class—or is it vice versa? Episcopalians, sometimes known to their more abstemious or hypocritical neighbors as "Whiskeypalians," tend to drink after funerals, for example—and often before, as well. The authors tell of their friend Anne Dudley Hunt, who was bravely dyeing Easter eggs one Easter Saturday despite horribly bruised knees and wondering aloud: "I just don't know. Did I hurt my knees yesterday afternoon doing the Stations of the Cross? Or did I do it falling down drunk last night?" Methodists are less anchored in the Cavalier tradition. And we will not speak of Baptists.

Anyway, the authors distinguish between "haute funeral food, which includes aspics, homemade mayonnaise, and dainty homemade rolls," appropriate for Anglican kitchens, and a "second tier" of dishes based on elements of what they present as "The Eternal Pantry"—stuff like canned artichoke hearts, canned French-fried onions, and cream of mushroom soup ("if you must") that should always be kept on hand for immediately required funeral food. Quoting Brillat-Savarin, who once said, "Tell me what you eat, and I will tell you what you are," they remark that "it's a pretty safe bet that nobody ever replied, 'Green-bean casserole with Campbell's soup and onion rings fresh from the can'" and observe that the poor Frenchman didn't know what he was missing. Episcopalians may eat these dishes, indeed with gusto, but they seldom prepare them. This is the stuff of the aforementioned "Methodist cooking," high in sodium but good for the soul, if not for the heart. Reading about it brings to mind the old joke about how Methodists believe that to get into heaven you have to bring a covered dish—and some of these dishes could get you there sooner rather than later.

Even this, however, is ladies' food (although *Being Dead*'s bing cherry and Jell-O salad with Coca-Cola strikes this Episcopalian as verging on trashy, redeemed only by the stipulation that it must be made with bottled Coke). In the lower reaches of Southern cuisine lurk dishes like Freda's Five-Can Casserole or, God help us, Tutti's Fruited Porkettes (Tutti's own granddaughter observes that you can't get trashier than a Hawaiian recipe with Southern ingredients), and for these one must turn to Ernest Matthew Mickler's classic *White Trash Cooking*.

I should note that the ladies who wrote this book are from Mississippi, and not just any old part of Mississippi. They're from the Delta, south of Memphis—what historian Jim Cobb has called "the most Southern place on earth," a place that offers a double-distilled version of a good many Southern ways—and their book reflects that. Moreover, it's not just Delta-centric, but resolutely Caucasian. When the authors write "Southerners" they really mean white Mississippians like themselves. Nevertheless, well-bred Southerners from other races and other parts of the South will recognize this ethnography as an only slightly exaggerated version of the ancestral wisdom. I'm an East Tennessee hillbilly myself, but when I read passages like this, I hear my grandmother's voice:

> A leafy green salad just doesn't seem right when someone has died. Sarah Jones thought her niece, who'd come from California for Aunt Bitsy's funeral, was just about the rudest person she'd ever met because she failed to grasp this basic rule. The niece not only talked like a Yankee, she said she'd eaten enough Velveeta and mushroom soup to last her until her own funeral. She said she wanted a Cobb salad. A Cobb salad? When somebody has died? Frankly, none of us could believe our ears. Sarah wrote her niece out of her will. Somebody so un-Southern wouldn't have the foggiest notion what to do with family silver.

That's pretty near perfect pitch.

I'll be stealing some of this book's throwaway lines. I've always needed a description of someone "whose ancestors could have come over on the Mayflower if they hadn't belonged to the Established Church." And it is true that for a really good turnout at your funeral it helps to have "dual membership"—in the Episcopal church and Alcoholics Anonymous. And I'd really never thought of it before, but yes, funerals do "cry out for canned asparagus."

Just one minor complaint, ladies: I don't think Emily Post would have approved of the missing apostrophe in your book's subtitle.

ASPECTS OF
THE SOUTH

OK, this section is something of a grab bag. Race relations and religion, good old boys and bad men, Hank Williams and Bill Clinton, Appalachia and Chapel Hill and the French Quarter. . . . What can I say? The South is sort of a grab bag, too.

I found it disconcerting to realize that these pieces come from six different decades, but time flies when you're having fun.

A NOTE ON THE "LONG ISLAND CAVE MYSTERY" MYSTERY

This early attempt to dispel Yankee ignorance and provinciality was written at a time when I was supposed to be studying for my graduate-school comprehensive examinations and was reading all of the Sherlock Holmes stories and novels instead. (It was published in the Baker Street Journal *in June 1969.) Who'd have thought that an East Tennessee upbringing would let me make a modest contribution to Holmesian studies?*

• • •

As "The Adventure of the Red Circle" drew to its close, Sherlock Holmes and Dr. Watson encountered Inspector Gregson leaning on a railing at the doorway of the Howe Street flat in which, unbeknownst to them, Black Gorgiano lay dead. After some chitchat and an exchange of compliments, Gregson

> struck his stick sharply upon the ground, on which a cabman, his whip in his hand, sauntered over from a four-wheeler which stood on the far side of the street. "May I introduce you to Mr. Sherlock Holmes?" he said to the cabman. "This is Mr. Leverton, of Pinkerton's American Agency."
>
> "The hero of the Long Island cave mystery?' said Holmes. "Sir, I am pleased to meet you."

This mystery, mentioned only in passing, has occasioned some puzzlement. The real mystery, the late Christopher Morley observed, "is that there are no caves on Long Island."

I suggest, however, that there is less mystery than meets the eye. Mr. Morley, with the charming parochialism that New Yorkers exhibit on occasion, seems to have assumed that Holmes had reference to the Long Island which abuts New York City, the Long Island of the Hamptons, Oyster Bay, Far Rockaway, and Bedford-Stuyvesant. Puzzled New Yorkers and others should know that near the present town of Kingsport, in upper East Tennessee, the Holston River, a tributary of the Tennessee, forms two channels. The smaller, known locally as The Sluice, runs its independent course beneath an intermittently sheer limestone face for three or four miles before rejoining the major channel. Scattered about the limestone face are the entrances to a number of smallish caves in which, as a lad, I undertook—as had my father thirty years before—various speleological and archaeological researches. From most of these cave mouths one can look out over the island formed by the forks of the river, an island known since the coming of the white man as Long Island.

The island and its caves have a fascinating history which I must, with reluctance, pass over here. Assuming, however, that this is the Long Island of Leverton's adventure, the question remains, what happened in this remote corner of Tennessee that was dramatic enough to come to Holmes's attention? I have no definite answer, but I would like to share my conviction that the mystery involved either the area's moonshine whiskey industry (which to this day often employs caves for both production and storage) or some later ramifications of the Confederate nitrate-mining operations in other caves nearby. This latter speculation may be buttressed by the fact that Allan Pinkerton, founder of the detective agency that bore his name, served during the Civil War as head of the Union Intelligence Service.

CAN THE SOUTH SHOW THE WAY?

This is another early piece, my first venture in op-ed journalism. It was written for National Review *in 1972, so long ago that the preferred word for African Americans was still in transition from "Negroes" to "blacks." For writing it, I got twenty-five dollars and a handwritten note of commendation from William Buckley.*

. . .

A recurrent dream for a minority of Southern whites, a dream remarkable for its staying power in the face of adverse evidence, has been that the South might someday show the world how an equitable biracial society could be achieved. Not a few white Southerners have been tempted to hope that the South could do more than catch up with the Northern pattern of race relations—that it could break through to an accommodation qualitatively different from and superior to that displayed in, say, Philadelphia or Cicero. If this should come to pass, "the South, which has always felt itself reserved for a high destiny," as Yale law professor Charles Black observed, "would have found it, and would have come to flower at last. And the fragrance of it would spread, beyond calculation, over the world."

Southern black leaders, from Martin Luther King to Charles Evers and, most recently, James Meredith, have entertained a similar hope for their region. Howard Lee, the black mayor of Chapel Hill, North Carolina, argues, for instance, that white Southerners are at least aware of black people's existence, which makes them easier for Negroes to deal with than Northerners. Writer Louis Lomax's assessment of the prospects for his hometown of Valdosta,

Georgia, was a little less backhanded: "Valdosta will make it peacefully into tomorrow, partly because the whites themselves are slowly changing, partly because the Negroes are not really pushing. Time nudges them both along."

Lomax was right: Southern whites *are* changing. Public opinion polls in 1942 showed 98 percent of white Southerners favoring absolute segregation in the public schools; by 1963, the proportion had dropped somewhat, to 68 percent; by 1970, only 16 percent of Southern whites said they would object to sending their children to schools with "a few" black children. These same polls show a leveling off of non-Southern support for desegregation during the 1960s, so that South and non-South are now more alike in their racial attitudes than at any time in the recent past.

The pattern of faster change in the South than outside is repeated when we turn from white attitudes to black economic circumstances (although here again the Southern black is still worse off than his Northern confrere). The question is what the limits of these changes are to be. Straightforward extrapolation suggests that Southern blacks will soon be better off, both relative to the ambient whites and absolutely, than Northern black people; cynicism suggests that this is too much to hope for, and that Southerners (white ones at least) should be content with a pattern of race relations and racial inequalities no worse than that found elsewhere.

But there are other grounds for hope. Lomax pointed to the attitudes of Valdosta's blacks as a beneficial element in the situation, and again his observation applies to most of the region. During the past ten years, many studies have been made of the racial attitudes of American Negroes. One constant finding in a changing decade has been that Southern blacks are less resentful, more hopeful, and less alienated than other black Americans. This forbearance, however undeserved, gives Southern communities the opportunity to prepare for change and to make it gracefully, in an atmosphere relatively free of urgency and acrimony. Although little in our region's past leads one to expect that we shall use the opportunity, it is there, and perhaps we shall surprise the cynics yet.

What grounds are there for hoping that racial change, as it is coming and continues to come, might lead to a happier situation in the South than elsewhere? Why would anyone suspect that blacks and whites might be able to get along better in the South?

Some have argued that there is a cultural similarity between the races in the

South, a similarity lacking elsewhere. We-all understand each other's accents, sing the same hymns, eat the same odd foods, go fishing when we get the chance, and so forth. This similarity, however perfectly obvious from Cambridge or New York, is somehow less so on the scene. Unfortunately for the theory, similarity is very much a contrast phenomenon; it takes a dissimilar third party to bring out the similarities, and such a useful group is conspicuously absent from most Southern communities. Even if it were feasible, overcoming ethnocentrism through ethnocentrism (which is what this amounts to) would be a dubious proposition. Moreover, cultural similarity is neither necessary nor sufficient for intergroup cooperation and mutual respect, as any historian could have told us.

A somewhat more promising line of reasoning goes like this: Southern whites and blacks have been in contact with one another for three and a half centuries. For better or for worse, we are not strangers to one another, and may even have come to understand each other. However, leaving aside the question of whether our grandfathers understood each other (I think there is a case to be made for black grandfathers having understood white ones, although not necessarily vice versa), it seems to me to be becoming painfully obvious how much in fact we have been strangers to one another. Social psychologists tell us that for interaction to produce positive feelings it must be interaction between persons of similar status, and this of course is precisely what Negro-white interaction in the South has not been. As William Styron observed some time ago: "To assume that anything more than a rare and sporadic intimacy on any level has existed in the modern South between whites and Negroes is simply to deny . . . the monstrous effectiveness of that apartheid which has been the Southern way of life for almost three-quarters of a century." (It is sad that as a higher proportion of interracial interaction becomes equal-status interaction, the overall amount of interracial interaction in the South may well be decreasing. The emerging Southern city seems to be about as segregated as its Northern counterpart, and it is possible today for a young Southerner to grow up without more than casual contact with the other race—a rarity as recently as forty years ago.)

There is a third reason, however, for hoping that the South may come out of the current turmoil in better shape than the North: The emergent themes in black rhetoric may strike a more responsive chord among white Southerners than among other white folks. "Black pride" translates as the proposition that a man should be proud of what he is—which might appeal to a people as idiosyncratic, and proud of it, as white Southerners. "Black power" can mean simply self-determination and freedom from outside meddling—another down-home note. And the abandonment of nonviolence seems to mean that if someone is pushing you around, you hit him—the time-honored Southern white response, and one that may strain our empathic powers less than did saintly self-restraint.

A nonviolent and assimilationist ideology was demonstrably effective in overcoming legal barriers to equality, but when it comes to getting Southern whites to respect those newly won rights and their holders, it may make more sense to talk in terms which we can understand. After three hundred years of exposure to us, black folks seem to have learned their lessons well. As long as they keep their message pure and simple, Southern whites may come to see its reason and justice.

TRUE BELIEVERS, AND OTHERS

This is another effort to promote inter-regional understanding, written for Brightleaf, *when that magazine was brightening the literary skies at the turn of the century. It tells Yankee newcomers to the South why they shouldn't mind being asked
about the state of their souls.*

. . .

The other day my buddy Norman came by to see me. Norm is a Yankee mi-
grant to Chapel Hill, a secular humanist of indeterminate extraction, and he
was real upset because he'd read about a survey showing that 66 percent of
North Carolina Christians say that they've been "born again." Norm's exposure
to North Carolina is pretty much limited to the Research Triangle and Charlotte—the "occupied territories," as they're known in some circles—and that
statistic plainly reinforced his image of the rest of the state as a place crawling
with *Deliverance*-style hillbillies who like to capture folks like him, tie them
up, and witness to them.

I tried to soothe him. I told him it's unlikely that he'll be forcibly evange-
lized—and not only because he's presentable enough that most folks probably
assume that he's already saved.

I told him a story.

At a conference in Italy back in the 1980s, I met an East German "sociologist" named Lothar. I put "sociologist" in quotes here because Lothar was
no scholar. He was first and foremost a Communist, and a real Party animal:
that he was allowed to travel in the West without an escort proved that. He

was also one of the most cynical human beings I have ever met. Maybe he had been idealistic in his youth (who knows?), but by the time I met him he was an apparatchik in his late thirties who drank too much and lied for a living. I couldn't help liking him.

He lied. I knew he lied. He knew I knew he lied. He knew I knew that, too (if you can follow that). We understood each other very well. But he went on lying anyway. It had become second nature to him. Usually he delivered the party line deadpan, with only a certain flatness in his speech and something in his eyes to let me know he was just doing his job. And usually I let his lies go by with nothing more than a smile, just to let him know I wasn't buying. But one evening several of us were sitting, talking, drinking, when someone asked him about some East German dissidents who had been in the news. Without batting an eye he explained that all of the seditious elements in the GDR were on the CIA payroll. Well, that was just too much. I said I'd just read that the American Communist Angela Davis was getting ten thousand dollars a speech on American campuses, and I didn't think it was fair that we had to support their dissidents and ours, too. Lothar laughed the hardest of anyone.

When the conference was over, he and I went to the train station together. It was early morning, but he had already been hitting the schnapps. As I headed for my second-class carriage, he stopped me. "We part here," he said. "I'm in first." He grinned. "Only the best for the working class."

I do wonder what became of him. There's not much demand for Soviet apologists in reunited Germany. If he was lucky, his liver gave out before his government did.

Anyway, the point of the story, I told Norm, was that Eastern European Communists weren't like the American variety. Whatever else you might say about them, American Communists were sincere. It's like Senator Olin D. Johnston of South Carolina said about his colleague Strom Thurmond, when Strom was filibustering a civil-rights bill in the Senate: "Listen to ol' Strom. He really believes all that shit." You didn't become a Red to advance your career. You really had to believe all that shit. In Eastern Europe and the Soviet Union, though, Communism was the state religion: it enlisted opportunists, conformists, the temperamentally conservative, and the merely prudent. Sooner or later, state religions do wind up that way. Their functionaries are no longer zealots who are ready to be martyred for their beliefs. They're like the bishops of the Victorian Church of England, of whom a critic observed, "In no case does their devoutness rise to such a pitch as to clash with the conventional usages of society [nor] is it in the least degree likely . . . that any one aspiring to saintliness would deliberately model himself on any one of them as an example."

Context is everything, I told Norm. Where he comes from, being born again makes a statement, because not many Yankees have been. Up yonder, if someone tells you he's regenerate you'd better check the exits if you don't want to experience some witnessing. Down here you'll hear that more often—66 percent of the time, apparently, if you ask—but it doesn't mean the same thing. Evangelical Protestantism is the Southern Establishment, and being "born again" often just means you've made an adult religious commitment, that you adhere to the state church.

Look, I told Norm: I'm not saying that's good. I'm not saying it's bad, either. I'm just saying it's different. You don't have to love it or leave it, but you might as well get used to it.

OLD BOYS, GOOD AND BAD

This is another column for Brightleaf, *an attempt to instruct non-Southerners about the proper use of the phrase "good old boy."*

• • •

When one of my students took a trip to the North, she came back complaining that people were always asking her to talk because they wanted to hear her Southern accent. "I don't ask them to talk," she observed. Well, yes, I told her, but Yankees are going to talk whether you ask them to or not. And they're going to talk about the South. And they're going to get it wrong.

A case in point is what has happened to the phrase "good old boy." For decades this label served Southerners well as a term of approval. Examples of its unselfconscious use can be found embalmed in the fiction of Walker Percy and—as I recall, although I can't find it now—Eudora Welty. Although often prefaced with the word "but" (for instance, "He's bad to drink, but he's a good old boy"), the phrase itself was wholly complimentary. Affixed to a Southern white man of any age, it meant that he had the qualities of competence, independence, a modicum of courage, and self-deprecating humor that Southerners admire. As Roy Blount once observed, "good old boy" used to be just an innocent Southern equivalent of "mensch."

That lasted until Tom Wolfe—a Southerner himself!!—took this good vernacular term and gave it to an undeserving world in a 1965 *Esquire* article on the stock-car racer Junior Johnson. What followed was remarkable. Within a very few years, with Sam Ervin in the Watergate hearings, Burt Reynolds on the nation's movie screens, and Jimmy Carter coming out of nowhere to win the presidency, all sorts of people who'd never actually had occasion to compliment a white Southern male began to talk about good old boys. "Suddenly," as Florence King remarked, "there was something called a Good Ole Boy instead of men who had always been called Good Ole Boys." Soon every Southerner with access to a typewriter was trying to make a Yankee dollar or two by explaining the concept to a clueless American public. (I did my share.) Nashville started producing country songs about good old boys. Madison Avenue used the term to sell things like Rebel Yell whiskey. Political commentators found it indispensable for analyzing the Carter White House.

Eventually, of course, the new wore off. Some of Carter's friends and relations gave the good old boy a bad name and the phrase its present connotations of cronyism and genial corruption. Southerners pretty much quit using it, except ironically.

But Yankees won't let it go. On a plane some time ago I was reading Delta's copy of John-John Kennedy's magazine when I came across an article by Paul Starobin about a female CIA officer who sued the Agency, alleging sex discrimination. The article said that after she filed suit National Public Radio piled on, with Nina Totenberg pontificating about the CIA's—wait for it—"good-old-boy network."

All right. Enough is enough. It's time to explain again.

Look. I've known a few CIA officers in my time, and not one has been a good old boy, either in the original or the present debased sense. FBI agents? Well, maybe a few. BAT guys? You bet. But our foreign intelligence service has always been staffed primarily by gentlemen who appear to have expensive educations and English tailors (even if these days they're more likely to come from Fordham or the University of Michigan than from Princeton or Yale).

There must be a technical term for the process by which words and phrases appropriate the meaning of other, unrelated words and phrases that resemble them. "Parameter," for example, was once a modest but precise term of art in mathematics; that it has become a fuzzy synonym for boundary or limit must have something to do with the fact that it sounds like "perimeter." Just so, "good old boy," a homely Southernism, has here been mindlessly conflated with the English phrase "old-boy network," which refers to the admiration and assistance extended to one another by the "old boys" of Eton and Harrow and other upper-class boarding schools.

It's true that the CIA used to draw on the American equivalent of the old-boy network. It may still. And it's also true that these informal fraternities usually exclude women. But they also exclude most men, including nearly all good old boys. So why is it that when the Agency allegedly discriminates the good old boy gets the blame? He didn't do anything. He was just minding his own business, repainting his pickup truck, whatever, and here he is taking the rap for a bunch of the Best and the Brightest.

I don't deny that there have been times and places when the good old boy was in the driver's seat politically (Georgia in the 1940s, for instance). If you use the phrase to mean any Southern white guy who isn't courtly enough to be a gentleman, maybe his hour has even come around at last in national electoral politics. And I'm not saying that some good old boys won't discriminate against women if it occurs to them and they get around to it. But if you think our intelligence establishment is run by good old boys—well, let's just say they're operating under very deep cover indeed.

FREE YOUR DOUBTFUL MIND

Hank Williams was not a good old boy; he was far too complex and troubled. I reviewed a book about him for the South Carolina Review.

• • •

When a Charlotte marketing firm put together a list of the twenty most influential Southerners of the twentieth century, right up there with Martin Luther King and William Faulkner, securely in the top ten, was a country boy from Alabama often known simply by his first name, not the "Hiriam" (*sic*) on his birth certificate, but another. When Waylon Jennings sings, "I don't think Hank done it this-a-way," few have to ask, "Hank who?"

Hank Williams died an untimely death in the back seat of a car somewhere between Knoxville, Tennessee, and Oak Hill, West Virginia, in the last hours of New Year's Eve, 1952, or the early hours of the next day, but if anything, he is better known and more respected as a singer and songwriter today than he was during his short and unruly life. Indeed, he has achieved the sure mark of country-music immortality with as many songs about him as by him. That's true for most of us, of course, but *The Complete Hank Williams* CD set offers 225 tracks—and one critic has complained that it left some out.

As Bill Koon demonstrates in his book *Hank Williams, So Lonesome*, there is also an enormous literature on the man, but only rarely has it risen above the fan-club level. In particular, despite all the recognition from the public and from his country-music peers, he has been largely ignored by scholars. Of course, this is just a special case of academics' disdain for country music in general. Although folklorists have studied the "pure" stuff, when it came to serious attention to the sort of thing played and sung on the Grand Ole Opry, for a long time it almost seemed that when you'd said "Bill Malone," you'd pretty much said it all. True, Koon gave us an English professor's take on Williams's life and work in a 1983 "bio-bibliography," but it languished in undeserved obscurity, so Koon returned to his subject in 2002 to bring the story and bibliography and discography into the twenty-first century.

The first part of Koon's book, "The Singer," gives a brisk overview of the facts of Williams's troubled life, adroitly disentangling them from the multitude of myths that have grown up around them, sorting out the sometimes conflicting accounts in the existing biographies, and adding the results of Koon's own interviews and documentary research. Williams's songs reflected his experience, if not quite in the spontaneous and unmediated way the legend has it, and Koon leads us through Hank's problems with liquor and with a succession of domineering women that started with his mother and included his first wife, the difficult "Miss Audrey" (she of the "Cold, Cold Heart"). Along the way, we encounter colorful characters like "Couzain Dud" LeBlanc, sponsor of the Hadacol Caravan, and watch as Hank upstages Bob Hope and intimidates Milton Berle.

Not to put too fine a point on it, the man's personal life was a mess, as were the lives of most of those around him. Koon provides a useful chronology in an appendix to help the reader keep things straight—which Hank himself had a hard time doing. Although he married his second wife, Billy Jean, three times in two days, for example, he overlooked the fact that her divorce was not yet final. (Nevertheless, in 1975 a judge decided that at least one of the marriages counted.) Things got even messier after his death, as lawsuits began to be filed, bodies were moved from grave to grave, and people's names kept changing. Hank's illegitimate daughter Antha Belle Jett, for instance, became Cathy Yvonne Stone, then Cathy Louise Deupree, and finally—as she undertook a show business career—Jett Williams.

Although Hank's biography often reads like something out of Erskine Caldwell, Koon recognizes that it would be of only limited interest if it had not somehow been transmuted into music and lyrics. In the second part of his book, "The Song," he looks thematically at Williams's astonishing output, ranging from good-timing party songs like "Hey Good Lookin'" and "Jambalaya" to the joyous gospel of "I Saw the Light," from amusing novelty items like "Kaw-

Liga" to heart-wrenching songs of love gone wrong like "Your Cheatin' Heart" and—well, at least a dozen more. Koon looks at the various pop music covers of Williams's songs, ranging from the insipid (Tony Bennett, Perry Como) to the inspired (Ray Charles, Jerry Lee Lewis) and concludes this section with a glance at those songs by other singers about Hank, after his death.

Finally, in a section called "The Resources," Koon presents a discerning review, now inevitably somewhat outdated, of the available recordings and critical summaries of the many books and articles about his subject. Since most of the latter are by relatives and fans, Koon's summaries will usually suffice. In fact, for most readers this book will provide all that they need to know about the man a *Down Beat* magazine poll named "the most popular country and western singer of all time."

THE MAN FROM HOT SPRINGS

Bill Clinton isn't a good old boy either. Like Hank, he's complex (if not as troubled as he should be). This column for Brightleaf *suggests that he overlooked a traditional Southern way to handle a sex scandal.*

• • •

Back in the spring of 1998, as the latest episode of the Clinton White House Follies unfolded, President Clinton was still denying everything and trying to change the subject, Hillary was standing by her man in the best Tammy Wynette tradition, National Public Radio was reporting that Clinton was going to "stick it out" (surely not the best way to put it), and the president's defenders had fallen back to the tacit line that, OK, he's lying, but it doesn't matter. Unexpectedly, the public at large seemed to agree, giving Clinton his highest job approval rating ever. The *New York Observer* had even rounded up a panel of ten Manhattan "supergals"—the likes of Nancy Friday and Erica Jong—to rave about how great it was to have a president who's "alive from the waist down."

It just wasn't fair. Poor Supreme Court Justice Clarence Thomas was raked over the coals during his confirmation hearings when all he was even *accused* of was talking trash with a grown woman lawyer who admitted that she didn't discourage him at the time. If old Billy Jeff's army rank had been anything less than commander in chief, or if he had worked for the University of North Carolina, he would have been looking for another job.

Anyway, for those of us with no partisan interest in whether Clinton was driven from the White House or not (and personally I could see the bright side of either outcome), this was all a great show. During the Watergate hearings, the eminent historian C. Vann Woodward came to lecture in Jerusalem, where I was teaching at the time. Wasn't it all horrible, an Israeli student asked him— wasn't it agonizing? "Naw," Vann said. "I wake up every morning, go downstairs with a spring in my step, pick up the paper, and say, 'Let's see what they've got on the son-of-a- bitch today!'" That's pretty much how I felt about *l'affaire* Lewinsky. We Southerners have always liked our politics to be entertaining, and this was every bit as good as World Championship Wrestling. But I'd like to suggest that, dramatically speaking, Clinton's performance could have been improved. Ponder the fact that Southern white voters disliked him (had it been up to us, he wouldn't have been president in the first place), and ask why.

His sex life wasn't the problem. After all, the South is the region that pro- duced politicians like Edwin Edwards, the randy governor of Louisiana known as "The Golden Zipper," and Big Jim Folsom of Alabama, the subject of many stories and at least one song (about an illegitimate child). At first it seemed that Clinton might be in this time-honored tradition, and we're attached to our traditions down here. I remember an old boy at the Southern 500 stock car race in 1992 telling the one about how Arkansas women are so fast that they had to put a governor on them. Everyone laughed understandingly. So Clinton backslides from time to time—well, which of us is without sin? But as we got to know the man, it became clear that he's not the kind of scoundrel we like. Southerners don't go in for nitpicking legalisms like "I didn't inhale." Clinton learned that sort of thing at Yale Law School, or maybe from the Je- suits at Georgetown—not growing up in Hot Springs.

No, the approved Southern style is confession. Youngsters these days may not recall it, but in 1976 even Jimmy Carter confessed to lust in his heart (in *Playboy*, of all places). That may not sound like much to confess, but give him credit for making the most of what he had. Edwards and Folsom had more to work with, so much so that when Edwards was running against David Duke, a former Grand Wizard of the Ku Klux Klan, he refused to talk about Duke's past because, he said, "he might talk about mine." And Folsom—well, he told a campaign crowd once that a friend, a judge, had warned him that his enemies were going to use a good-looking woman to trap him:

> I said, "Judge, you mean she's built like this?" He said, "That's right." I
> said, "All up and down and every whichaway?" He said, "The most perfect

figure you ever saw in your life." I said, "Judge, you've just got to go back and tell 'em that if they set that trap, and if they bait it with that kind of bait, they're going to catch old Big Jim every time, every time."

Clinton could learn from Big Jim, who once said, "Ain't no use of denying it if they're accusing you of something. . . . You go to denying something, they'll say, hell, he's guilty." What if the president had come on television, looked us soulfully in the eye, and come clean? I don't know how "They're going to catch old Bill every time" would have gone down with the *Washington Post*, but apparently Erica Jong and Nancy Friday would have bought it. So would a lot of Southerners. And if he'd said he was in therapy, he'd have locked up some Californians, too.

A POLITICAL PARABLE

This essay, written for the American Enterprise *shortly after Clinton's presidency ended, pointed to some eerie parallels to an earlier president. I've expanded it a bit. Readers who don't remember Travelgate and Vince Foster may have to do some hasty Googlework.*

. . .

Now that Bill Clinton is out of office (albeit in a way that brings to mind the apocryphal song "How Can I Miss You If You Won't Go Away?") the question of his place in history inevitably arises. No doubt it will be years before a consensus emerges, and even that will be subject to revision, but a comparison to his predecessor Warren G. Harding may suggest an answer. So far the parallels have been remarkable.

Like Clinton, Harding was a man of humble small-town origins, a fact he used for political advantage. A Baptist layman and an enthusiastic amateur musician (who claimed that he had played every band instrument except "the slide trombone and the E-flat cornet"), he pursued an undistinguished career in Ohio state government, until he lost a race for governor in 1910, at which point his political career seemed to be over. Six years later, however, he was back holding office (as a United States senator) and the keynote speaker at his party's national convention. Four years after that the party nominated him for president.

Clinton, of course, is a Baptist layman from humble small-town origins who plays the saxophone, lost a race for governor, and gave the keynote address at the 1988 Democratic national convention.

Harding got the nomination because he was an affable man with a knack for public speaking and no inconvenient principles. He had ducked crucial Senate debates on Prohibition and women's suffrage, for example, and waffled and deliberately obfuscated his position on the League of Nations. This ambiguity made him attractive to party regulars, who were eager to regain the White House.

Sound familiar?

Harding's rhetoric was that of a second-rate John Kennedy—"We must have a citizenship less concerned about what the government can do for it and more anxious about what it can do for the nation"—but he seemed to offer a new generation of leadership: No previous president had been born after the Civil War. Harding's influential show-business friend Al Jolson campaigned for him across the country.

Clinton was the first president to have been born after World War II, and his show-business supporters included Barbra Streisand, Aretha Franklin, Barry Manilow, and Michael Jackson, all of whom sang at his inaugural gala.

A handsome charmer of a man, notorious among his aides for plunging into any available crowd of voters to shake hands, Harding won in a landslide. Although there were no public opinion polls to document a "gender gap," his victory rested in part on the votes of women newly enfranchised by the Nineteenth Amendment. (He was the first president of his party to support women's suffrage, which he had welcomed in his speech accepting his party's nomination.)

Clinton, notoriously affable, was in a dead heat with Bob Dole among male voters in 1996, but was 15 percentage points ahead among women.

In office, Harding surrounded himself with cronies from his home state, who brought their corrupt statehouse ways to D.C. The secretary of the interior, for example, eventually went to prison for taking bribes. The director of the Veterans Bureau was jailed, too: he took payoffs from builders and sold hospital alcohol and drugs to bootleggers and dope dealers. The head of the FBI used agents to harass critics of the administration. The attorney general was indicted twice for fraud. One of the attorney general's friends died under suspicious circumstances of a gunshot wound to the head: the verdict was suicide, but rumors persisted that he had been murdered.

Can anyone say "Webster Hubbell"? "Travelgate"? "Filegate"? "Jim and Susan McDougal"? "Vince Foster"?

The president's strong-minded and independent wife had earlier proved herself to be an efficient, if domineering, businesswoman, and although her outspoken feminism sometimes embarrassed the administration, it was generally recognized that she had largely engineered his political career.

She was known to consult a noted Washington psychic, but she didn't need a séance to talk with Eleanor Roosevelt (as Hillary did, according to Bob Woodward); she could just ring her up: Eleanor was one of the group known as "Flossie's gang."

Flossie became the most public First Lady the nation had known, dealing directly with the press—even holding her own press conferences for women reporters. She reveled in the role, demanded and got her own Secret Service protection, met constantly at the White House with women's groups, advised her husband on everything from protocol to policy, and sometimes even drafted his speeches.

I don't think the parallels need to be spelled out. In fact, you're on your own from here.

The Harding marriage was largely one of convenience. The president resented his wife's imperious ways, and sarcastically called her "the Duchess." For her part, she despised his weakness and resented his philandering, which continually threatened to erupt in public embarrassment. One old flame, the wife of an Ohio friend, threatened during the presidential campaign to publish letters documenting their love affair, even though she had already been given a Cadillac and offered five thousand dollars a year. His campaign manager kept her quiet with another twenty thousand dollars and a round-the-world cruise for her and her husband.

But the president's most notorious escapade involved a young Ohio woman—thirty-one years younger, in fact—with whom he had begun a liaison while a senator. (He found her a job in Washington.) After he became president, he arranged for the Secret Service to smuggle her frequently into the White House, where the two made love in a closet down a short passage from the Oval Office. The infatuated woman stalked the president, making a point of showing up at public occasions where he was present. Apparently she hoped that the president would divorce his wife and marry her. She had a child, which the president supported with payments hand-delivered by the Secret Service (although it is not clear that it was actually his).

The president and his wife entertained special friends in the private quarters of the White House (serving illegal alcohol, which went on the books as medical supplies), but the president most enjoyed getting away from his wife to smoke and drink and play poker with his cronies, or to play golf with them at the Chevy Chase Country Club. He also loved to travel—maybe to get away from home—and became one of the most peripatetic presidents to date.

He seems to have been genuinely concerned about the plight of black Americans (although, of course, he also belonged to a party that depended on the black vote for its majorities). In office, he supported federal anti-lynching legislation, ended President Wilson's exclusion of blacks from federal offices, and once courageously addressed an audience of thirty thousand Alabamians on the iniquity of segregation.

In fact, it was often said that he was the nation's first black president—and not just figuratively speaking. The hometown rumor that his father was of mixed race was given national currency during the presidential campaign in a book by an Ohio college professor, and hundreds of thousands of pamphlets were distributed door-to-door and on trains, including pictures of the White House labeled "Uncle Tom's Cabin." The editor of a black newspaper in Cincinnati claimed that when the candidate was first running for office in Ohio he had told black audiences that he was a Negro. The president never denied it: "How should I know?" he is reported to have said. "One of my ancestors might have jumped the fence."

Harding's presidency coincided with an unprecedented economic boom, fueled by record consumer spending and 2 percent unemployment, but despite the general prosperity and his personal charm, his party suffered serious reverses in the off-year congressional elections two years into his term as president, and his presidency began to unravel.

But here the parallels to Clinton end. As rumors of corruption swirled around them, the Hardings left Washington for a cross-country tour. In San Francisco, the president was taken ill and died, while alone with his wife. Later, a former FBI agent wrote a book claiming that the First Lady had poisoned him, to avoid impending disgrace. (For whatever reason, she refused to allow an autopsy.)

Dying when he did was probably a good career move for Harding: The nation mourned him deeply and the old comparisons to Abraham Lincoln were dusted off for the occasion. But Harding's reputation has not worn well. In fairness, he does not seem to have been personally corrupt, but most historians have nevertheless rated him as the worst president in the twentieth century.

BAD MAN IN THE MOUNTAINS

Like the good old boy, the "bad man" is a well-established social type, and this fore-word to a book by Tom Burton discusses him. Tom taught for many years at East Tennessee State University, and we were colleagues when I taught there in 2002.

• • •

In *Beech Mountain Man,* English professor Thomas Burton has transcribed and edited the spoken memoirs of a mountaineer named Ronda Lee Hicks. In his introduction Burton says that Hicks is "a man you don't meet everyday," and after only a few pages of this disturbing but gripping book I was glad that I don't. This secondhand encounter is plenty, thank you.

Of course, city police and rural sheriffs run into the likes of Ronda Lee Hicks all too often, and many of us who grew up in Appalachia have at least known *of* someone like him, but most readers of university press books encounter such characters only in fiction. They do encounter them there, though, because Hicks is a classic example of a well-known type that we can call the Bad Man. The Bad Man may not be bad in all ways (and he's only usually a man—there is a female version), but this is definitely someone you don't want to cross or even seriously annoy, because he is likely to respond with abrupt, brutal, and overwhelming violence.

Readers should resist the temptation to see Hicks as an escapee from some hillbilly freak show. When Jim Croce sang about "Bad, Bad Leroy Brown" ("Badder than old King Kong / And meaner than a junkyard dog") he was evoking an African American Bad Man celebrated in song from "Stacker Lee" and "Railroad Bill" to the latest rap video. Irish Americans and Sicilian Americans have had their own hard cases as well, familiar to viewers of movies like *Gangs of New York* and *The Godfather*. The *cholo* variety can be found in the mean streets of East Los Angeles.

The point is that the Bad Man is by no means unique to Appalachia, and few Americans have any reason to be smug on ethnic grounds.

It should go without saying that Bad Men exist on the fringes of groups made up for the most part of hardworking, churchgoing, respectable people, and that they grotesquely exaggerate otherwise admirable values—a tradition of honor, for example, or an ethic of self-reliance developed in response to a hostile and dangerous environment. All of this is true in Appalachia, as well. That said, however, homicide rates suggest that Bad Men are more common in Appalachia than in, say, New England or Minnesota. In fact, they seem to be more common in the South as a whole—one of many cases, perhaps, where a Southern trait can be found most extensively among black Southerners and mountain whites. Listen to W. J. Cash, writing in *The Mind of the South* about the white male world of the antebellum plantation South: "[It] was full of the chip-on-the-shoulder swagger and brag of a boy—one, in brief, of which the essence was the boast, voiced or not, on the part of every Southerner, that he would knock hell out of whoever dared to cross him." Cash saw this trait as a manifestation of a more general "individualism"; into the twentieth century, he wrote, Southerners saw the world "as, in its last aspect, a simple solution, an aggregation of self-contained and self-sufficient monads, each of whom was ultimately and completely responsible for himself." Hank Williams Jr. sings that "a country boy can survive," and that is a common ideal, if only rarely a statement of fact.

Part of this ethic is a disdain for institutions. When it comes to getting right with God, Evangelical Protestants are—and believe they should be—pretty much on their own. As Tom T. Hall puts it in another country song, "Me and Jesus got our own thing going / Don't need anybody to tell us what it's all about." The same goes for redressing grievances—maybe that, too, should be done man to man, with no need for third-party mediation. Think about what Hicks is implying when he says, "You know, when somebody does somethin' to you, you don't think about goin' to hire you a lawyer." (Burton's faithful rendition of Hicks's speech may take some getting used to, especially for readers not accustomed to Appalachian dialect, but try reading this book aloud.)

Finally, according to Cash, the "ruling element" in this tradition is "an intense distrust of, and, indeed, downright aversion to, any actual exercise of authority beyond the barest minimum essential to the existence of the social organism." "Nobody controls me," Hicks claims, and his insistence on that point has made him an unsatisfactory soldier, employee, and husband. But he's only extreme in this aspiration, by no means alone.

So to understand Ronda Lee Hicks read *The Mind of the South*. Or, for that matter, read *Southern Honor* by Bertram Wyatt-Brown, or *Culture of Honor* by Richard Nisbett and Dov Cohen, or, maybe best of all (the author is from East Tennessee), *Vengeance and Justice* by Edward Ayers. And read sociologist Lonnie Athens's description in *The Creation of Dangerous Violent Criminals* of how Bad Men are made, a process in which violence, often originally deployed in self-defense, earns one a reputation as "crazy" or "dangerous," a sort of celebrity with rewards that may outweigh the obvious drawbacks. This process can play itself out in the biography of someone from any race, social class, or ethnic group, and for women as well as for men, but obviously some kinds of people—people in some regions, for example—are less likely than others to have other advantages or alternative sources of self-esteem. Some times and places are also more likely to provide the sort of "coach" that Athens argues is usually a factor, someone who insists that self-defense is a "personal responsibility which [the novice] cannot evade, but must discharge," "glorifies violence through storytelling," and "promotes violence through belittling and derision [or even] physical punishment" ("Stand up and fight, or I'll beat you myself"). The lesson, as Kenny Rogers puts it in yet another country song, is that sometimes you have to fight when you're a man.

I said earlier that a Bad Man isn't necessarily *all* bad, and Hicks does have his own standards. Notice, for example, that he carefully avoids profanity when speaking to the professor. He speaks respectfully of his parents. He has never dated more than one woman at a time ("even when I was married"). And he believes there's "somethin' wrong with your mind to start with if you kill a man just because you want his money." But he also believes that "If somebody does somethin' to you, I think you should always get revenge." In some circumstances, for some people, that lesson is well-nigh inescapable.

CHANGE AND DECAY IN ALL AROUND I SEE

These three elegiac reviews look back fondly to the South of the mid-twentieth century. That era's shortcomings are obvious, I suppose, but those of us who knew it do find things to miss. The first two pieces were written for Southern Cultures; *the last for the* Oxford American. *(I thought of the "Best Little Hair Houses" title too late to use when it was published, but better late than never.)*

• • •

Music from the Golden Age

One reason baby boomers are despised by their elders is that they think they're the first generation to have experienced everything. From sex, drugs, and rock and roll to aging parents and menopause, nothing happened until it happened to them. A case in point is the list of "The 100 Greatest Songs of Rock & Roll" compiled for a television special back as the twentieth century was stumbling to an end. A mere sixteen dated from before 1960 (and four of those were by Elvis). Almost as many songs were by the Beatles and the Stones as by all of the 1950s rockabilly, doo-wop, and R&B singers put together.

This is, to put it mildly, a ludicrous distortion. The 1960s were noisier, druggier, and more pretentious than the preceding decade, but the Golden Age of rock and roll lasted from 1954 until 1959. Period. I speak as someone who ran a program called *Rock and Roll Memory Time* on his college's student radio station in 1962.

If you want to know what I'm talking about, check out *Loud, Fast & Out of Control*, a four-CD compilation from Rhino. From the opening strains of

"C'mon Everybody" by Eddie Cochran to the last notes of the Viscounts' version of "Harlem Nocturne," it offers exactly what its subtitle advertises, "The Wild Sounds of '50s Rock," accompanied by splendid period photographs, *three* intelligent and entertaining introductory essays, and what are simply the best liner notes I've ever read. For example, from the notes to "Fujiyama Mama" ("When I start eruptin', ain't nobody gonna make me stop"): "Wanda Jackson insists that she really wasn't that kind of girl, but while other women singers were simpering about where the boys are, Wanda always sang as if they were in her hotel room."

Inevitably there's a Southern slant to this. Rock and roll was pretty much created by black and white boys (Wanda was an exception) from somewhere between Lubbock (Buddy Holley) and Norfolk (Gene Vincent), and even those who weren't Southern (Eddie Cochran, from Minnesota via California) sounded as if they were. The 1950s South is often seen as bland and repressive, and, well, it *was* bland and repressive. But say this for that decade: it gave young Southerners something to rebel against—and this music is one of the delightful results.

If you remember the 1950s, this music will bring them back. If you don't remember them, you'll wish you did.

Roadside Attractions

Among the many things we can blame the 1960s for is the end of the Golden Age of family automobile travel. Ten-hour days of being beaten by a hot, 55-mile-an-hour wind while trying to hear scratchy AM radio stations over the noise of the wind and the tires. Sticking hands out the open window to make airfoils, waving at porch-sitters who were watching the passing traffic (usually they waved back). Holding your breath over bridges, counting cows and horses (a white horse doubled your score), reading Burma-Shave signs, and arguing about where the exact middle of the back seat was. Anyone whose idea of summer vacation has been shaped by air-conditioned travel on limited-access, limited-advertising interstate highways with nothing to see but scenery—anyone, that is, who came to sentience in the 1970s or later—simply cannot imagine how it used to be. Actually, it was pretty miserable.

But American enterprise provided welcome breaks from the misery with innumerable "roadside attractions," most of them advertised on dozens of "[so many] miles to" signs that gave ten-year-olds plenty of time to nag their parents to stop. Most were done in by the triple whammy of those interstate highways, the rise of corporate "destinations" like Disney World (opened in 1971), and a blasé generation of children who had seen greater wonders on television. In *Dixie before Disney: 100 Years of Roadside Fun*, however, Tim Hollis, an Alabamian just old enough to remember, has produced a damn near comprehensive catalogue of the South's contributions to this midcentury American phenomenon. Hollis examines everything from the early days of Stuckey's and Kentucky Fried Chicken to the rise of tourist meccas like South of the Border, Rock City, Cypress Gardens, and Gatlinburg.

Many of these places drew on some version of local history (e.g., Confederama), local culture (Booger Holler), or local environment (countless Florida gator farms), and even those whose appeal appeared to rest on being exotic or strange had a certain provincial charm. (A Virginia snake and monkey farm. A house-that-defies-gravity in Florida.) Sure, the post-millennial South has plenty of tourist traps—think Pigeon Forge, Branson, Myrtle Beach—but these spots are somehow more meretricious than tacky, more Las Vegas than Rock City, and there's a bland placelessness about them: they could all have been brought to you by Erewhon Enterprises, Inc.

Hollis reminds us of what we've lost: simpler pleasures, simpler times, simpler selves. His breezy style suits his subject matter (a "cultural studies" approach would have been too dreary for words), but an impressive bibliography and chapter notes are tucked away discreetly in the back for anyone who wants to take this seriously. The book is lavishly illustrated with old postcards, brochures, and roadside signage.

My only complaint is that Texas gets short shrift, which means there's no mention of Aquarena Springs, one of my personal favorites, which used to offer a wacky underwater pageant involving Indian braves, mermaids, Glurpo the Clown, and Ralph the Diving Pig. Alas, it has been bought by Texas State University and turned into just another nature center. Ralph will dive no more.

Best Little Hair Houses in Dixie

When Stanford University aroused the ire of conservatives by offering a course on "black hair" a few years ago, the course's proponents argued that what people do to and with hair is a matter of great cultural import among African Americans and deserves serious attention. They may have been right about that, but like a great many "black" things in America, this hair business is something that has been shared by Southern whites, albeit in a somewhat paler version. The beauty parlor, in particular, has been celebrated in song (although I don't recall any by former beautician Tammy Wynette) and story (including at least two novels: Sarah Gilbert's *Hairdo* and Sandra King Ray's *Making Waves in Zion*). When the Knoxville entrepreneur Chris Whittle published a special "Salon Edition" of *Southern Style,* his magazine for Southern women, he knew what he was doing.

Given all that, compiling a book like *The Beauty Box: A Tribute to the Legendary Beauty Parlors of the South* is, like many of the best ideas, obvious once you think of it. What it does is simply to provide fond vignettes of forty-two old-fashioned beauty shops, scattered from North Carolina to Texas. These aren't your newfangled shopping-mall operations with cutesy names like Mane Attraction or Curl-Up-and-Dye. They tend to have names like—well, like The Beauty Box, or Babette's Cut & Curl, or, at their most hoity-toity, Joseph's Coiffures. Some of these establishments serve black customers, some white (apparently, as with churches and funeral parlors, self-segregation is still the rule), and a few have some male customers, although the word "unisex" isn't on their signs and probably isn't in their vocabulary. But all of them offer their regular customers a good deal more than hair care, as this book amply documents.

Don't let Fannie Flagg's blurb ("Hairlarious") or the publisher's back-cover label ("Humor") mislead you. This is not just another condescending look at the kooky South. There's plenty of humor in this book, some of it pretty raunchy, but most of it comes from the beauticians themselves, for whom amusing talk seems to be almost an occupational requirement. Whether lamenting the lost art of teasing or telling about memorable customers, these folks tend to be good talkers. Several argue that shops like theirs are an endangered species, and to judge by the average age of the customers pictured in Karim Shamsi-Basha's photographs, they may be right about that. All the more reason to be grateful, then, that Shamsi-Basha and author Kathy Kemp have recorded this vanishing institution for posterity.

THE FRENCH QUARTER RENAISSANCE
OF THE 1920S

My book Dixie Bohemia *was based on the 2011 Fleming Lectures at LSU. I like to think that project was a serious scholarly enterprise, but it was also a jeu d'esprit that let me and Dale live in the Quarter for a couple of months. This is sort of a précis of the book, written as an entry for KnowLA.org, the* Digital Encyclopedia of Louisiana.

• • •

In the 1920s a Bohemian scene emerged in the French Quarter of New Orleans that the *Double Dealer* magazine hailed as "the Renaissance of the Vieux Carré." Some of the writers, artists, poseurs, and hangers-on involved were consciously trying to replicate the better-known Bohemias of Paris and New York City, and in many respects they succeeded. With the support of local patrons, they created a number of cultural institutions, some short-lived but others more enduring, and contributed to the historic preservation and commercial revitalization that turned the French Quarter from a slum into a tourist destination and a center for nightlife, with housing for elements of the upper-middle class. Ironically, this transformation drove out many of the working artists and writers who had helped to bring it about.

Origins
Anthropologist and novelist Oliver La Farge described the French Quarter of the 1920s as "a decaying monument and a slum as rich as jambalaya or

gumbo." Most of its once-elegant buildings had been divided into tenements rented to the poor, notably to the first- and second-generation Sicilian immigrants who by one estimate made up 80 percent of the resident population in 1910. In the years during and just after World War I artists and writers began to move into the area immediately around Jackson Square, attracted by the cheap rents, faded charm, and colorful street life.

Although a few of the Quarter's new residents were native New Orleanians, most came from elsewhere. Several wrote for the city's daily newspapers and encouraged the developing scene by reporting on it. Lyle Saxon, for example, one of the first to adapt a historic building in the Quarter for his own use, used his platform at the *Times-Picayune* to encourage artists and writers to do likewise. Natalie Scott, a society columnist for the *States*, chronicled and promoted the Bohemian goings-on in the Quarter, bought and restored several buildings, rented apartments to artists and writers, and lived in one herself.

Another source of aspiring Bohemians was Tulane University. Its architecture students had for some time been making measured drawings of the Quarter's old buildings, and art students from Sophie Newcomb College, the university's college for women, had been painting and drawing the picturesque ones. Graduates and faculty members from both programs established studios in the Quarter, showed their work in its galleries, and even moved there to live and to socialize. Other Tulane people did so as well: Frans Blom and Oliver La Farge from the university's Middle American Research Institute, for instance, who helped to establish a continuing Mexican connection that brought Mexican artists and writers to town and sent New Orleanians south for summer visits and, in a few cases, for good.

Business interests have often been cast as the villains in the story of the Quarter's revival, and it is true that some shortsighted developers were eager to raze it and replace it with clean and modern buildings. But it should be noted that many businesspeople saw the unique neighborhood's commercial potential. In fact, the first practical proposal for large-scale renovation came from the president of the Association of Commerce, who suggested in 1919 that the old Pontalba buildings should be converted to studios and living space for artists. Looking back, photographer William "Cicero" Odiorne observed that "the revival of the old Quarter was a sort of civic project." Uptown New Orleanians were interested in "French Quarter Bohemianism," he said, because people like him were "useful."

Personalities and Social Life

One of the Quarter's best-known figures at this time was William Spratling, a young artist on the architecture faculty at Tulane. In 1926 he and his apart-ment-mate William Faulkner (not yet a famous writer) self-published a slim book entitled *Sherwood Anderson and Other Famous Creoles,* described later by Spratling as "a sort of mirror of our scene in New Orleans." Comprising sim-ply Spratling's drawings of their friends and an introduction by Faulkner, the book gives an idea of the sort of creative figures involved in the Renaissance. It included painter and teacher Ellsworth Woodward, lithographer Caroline Wogan Durieux, photographer "Pops" Whitesell, architects N. C. Curtis and Moise Goldstein, and Mardi Gras designer Louis Andrews Fischer, as well as pianist and composer Genevieve Pitot, activist and preservationist Elizabeth Werlein, and Tulane cheerleader Marian Draper. The best known of the "Famous Creoles" today, however, are undoubtedly some of the dozen or so writers, in-cluding the young Faulkner, the even younger Hamilton Basso, and, of course, Sherwood Anderson.

Anderson first visited New Orleans in 1922, found it "surely the most civ-ilized spot in America," and returned to take up residence in 1924 with his new (third) wife, Elizabeth. Already a celebrated writer, Anderson quickly became, in Spratling's judgment, "the Grand Old Man of the literati in New Orleans." The Andersons were at the center of the Quarter's busy social life in the mid-1920s, their apartment in the upper Pontalba building the scene of almost nightly gatherings, and their Saturday dinner parties occasions for introducing locals to visitors like writers Carl Carmer, Anita Loos, Edmund Wilson, Edna St. Vincent Millay, and John Dos Passos, and publishers B. W. Huebsch and Horace Liveright.

Contemporary accounts and memoirs make it clear that most of the Quar-ter's new residents enjoyed what Elizabeth Anderson recalled as "a social and congenial time." Even impecunious young Bohemians (all of them white, in Jim Crow Louisiana) could usually afford (African American) "help"—Faulk-ner, Spratling, and La Farge, for example, shared the services of a cook, who washed and cleaned as well—which made the frequent dinner parties and other entertaining possible. The Quarter also offered cafés for midday coffee and conversation, inexpensive Creole and Italian restaurants, and an abun-dance of speakeasies (at one point Elizebeth Werlein counted seventy-four in a nine-block radius). The ordinary social round was punctuated by special events like the racy, more or less annual "Bal des Artistes" to benefit the Arts and Crafts Club, or an ill-starred cruise on Lake Pontchartrain that Sherwood Anderson organized (immortalized, after a fashion, in Faulkner's novel *Mosquitoes*), all of it fueled by a flood of illegal alcohol. Elizabeth Anderson recalled, "We all seemed to feel that Prohibition was a personal affront and that we had a moral duty to undermine it." Certainly bootleg liquor was as easy to find and as emblematic of the scene as marijuana would be for a later generation of rebellious young people.

New Institutions

Several new institutions contributed to this flourishing of cultural activity, and benefited from it. All were largely bankrolled by business people and philanthropists who were not themselves "Bohemian," but who valued the presence and enjoyed the company of those who were.

The *Double Dealer* was a literary magazine founded in 1921 by two young men from prominent New Orleans Jewish families. For its five years of existence, it provided a gathering place and rallying point for the literary component of the Renaissance. Although its office was actually across Canal Street from the French Quarter, its staff, contributors, and hangers-on were very much a part of the Quarter scene, gathering most afternoons at the Pelican Bookshop on Royal Street for wine and salami sandwiches. Sherwood Anderson dropped by the office shortly after he arrived in New Orleans, and stayed on to become a mentor and frequent contributor.

The Arts and Crafts Club was for artists what the *Double Dealer* was for writers. Its lectures, classes, exhibits, and salesroom were open to the public, and its activities received extensive coverage in the local newspapers. The club was largely bankrolled by Sarah Henderson, a sugar-refinery heiress, and its activities appealed to a mix of working artists, serious amateurs, and the merely "artsy."

Le Petit Theatre du Vieux Carré, which began as the Drawing Room Players uptown but moved in 1919 to the Quarter (where it remains today), also provided a setting in which "Society" mingled with Bohemia. Many of the Quarter's artists, writers, and musicians were involved in production and design; the theater's founders, its management, and most of its audience were drawn from more privileged circles; and both groups participated as actors.

Uptown society people were also brought to experience the Quarter's romance and squalor firsthand when organizations like the Daughters of 1776–1812, the Quartier Club, and Le Petit Salon renovated historic properties to use as clubhouses. Though by no means Bohemians themselves, members of these elite women's groups invited the more presentable artists and writers to be speakers and guests, and allied themselves with the Quarter's artistic element in the nascent historic preservation movement.

Transformation and Decline

Once a critical mass of artists and writers was reached, related businesses began to appear. As early as 1922 a walking tour suggested in the *Double Dealer* pointed out the Quarter's "restaurants, auction marts, antique shops and book stalls," including such Bohemian hangouts as John and Grace McClure's Olde Book Shoppe and the Arts and Crafts Club's galleries. That same year, a *New York Times* article headlined "Greenwich Village on Royal Street" observed that the Quarter offered "the usual teashops and antique shops and book-shops." The new cultural and commercial activity meant that uptown New Orleanians who might never previously have set foot in the Quarter began to venture into it for lunches and shopping, for exhibits and classes at the Arts and Crafts Club, and for plays at "Le Petit." Visits to the French Market for coffee became a common post-party activity.

Some uptown visitors liked what they saw so much that they purchased houses as rental property or for pieds-à-terre. Some of the more adventurous even moved into the Quarter themselves, many of them what would later be called "fauxhemians," like the fashionable young couple whose "impromptu studio party" led a society reporter to gush, "That's one of the advantages of being an artist . . . , you can give such wonderful parties!" This sort of thing led more than one real artist to grouse that the Quarter was filling up with the kind of people "who rent an ordinary furnished room and call it 'my studio.'" The *New York Times* observed that "the French Quarter has suffered the fate of such quarters. It has become a fad. It has become, in a way, fashionable."

Inevitably, the Quarter's new appeal was soon reflected in rising rents and real estate prices. When Natalie Scott sold a St. Peter Street house she had owned for only sixteen months, she tripled her investment, and the value of Le Petit Salon's clubhouse almost quadrupled in six years. The days when Lyle Saxon could rent a sixteen-room house on Royal Street for sixteen dollars a month would not come again.

The Quarter was also discovered by tourists. In 1924 Saxon published a walking tour of the Quarter in his newspaper column, but he was dismayed by how many people took his advice to come have a look. He wrote later that the place had become a "mad house," with "a horde of tourists everywhere, and people riding around with horses and buggies, sight-seeing."

Increasing rents meant that fewer working artists and writers could afford to live in the Quarter, and the influx of tourists and of businesses catering to them meant that fewer wanted to live there anyway. By the 1930s most of those depicted in *Sherwood Anderson and Other Famous Creoles* had decamped. Faulkner went home to Mississippi and the Andersons left for the mountains of Virginia; others went to New York, or Paris; some went to Taxco in Mexico and Santa Fe, New Mexico (where they got to see the same process repeat itself). Although some vestiges of Bohemia and even a few actual Bohemians remained in the Quarter, its Bohemian moment had passed.

A LAST LECTURE

In 1998 a University of North Carolina student group asked some faculty members to give "last lectures," and for me it wasn't just pretend: I was about to retire. My lecture drew heavily on an address I'd given at a recent commencement, and it won't hurt you to read the rah-rah stuff about Chapel Hill. UNC may have disgraced itself chasing athletic glory, but I still think it's a special place.

• • •

I found myself wondering the other day why I had agreed to do this. Not that it's a burden—quite the contrary, it's an extraordinary honor and privilege—but even for someone who has stood up in front of classes several times a week for three decades it feels grossly immodest to put myself forward this way. Y'all are not obliged to be here: none of this will be on the test. What can I say that will make it worth your while to have come to hear me?

As I was thinking such thoughts, I happened to come across a commencement address by the distinguished Presbyterian divine and Confederate apologist Robert Lewis Dabney. Addressing the graduates of Hampden Sidney College in 1882, the Reverend Dr. Dabney began much as I just did, by confessing his unworthiness for the task, but he added: "We who are passing off the stage of public action owe a sympathy to the young who are entering on it, which should forbid our withholding any service or evidence of affection they may ask of us. It is this which has forbidden my saying No to your request."

In other words, if I'm wasting your time, it's your fault for asking me.

Dabney and I share something besides impending departure from the stage and feelings of inadequacy, and that's a devotion to the South and concern about where our region is going. The title of Dabney's address was "The New South," and that's sort of what I'll be talking about this evening—the latest New South, and what the University of North Carolina at Chapel Hill has to do with it.

I've spent my entire academic career, ever since I left graduate school in 1969, at Chapel Hill. Several times I've had opportunities to leave, twice I thought seriously about it, and once I almost did, but when push came to shove I just couldn't do it. And I've never regretted not going. UNC is a very special place; for someone with my interests, there's no better place in the world. What makes Carolina so special? How is it different, and—let's not be modest, not among ourselves—how is it better than any of a hundred other universities we could name?

It is, famously, the First State University. With the enlightened and generous support of the taxpayers, UNC has served North Carolina well: educating its young people, training its leaders and public officials, studying its history and culture, addressing its problems through research on everything from hemophilia to highway safety. We can be proud of that.

Carolina is also a great center of scholarship, with a national—indeed, an international—mission, and reputation, and influence. We rank among the top thirty or forty universities in the country. A few individual departments and schools are within shouting distance, if not within measurement error, of the very best in the world. When it comes to research and advanced study we're playing in the Big Leagues, and we can be proud of that, too.

But neither of these understandings of UNC—as a state university or as a contributor to the world of scholarship—neither of these touches on what makes Carolina unique. There are other great state universities. These days there are even some half-decent ones elsewhere in North Carolina. And certainly there are other world-renowned centers of research. There's a pretty good one of those in our neighborhood, too.

But UNC has had a third role, an intermediate one, and it's the one that I think has actually made Carolina unique. At least since the 1920s UNC has been a great *Southern* university, training many of our region's leaders, studying and serving the South to an extent no other institution can rival. Chapel

Hill has also nurtured scores of accomplished students of the South, men and women who have devoted their lives to describing and interpreting the South to itself and to the world. Our sociology and anthropology departments have housed a dozen, notably under the thirty-year leadership of Howard W. Odum. Our history department compiled an equally notable record of scholarship, while training the better part of two generations of Southern historians. Scholars in our English department largely defined Southern literature as a subject for study, while writers in the same department were producing some of the best of it. Our political scientists analyzed black and white Southern politics in a time of dramatic transition. Our university press built its considerable reputation largely by publishing studies of Southern history and literature and folklore, white and black, side by side with surveys of the South's many social and economic problems. It's this record of regional scholarship and service that led historian John Egerton to characterize UNC in the 1930s as "the light of the South and a place of national significance."

This tradition is still alive. It's simply a fact that you can't seriously study the history or culture of the South without, sooner or later, coming to Chapel Hill to do it. Studying the South is one thing—maybe *the* one thing—that we do better than anyone else in the world. Dozens of faculty members across the university take the South as their subject. The Southern Oral History Program captures the opinions and recollections of both famous and "ordinary" Southerners. Our magnificent library is systematically documenting the South from its prehistory to the present, and making that documentation available on the Internet. Two fine quarterlies, the *Southern Literary Journal* and *Southern Cultures,* are edited here. The Howard Odum Institute for Research in Social Science is the principal repository for studies of Southern public opinion. The Southern Historical Collection and the Southern Folklife Collection are research archives simply not equaled anywhere else. When UNC established a new Center for the Study of the American South in the 1990s, we were building on the fact that Carolina was not just *a* great Southern university, but arguably *the* great Southern university.

But some may say, wait a minute, isn't it provincial to think of UNC this way? Well, of course, if the South is a "province," that's true by definition. But to study and to serve your homeplace needn't mean that you're parochial or narrow. Nobody thinks less of St Andrew's because it's a great Scottish university, or of the Sorbonne because it's French. No, what that objection usually conceals is an assumption that defining something as "Southern" makes it somehow second-rate. Unfortunately some Americans, even some Southerners, still think of the South as a sort of down-at-the-heels country cousin, or maybe a shabby-genteel maiden aunt, always nattering on about the past.

But people who think that way are the ones living in the past. Consider the "province" that a Southern university serves these days. Southern literary and musical excellence is a relatively old story. Everyone knows about that, or should. But now the South seems also to be taking the lead in America's political and economic life, and that's something that we haven't seen for a long time. Stop and think about it: If the Arkansas boy now in the White House resigns, we get Al Gore of Tennessee. If he resigns, we get Newt Gingrich of Georgia. And if he goes? Uh-huh: Strom Thurmond of South Carolina. (At last.) And it's not just the line of succession to the presidency, not just the leadership of both houses of Congress, who have these . . . funny accents. So do cabinet officers, national party leaders, and scores of lesser officials. Even the chairman of the National Endowment for the Humanities is a Southerner, from Mississippi, and the chairman of the National Endowment for the Arts is a Tennessean, former director of the Country Music Foundation no less. As Bob Dylan put it once, "You don't need a weatherman to know which way the wind blows." (Dylan, a Minnesota boy trying to sound like an Okie in the 1960s, was ahead of the curve.)

And that's not all. Recently the *Economist* magazine, of London, concluded in a special issue on the South that it has become "a locomotive powering the American economy." For better or for worse, Southern companies like Walmart and the Hospital Corporation of America and Southwest Airlines have completely changed the way of doing what they do. Companies like CNN and Federal Express have invented entirely *new* things to do. The South is the home of market leaders in a dozen fields, from Compaq Computers to Delta Airlines to TCBY yogurt. NationsBank, First Union, and Wachovia are some of America's largest banks, and Charlotte is about to surpass San Francisco as the country's number-two banking center, second only to New York City. The South's economy is now generating half of America's new jobs, North Carolina and Mississippi are the nation's most industrialized states, and an article in the *American Spectator* magazine talks about the ongoing Great Migration from the Northeast to "more economically robust and culturally normal places like Georgia, North Carolina, Florida, and Texas."

Now, anyone my age must be astonished to hear a national magazine, even a conservative one, call the South "economically robust," not to mention "culturally normal." It hasn't been that long since President Roosevelt characterized the South as "the nation's number-one economic problem." For so long the South has been treated as an embarrassment and a national whipping boy that many of us have trouble thinking of it as a leader and a good example. But the dynamism of the South's economy is making it an increasingly important component of the global economy. We hear a lot about "globalization" these days, and, sure, a lot of what we hear is what Clare Booth Luce called "globaloney." But one thing globalization means, when it means anything at all, is that regions all over the world, from Quebec to Catalonia, are being taken seriously, as markets, as locations, as competitors—taken seriously in their own right, not just as parts of larger nation-states. That's why Southern studies are flourishing at the University of Kyoto: The Japanese know a market when they see one; they know that if the South became a separate country today, it would have the fourth-largest economy in the world.

In a country song recorded in 1976 Tanya Tucker sang, "I believe the South is going to rise again, but not the way we thought it would back then." And so it has.

We still have a way to go. We all know that. And progress brings its own problems. Increasingly we have the same problems as the rest of the country, the problems of an urban, industrial society. Moreover, as the Reverend Dr. Dabney warned those Hampden Sidney students in 1882, it's spiritually dangerous "to make the appliances of production the all in all, to exclaim as so many do of factories, and mines, and banks, and stock boards, and horse-powers of steam, and patent machines, 'These be thy gods, O Israel!'" I could have given you that lecture this evening: I can preach it either way. But, as Scarlett O'Hara might have said, let's think about it tomorrow. My present point is that, despite setbacks and frustrations, Southerners are now citizens of no mean city. There was a time, not long ago, when being a "great Southern university" might have sounded like a joke in poor taste. But that time has passed.

Writing in 1940, W. J. Cash observed that the South has been "not quite a nation within a nation, but the next thing to it," and, like it or not, Atlanta has become our semi-nation's capital. It's where many Southern movers and shakers go to move and shake these days. UNC is well represented there, as we should be. We have thousands of alumni in Atlanta: journalists, academics, corporate lawyers, bankers, leaders in business and commerce. Some of them recently gave several hundred thousand dollars to endow a professorship in Southern studies (bless their hearts). We threw a party in Atlanta to thank them, and I gave a little talk. I talked about Atlanta as the South's de facto capital, and I urged them to think of Carolina as a sort of Harvard to Atlanta's New York, Oxford to its London, Athens to its Rome. . . . Well, maybe I got carried away. But to be the South's "national" university, to be a Southern Sorbonne or St Andrew's, is not a shabby ambition, and it's not an unrealizable one, either. It's something we almost do already, and something we will continue to do, whether we work at it or not—whether we even think about it or not. But imagine what we could do if we accepted that role deliberately, rejoiced and were glad in it, invested in it and built on it.

Carolina's regional leadership isn't in conflict with our other roles. Indeed, historically, it has been inseparable from them. Much of the UNC's service to North Carolina has been a by-product of its focus on the region, and its world-wide reputation has been largely built by scholarship and research in the South, and on it. There's little danger that we'll forget or neglect either of our better-known roles. Our special relation to the state of North Carolina is sometimes troubled, but it's never seriously in question. And our faculty won't give up their national and international orientation and aspirations without a fight. But I hope we won't forget our regional role, either.

Let me close in the approved Southern fashion, with a story. In 1938 Jonathan Daniels of the *Raleigh News and Observer* was in Marked Tree, Arkansas, talking with a country lawyer. When Daniels said he was from North Carolina, the lawyer pointed to a shelf of books on the South, many of them from the UNC Press, written by UNC authors like Howard Odum, Rupert Vance, and Arthur Raper.

"Do you know Odum?" he asked. Daniels said he did.

"And Vance?" the lawyer asked. Daniels said "yes."

"Have you read Raper's *Preface to Peasantry*?" Daniels nodded.

"I've got 'em all," the lawyer said. "That's a great university at Chapel Hill."

It is a great university. A great *Southern* university. As I pass off the stage, I'm proud to have been a part of it, and I thank you for the chance to talk about why.

SURVEYING
THE SOUTH

I was honored, if somewhat apprehensive, when *Southern Cultures* marked my retirement by commissioning my friends, the noted historians of the South Elizabeth Fox-Genovese and Eugene D. Genovese, to interview me for its Spring 2001 issue. You'll see why it's immodest for me to include that interview here, but I can live with that.

SURVEYING THE SOUTH
A Conversation

On a Saturday afternoon in August 2000, I sat down for a conversation with Betsey and Gene Genovese at their home in Atlanta. The tape recorder was turned on—

• • •

JOHN: Aren't you supposed to read me my rights?

BETSEY: I'd like to start with what you mean by the South. You've written a lot about the South. You do all this mesmerizing stuff with how many more people eat Moon Pies down here than in other parts of the country, or go to church, or what have you. But what's beyond that, beyond what those numbers add up to?

JOHN: As I've often said, I'm less interested in the South than I am in Southerners. I'm less interested in the region than I am in the group. And social psychologist that I am, I see the group as defined by identification with it. Basically, the question arises: Who are these people who describe themselves as Southerners? And what does that mean? How has it changed? How is it changing? I don't see Southern identification as some sort of Platonic ideal to which people are in some sort of approximation. I see it as defined on the ground by the folks who choose to affiliate. And this means that the group is open to attrition and infiltration. It doesn't mean the boundary doesn't exist, it just means people cross it. What that boundary contains can change and has changed. What it contains is an empirical question.

BETSEY: Then why do you think, as I do myself, that history seems to be so important to people's sense of what it means to be a Southerner? History, place, continuity in place, family, all of those things.

JOHN: I agree with you that history has been and still is important, and that one way many groups define themselves is by a shared history transmitted through ancestry. It's not the only way groups define themselves. Social classes are defined by what they have in common in the present, although they have histories, too. But it's a shared predicament in the present that gives rise to class consciousness.

GENE: Let me press a bit further on the question of identification as Southerners. That identification surely has an objective basis historically. You suggest it has been a changing basis, but then it seems to me necessary to trace the main lines of that basis. What over time has made the South a distinct region, understanding that it has not been static? It seems to me implicit in your work that there is something that could legitimately be called a tradition, which again would distinguish the South and Southerners from other Americans.

JOHN: Well, you historians tell me the South emerged as a self-conscious region in the sectional conflicts of the early nineteenth century. These were over slavery. And I don't have much patience with folks who say the Civil War was not about slavery. It certainly wouldn't have happened without it. It's true that most white Southerners weren't slaveholders, but a good many of them would have liked to be. Folks up in the hills where I come from used to sing, "All I want in this creation's a pretty little girl and a big plantation."

But just as plainly, Southern identification is not about slavery anymore. For a long time it was about Jim Crow. That's what Ulrich Phillips said in the 1920s: The "cardinal test of a Southerner" was the commitment that the South be and remain a white man's country. That was a glaring and obvious distinction. The minute you crossed into the South you were under a different system of laws. Ninety-eight percent of white Southerners in 1942 thought black and white children should go to separate schools. But that's not what the South's about anymore. These days Southern identification is not so much a matter of shared history as a shared cultural style—some cultural conservatism, religiosity, manners, speech, humor, music, that sort of thing.

I don't think many Southern blacks at the turn of the century referred to themselves as Southerners; Booker T. Washington was perhaps the major exception. That's changed. [Political scientist] Merle Black and I looked at survey responses between 1964 and 1976, and Southern blacks' ratings of the word "Southerner" went from sort of tepid to quite warm. I think what changed was that they began to think of that word as applying to themselves. And certainly there are plenty of examples now of Southern black politicians saying, "We Southerners," or "We in the South." That's a major change. And if you have a group defined on the basis of cultural style, it's open to both blacks and whites. It's also open to migrants who acquire the style, or to their children (whether they want it or not), in a way that an ancestry-based group isn't open to outsiders. To those of us who like to have Southerners around, this is a cheering development. To be a Southerner in 1900 meant standing up for Dixie and saluting the flag, and venerating the Lost Cause and its heroes, but the Confederate heritage, for all that it's making a lot of noise these days, is one that's shared by fewer and fewer residents of the South in each generation. We did a survey a while back: roughly a third of white Southerners have Confederate ancestors and know it, a third didn't know whether they did or not, and a third knew they didn't. So, that's not what the South's about, these days.

GENE: And tradition?

JOHN: Tradition. There are several different Southern traditions, and one of them is the one that you all have written and talked about. It's an aristocratic tradition that came out of Virginia and Low Country South Carolina and got transplanted to places like Alabama and Mississippi. Another is the one that I grew up in, up in East Tennessee. It has more to do with Davy Crockett than with James Henry Hammond. It's a boisterous sort of individualistic frontier tradition. It lasted a long time in my neck of the woods. Those two things coexist—maybe with different emphases in different parts of the South, but they're both Southern traditions. One gave us country music and stock car racing, and the other gave us—whatever it is it gave us.

BETSEY: But here you have, with more charm, intelligence, and wit than almost anyone I can think of, with the possible exception of Florence King, defended that boisterous frontier tradition. It demonstrably is not your own.

You are MIT and Columbia educated. You are urbane. You may enjoy country music, but you remain a member of the Episcopal Church. By any, by all, of your favorite objective sociological criteria, you would come across as upper class, not as boisterous frontiersman, East Tennessee or not.

JOHN: That's a class thing, I suspect. I'm upper middle class. I grew up in a surgeon's family in East Tennessee. But I did grow up in East Tennessee and I did go to public schools. And one aspect of this tradition is egalitarianism, at least among men. Rank is settled more by athletic ability and physical prowess than by wealth or education. So I can talk that talk, and in a sense it is my tradition. I come from it, and on my father's side, I'm only a couple of generations removed from it. My grandfather was an upward-mobility story. He was an orphan boy in southwest Virginia who taught school for a while and then went to medical school. So I don't feel alienated from that tradition. I've done other things as well, but I'm not a stranger to it.

BETSEY: How would you feel, for example, about the current battles over the Confederate flag? And how would you come down relative to other people from that hill country?

JOHN: That hill country tradition was ambivalent and conflicted in the 1860s. I had relatives on both sides of that war in the same county, probably burning each other's barns. And I don't think they stopped fighting in 1865.

BETSEY: But both sides were probably racist?

JOHN: Both sides were racist—probably in a pretty theoretical way because there weren't many black folks up there, but they would have liked to keep it that way, I expect. As far as the Confederate flag goes, I have no problem with people who honor it and see it as a symbol of valor and devotion to duty and heritage. No problem at all. And they mean by it what they mean by it, and not what the NAACP understands it to mean. And they're entitled to their interpretation. On the other hand, my own view is that it doesn't belong as an official state symbol because those symbols should belong to all or at least most of the citizens of a state. Now that black folks are full citizens of the commonwealth, their views should be taken into account, even if you believe their views are mistaken, as my Sons of Confederate Veteran friends think they are. So, partly for political reasons, partly for temperamental reasons, I'd like to see us get the state out of the business of venerating Confederate symbols and let individuals do that if they feel like it.

BETSEY: Do you think that the current move, at both the state and the federal level, is toward letting individuals do what they choose to do, especially honoring the Confederate flag? Is that the trend in expressing religious views?

JOHN: I'm not sure I'd go that far. In fact I think some views are being defined as unacceptable. I don't think there is a strong libertarian tide running in every respect today.

BETSEY: But that does cast a light on saying cheerily, "Well, we'll get the state out of the business of defending the Confederate tradition." It's like saying we'll get the state out of the business of religion. We'll get the state out of the business of letting boys play football. There are lots of things we can get the state out of that aren't anywhere near as neutral as you make them sound.

JOHN: I'm not a thoroughgoing libertarian, although I'm probably more of one than most of my friends. But I think you have to deal with this on a case-by-case basis. In other words, I'm not consistent. One alternative is to honor all traditions and support all religions, including Wicca. The other is to do none. It seems to me those are the two alternatives when you've got a pluralistic society, and which you do in a particular case is a political decision. Virginia tried to combine Lee-Jackson Day with Martin Luther King's birthday, and that's one way to do it. Probably not stable, but worth a try. Another way is to not honor anybody at all.

BETSEY: Do you think not honoring anybody at all poses any kind of problem?

JOHN: Well sure it does. A nation, any society, needs heroes. But it's not necessarily the case that the state has to identify them, not if you've got a robust nonstate sector. Ours could use a little "robusting."

GENE: When Zell Miller was governor here in Georgia, he raised the question of getting the state out of the flag issue in the most extraordinarily hypocritical way. He wanted to return to the former state flag, which of course was another Confederate flag. Incidentally, if that had been done honestly it would have made a good point. It's one thing to honor the Confederate tradition, what was positive in it. It's another thing to use the battle flag, which was imposed by the segregationists in a specific moment. But the main line that the established political opponents took was that we have to take the flag down because it's costing us money. That with the Olympics coming on and this and that, the Yankee money won't come in. Now I was astonished when I heard this. I wasn't prepared to believe that the majority of the people in Georgia, black or white, were prepared to announce that they were whores, but the governor thought differently. My point here, however, is to say that when you take the state out of this, you move the corporate entities in.

JOHN: In some moods I share your view that this is contemptible. On the other hand, we've got a republic here that's explicitly devoted to the pursuit of happiness, which these days typically means the pursuit of prosperity and wealth. And Samuel Johnson did say once that a man is seldom so innocently engaged as when he's making money. It's not a particularly edifying thing to watch, but compare it to the alternatives. Atlanta used to call itself the city too busy to hate. Fred Hobson said once that that's a pretty sorry reason not to hate. But if the choice is between that and hatred, I'll take that.

GENE: Let's sit back a little bit on this question of the South as a region. You've been coeditor of *Southern Cultures,* very good journal, but the name has always bugged me. Every region is made up of alternative cultures, and, as you pointed out, alternative traditions, but if one is going to speak about the South distinctly, then there has to be a meaningful way to speak of Southern culture, taking full account that it embraces as wide a range of variations as any other regional or national culture. So what exactly were you chaps up to?

JOHN: I fought that battle and lost. I wanted to call it *Southern Culture.* My coeditor, my esteemed coeditor [Harry Watson], felt it should be plural, and more to the point our publisher (who at that time was Duke University Press) thought it should be plural. And basically I was outvoted. I had the choice of walking out or living with it, so I decided to live with it. Since then I've come around a bit. It does give us a flexibility that we might not have if we had called it *Southern Culture.* I solicited an article not long ago, for example, on black Baha'i in South Carolina. You can run that piece in a journal called *Southern Cultures.* It's a little harder to do in one called *Southern Culture* because this is such an eccentric topic. But it's an interesting one. Personally, I think there is a Southern culture. I think it's shared to a great extent, as I said, by both blacks and whites, and Protestants, Catholics, and Jews, and about any other way you want to slice the Southern cake. I once wrote a piece on Southern Jews who within the American Jewish community look very Southern. Within the Southern community they look pretty Jewish. Same story with Hispanics. I was reading a piece not long ago showing that Mexican Americans in Texas actually look like Texans compared to Mexican Americans in California, who look like Californians. But I had to conclude that the name of the journal was a lost cause, and I've had enough of those.

GENE: I, myself, would capitulate on the question of *Southern Cultures* when you run an article on Southern Sicilians, but not before that.

JOHN: Why don't you write it for us?

GENE: I don't know enough about it. But, seriously here, you mentioned cultural conservatism as one of the hallmarks of the South. And that, too, certainly has changed radically over time. To what extent do you think the South today is significantly more conservative culturally than other parts of the country and why?

JOHN: There is this individualistic streak that we were talking about earlier that complicates things, because it's not Allen Tate's kind of conservatism exactly. But just at the level of the survey data I spend a lot of time looking at, you find a more skeptical attitude toward feminism, for example. A less tolerant view of homosexuality. Fewer people drink liquor. Fewer people are cremated. This conservatism crops up in peculiar ways, but basically it's just more resistance to change. Now I'm not saying that things aren't changing. Plainly they are. But the South remains relatively conservative. In 1919 the issue was women's suffrage. Most Western states had it. Most Southern states didn't. Mississippi didn't ratify the Nineteenth Amendment until 1984. But when the Equal Rights Amendment came along, the states that held out against that were primarily Southern states and Utah. The issues change, but the South remains relatively conservative. And this is not just a Southern white thing, incidentally. On matters other than race relations, black Southerners are more conservative in many ways than white Southerners.

GENE: My impression is that the black community in the South is much more culturally conservative than is generally appreciated, and that in that respect it is well out of step with its political leadership. I don't suggest here that the politicians are manipulating their people. I don't think that. What I do think, however, is that black people have their own priorities and are prepared to remain relatively silent while their political leaders cut their deals. Nonetheless, in a few polls I've seen on specific issues they send a message saying, "We really don't like this."

JOHN: I think you're absolutely right. Of course, the paramount issue for black Americans, especially black Southerners, has been civil rights and race relations. And as long as there is any question of whether that's settled, they're understandably going to remain with the party that's more liberal on that issue. And that means they're willy-nilly staying with the party that's more liberal on other issues as well. But if you look at data on things like abortion or homosexual rights, the black community—and not just in the South but especially in the South—is pretty conservative. It's just that these issues aren't central at this time.

GENE: You contributed an article to a book by fifteen Southerners [*Why the South Will Survive*] in which you compare the rough individualism of the up-country yeoman, to which you have recently alluded, with the genteel tradition that was conservative in a socially organic sense. Your discussion in that essay was the best I've ever seen anywhere, but problems remain. As a historian, I think the one problem that needs a great deal more attention is the extent to which in the Old South that antagonism was transcended. The slaveholders exercised hegemony, but they exercised hegemony by making major concessions to that pressure from below. Now it does seem to me here that one of the unifying forces was this strong commitment to republicanism, and that is what separated the most hardened traditionalist conservatives from their European equivalents. Obviously, slavery provided a framework that permitted a certain kind of ideological transcendence. I would be interested in hearing your thoughts about how that has worked out over time. The same tensions clearly exist today.

JOHN: I'm not sure I've got anything intelligent to say about that, but let me vamp for a while. I agree with you that the slaveholders exerted hegemony in most places. I grew up twenty miles from where Andrew Johnson grew up, and he was elected to Congress by running against the stuck-up aristocrats of

West Tennessee. But we know what happened to Andrew Johnson. And Parson Brownlow and these folks weren't hegemonized, but they were certainly marginalized. In any case, I think most nonslaveholding whites, as I said, aspired to be slaveholders. A good many of them were related to slaveholders. There was a reasonable prospect that they or their kids might someday be slaveholders. So they certainly weren't interested in emancipation, whether they were slaveholders or not. When push came to shove, these folks turned out and the poor man fought for the rich man for a good long while. These days, I think individualism has probably triumphed. I don't see too many signs of the old organic conservatism around. It's hard to find too many people that actually embody the Southern conservative tradition these days. We have Southerners who are conservative, who call themselves conservatives, but Newt Gingrich is not the kind of person you're talking about. It's an individualism that's translated increasingly into economic ideology. The South was a solid part of the New Deal coalition not because folks were organic conservatives but because they were desperately poor. Now that we're not so poor anymore, folks are beginning to think that people ought to be able to hang on to what they've earned. Government shouldn't tax it away. That sort of libertarian economic thought is probably the natural expression in the economic realm of this strain that's always been there.

GENE: What you seem to be suggesting, and I'm not fighting you on this at all, is that the South in effect, as liberals have been saying for a century, is becoming just another part of the United States. It's remarkable how many new New Souths we have had since 1865, and much of your work has cautioned against exaggerating this. You're now suggesting, however, that the culture of the South is now a culture of industrialization. Do you then think, however unpleasant the thought may be, that at this point in time, a much stronger case can be made that the differences—the regional differences, the cultural differences between the South and the rest of the country—are disappearing?

JOHN: Certainly when it comes to economics they are. And for the most part, good riddance. Not too many people are nostalgic about hookworm and pellagra. The South is now the most industrial region of the country. North Carolina and Mississippi have the highest percentage of their labor force employed in industry of any states in the country. The Agrarians' nightmare has come to pass. As usual we're kind of lagging in things because we're getting into heavy industry just as everybody else is getting out of it. That difference is gone with the wind, but there are other differences. I mean the solid religious South preceded the solid political South, and to a great extent it still is an evangelical Protestant region. Leave Texas and Florida with their big Hispanic populations out of it, and 90 percent of Southern whites and blacks are still Protestant. Slightly more than half of those are Baptists of one kind or another. Speaking of individualism, by the way, here it is in the religious realm.

GENE: You've done an enormous amount of work on a wide variety of problems, not only concerning the South, but also your more recent work on the Anglican church [in the book *Glorious Battle*]. Several questions occur to me. One is what you see as the unifying theme in your work. Or perhaps to put it another way, am I wrong in thinking that certain large questions were with you early in your career, and you have been working them out along different lines? Second, I will ask you the question that nobody wants to be asked and everyone is incensed when asked. What do you consider to be your most important contribution to scholarship, your intellectual work, and what is your favorite work? The two are not necessarily the same.

JOHN: Let me answer the second and third questions first because they're easier. If I've made a contribution at all, it's been working out the implications of viewing Southerners as a sort of quasi-ethnic group. It wasn't an original insight. Other people said it. But I think what I did first was to take that seriously and to ask some of the same questions about Southerners that had already been asked for a long time about racial groups and immigrant ethnic groups. Questions about identity, consciousness, boundary maintenance, stereotyping, all of this social-psychological stuff. And that really runs through a good many of my writings, particularly my early work. Probably the most explicit treatment of it is in a little book called *Southerners: The Social Psychology of Sectionalism*. I really tried to take that seriously, and a lot of people have said they find this a useful way to look at things.

My favorite work is probably the book Dale and I wrote together called *1001 Things Everyone Should Know about the South,* not just because it sold the most copies and made the most money, although that's nice, but because it reached the largest audience and did say some stuff that is important. I don't think it's a trivial book. It's not a scholarly book, but it's informed by a good deal of scholarship and it's been well received. It's taught a lot of people a lot of things they ought to know about the South. And it was also fun to write. Dale and I had a good time with that one.

Now, to the question about common themes. The easy answer to that is that both the work on the South and the work on the Church of England reflect my biography. I am a Southerner and I am an Episcopalian, and I'm curious about both of those heritages and what it means and how it became what it is. And I've been lucky enough to be able to explore that. It's sort of working out psychotherapy in public. That's the obvious answer. And it may be the actual answer, but I think you can find some common intellectual themes as well that have to do with tradition, how it's viewed, how it's created.

I really got interested in the Anglo-Catholics when I discovered that that species of Anglicanism was not, as I had always assumed, simply a fossil remnant of the pre-Reformation English church. In the nineteenth century, it was an innovation, a conscious turning back the clock. That got very interesting. All of a sudden here were people who decided they were going to roll back the Reformation. At some level this concern with tradition and how it is manipulated and used and how it shapes the way people think about themselves is the common thread there intellectually.

GENE: Have you considered the work you've done on that subject directly in relation to the Southern experience where high church Episcopalianism did not fare well?

JOHN: You're certainly right that there hasn't been a high church Episcopalian tradition in the South. Southern Episcopalianism has been very much eighteenth-century Anglicanism, low church. That's the church of Robert E. Lee and William Faulkner and Booker T. Washington. (You want to ask what those three had in common? They were all buried by the *Book of Common Prayer*.) But I haven't explored that.

GENE: I was wondering if you thought you might down the road?

JOHN: One of the things that I have been interested to learn was that the Anglo-Catholics in England were prominent among the English supporters of the Confederacy, which may not surprise you. Dale and I were just in Richmond at the Museum of the Confederacy, where they had an exhibit on Robert E. Lee with a Bible that was sent to Lee by his English admirers, who all turn out to be in my book—prominent Anglo-Catholics. But the Southern Episcopal tradition has been very Protestant and looks very much like some species of Presbyterianism. Incidentally, that's the tradition I was raised in, sort of low church.

BETSEY: I was going to ask about your sense of the relations among the different parts of your work, because this is something that people throw at me a lot, that I deal with very different kinds of subjects and topics. And the Anglo-Catholicism is a nice segue into it. Obviously, you're very well known for your insightful and witty essays. You have done a great deal of statistical work on polling data on the nature of the South and how people define themselves as Southerners. There's the Anglo-Catholicism. . . .

JOHN: Yes, the one thing that all of this work has in common is the biographical angle. I've been extraordinarily privileged, most college professors are, to be able to explore things that I'm interested in. Every time I've had an interest I've been able to go out and pursue it. And the interests and their commonalties have to do with my biography, so maybe there's some sort of intellectual coherence. Certainly since I got tenure, I've been free to do exactly what I wanted to do. And that's what I've done. It's a rare privilege, and those of us who have had it should all be thankful.

GENE: I'd like to ask two related questions. One is that of all those who have spoken frankly as Southern conservatives and have remained true to their principles, you may be the only scholar—academic at any rate—who has managed to achieve a large respectful audience outside of your own club. Much of that has to do with your talent and your style. But without taking anything away from that, when one thinks of the short shrift given to first-rate men like Richard Weaver and M. E. Bradford, among others, something else is going on here, and I wonder if you have any thoughts about it? The other question is, your sociological work has always had political implications that you have frankly suggested but that have not been your main focus. Would you share your thoughts with us as to where the South is going politically in relation to other regions, and what trends you think are particularly strong?

JOHN: Part of the reason that I've reached a broader audience than some of the people you have in mind is that I've tried to. In my early years I was a careerist.

I wanted to succeed. I wanted a good job, so I tried to publish my work in mainstream journals. I didn't send my books to conservative publishers. I got them into university presses. I didn't write for the choir. I was writing actually for other academics whose opinion was going to determine my future. It may just be a matter of politics and diplomacy. I may just be more concerned with that stuff. But I've always been, at least since my grad school days, in an ideological minority, and if I was going to have any friends at all I was going to have to talk to liberals or radicals. You learn to get along with these people. The alternative is oblivion.

BETSEY: I'm now borrowing from what I can imagine might be some of your more bunkered colleagues' views. Looking back, do you feel you've sacrificed anything for that?

JOHN: Some of my old bunkered colleagues also see me as squishy soft. And in point of fact, I am. If I were being defensive, I'd say I'm not as doctrinaire as they are. You might say I'm not as consistent as they are, or as hard-core as they are. I'm perhaps a little too ready to see other people's points of view. Now, if you're trying to talk to other people it helps to see their point of view. But it does kind of soften your rhetoric a little bit, and softens your edges.

BETSEY: No, but it's a real question, the balance between loyalty to one's convictions and the compromises necessary to coexist with the world. You have a unique talent and it's wonderful, but it's a mixed blessing. Of all your cohort, you surely are the one who has managed to make conservatism seem the least threatening to the academy at large. I can't help wondering if you ever have a feeling of frustration. Do these folks understand you have a limit?

JOHN: Part of it is having a sense of humor, which may sometimes mean that people think I don't actually believe what I say. And, in fact, some of it I don't believe. I overstate it for laughs. I'm not particularly comfortable being called a conservative. I don't mind being called conservative—adjective—but I'm not a movement kind of guy. I never have been. My species of conservatism, if that's what it is, is sort of Epicurean. I'll try to live a good life and be a witness of various kinds, and if anybody is persuaded by that, fine. But I'm not really out to change the world. I don't have any great belief that I'm capable of that. A lot of my colleagues in sociology in particular went into it because they wanted to improve things some way or other. I wanted to explore my interests and learn things that I was interested in. And occasionally I've wanted to entertain and amuse other folks. But my function is more ornamental than anything else. At least that's how I've seen it.

GENE: So what's your thinking on the political position and the course of the South?

JOHN: Well, that's getting muddy. The Solid South is no more. But the South, along with the Mountain States, is becoming the most reliably Republican part of the country—although not as reliably Republican as it was once reliably Democratic. But in 1996, the South had 163 electoral votes? Something like that. And Dole got 104 of them.

GENE: I have a theory on that. Southerners are deeply sympathetic people, and they felt that Dole should get some votes.

BETSEY: You have lived with three strong, accomplished women. What is your take on feminism and its impact?

JOHN: Y'all work it out and let us know what you want. It's okay with me. One thing about living with three strong and accomplished women is you learn to let them tell you what to do, at least as far as women are concerned. I'm solid on equity feminism. I've got no problem there. I can't imagine anybody of any sense has any problem with that anymore. But as for the whole rest of the agenda, whatever I say I'm wrong, so I'm just going to lie low on that one.

GENE: I think we should make it clear that of these three strong women, only one of them is—

JOHN: Yes, I'm only married to one of them.

BETSEY: Two of them are daughters.

JOHN: The other two are daughters, yes. And I've got a mother, too, you know.

BETSEY: All right. You're someone who is very much engaged with culture and who reads broadly. There is a very strong move these days among Southern literary scholars to insist, not merely for the present, but when they can get away with it retrospectively, that maybe we shouldn't be talking about the South at all, or Southern literature, but of regionalisms. And the South is one regionalism among many. Now, could any other region produce a William Faulkner or a Eudora Welty?

JOHN: We've had similar discussions in sociology, and I presume you have in history. Sure, it's true to say that the South is one among many American regions. But it's equally true and obvious, I think, that it's the most distinctive. And one of the earliest. And certainly the most obstreperous and self-conscious. And, to my mind, the most interesting. But if somebody wants to study the literature of the Pacific Northwest, fine. There's not much of it, but . . . the literature of the Dakotas, I don't know. I guess there is some. Great Plains literature, I suppose you could do that.

BETSEY: Most of those are Native American.

JOHN: Right. I get increasingly impatient with this kind of definitional discussion. I think you ought to get on and talk about the literature. Talk about the subject that you're talking about rather than talking about how you're going to talk about it. But that's my growing anti-intellectualism.

BETSEY: Well, is it anti-intellectualism? Is it anti-theory? And as one who has written a lot of theory myself, I get pretty impatient with what passes for theory these days. Mainly because a lot of it's theoretically dumb.

JOHN: Yes.

BETSEY: I mean it's not interesting. But I want to end with this question: Do you really want to conclude with that level of agnosticism or empiricism that refuses to say that there is something about the South that matters, above and beyond your personally finding it the most interesting?

JOHN: In that volume that Gene mentioned by the fifteen Southerners, *Why the South Will Survive,* there's a splendid belligerent statement by Clyde Wilson in the introduction about how the South is as real as Hollywood and corn and capitalism and half a dozen other things. Sure it's a concept, and you can deconstruct it in various ways. But it's there on the ground, too. And the fact that there are people who, when you ask them, say, "Hell, yes, I'm a Southerner," is every bit as much a fact as the kudzu that's growing in your backyard here. Michael O'Brien is only one of many people who've basically called me theoretically naïve, and I don't mind that label. I was trained as a positivist, and I'm a number-crunching social scientist. I am an empiricist.

BETSEY: Yes. All of that. Just a poor country boy. That label says more about Michael than it does about you.

GENE: Measurably.

JOHN: Well, you know, the South's there. Southerners are there. I'm persuaded of that. You kick them, you hurt your toe.

ACKNOWLEDGMENTS

I am much obliged to Lee Sioles, Rand Dotson, and their colleagues at the Louisiana State University Press for their act of faith in bringing this book to print, and to Susan Murray, whose copyediting went far beyond checking my spelling and punctuation. I'm also in debt to those whose publications, conferences, and speaker series elicited or accepted these pieces in the first place. In particular I thank the following publishers and copyright holders for permission to reprint the material indicated.

American Enterprise
A Delicious Way of Death (Originally "The Southern Way of Death.")
A Political Parable (Originally "Bubba's Uncle Warren.")

American Journal of Sociology
The South the Plantation Made (Originally published in the *American Journal of Sociology* [March 1976]. © 1976 The University of Chicago Press.)

American Psychological Association
Why Has There Been No Race War in the South? (Copyright © 2001 American Psychological Association. Reproduced with permission.) The official citation that should be used in referencing this material is Reed, J. S. (2002). "Why Has There Been No Race War in the American South?" In Chirot, D., & Seligman, M. E. *Ethnopolitical warfare: Causes, consequences, and possible solutions.* (Washington, DC: American Psychological Association)

Atlanta History
Southern Culture—On the Skids? (Originally published in *Atlanta History: A Journal of Georgia and the South.* © 2001 by the Atlanta Historical Society. Reprinted with permission.)

Atlanta Journal-Constitution
Why a Southern Poll? (Originally "Southern Life Poll—Reports of South's Demise Greatly Exaggerated.")

Baker Street Journal
A Note on the "Long Island Cave Mystery" Mystery

BBQJew.com (Dan Levine)
BBQ & A

Brightleaf : A Southern Review of Books (David Perkins)
The Man from Hot Springs
Old Boys, Good and Bad
True Believers, and Others
We Shall Overeat

Chronicles (formerly *Chronicles of Culture*)
Clear-Eyed Southern Boy
We, the Natives

CKM Press
Two Alabamians (Originally the foreword to Chip Cooper and Kathryn Tucker Windham, *Common Threads: Photographs and Stories from the South.*)

Front Porch Republic
A Tale of Three Restaurants

Gulf South Historical Review
My People, My People!

KnowLouisiana.org, the Encyclopedia of Louisiana
The French Quarter Renaissance of the 1920s

National Review
Can the South Show the Way?

New York Times
The Third Rail of North Carolina Politics (Originally "The Politics of Barbecue.")

Oxford American
Best Little Hair Houses in Dixie
The Uses of Southern History

Raleigh News & Observer
How Hillary Got Smoked in North Carolina (Originally, "How Hillary Tumbled into the NC Barbecue Pitfall" [December 7, 2016]. Reprinted with permission from *The News & Observer* of Raleigh, North Carolina.)

South Carolina Review
Free Your Doubtful Mind (Originally "Hank Done It This-a-Way" [Fall 2003].)

Southern Cultures
[All pieces in "The Southern Focus Poll" section except the first]
Barbecue and the Southern Psyche
Forty Defining Moments of the Twentieth-Century South
Surveying the South: A Conversation
Surveyor of the Bozart
There's a Word for It: The Origins of "Barbecue"
The Twentieth Century's Most Influential Southerners

Texas Monthly
Contra los Herejes (Originally "The Barbecue Editor Disputes a Tar Heel." Reprinted with permission from the May 2013 issue of *Texas Monthly*.)

Times Literary Supplement **(London)**
Through the Southern Looking-Glass (Originally "Without the Magnolias," February 27, 1998.)

University of Alabama Press
A Good Thing from Auburn (Originally published in Gordon E. Harvey, Richard D. Starnes, and Glenn Feldman, eds., *History and Hope in the Heart of Dixie: Scholarship, Activism, and Wayne Flynt in the Modern South* [Tuscaloosa: University of Alabama Press, 2006]. © 2006 The University of Alabama Press.)

University of Georgia Press
Kitchen Windows on the South (Originally "Introduction: Southern Eats," in Anthony J. Stanonis, ed., *Dixie Emporium: Tourism, Foodways, and Consumer Culture in the American South*. © 2008 The University of Georgia Press.)

University of North Carolina Press
Barbeculture in the Twenty-First Century (Originally "Barbecue Sociology: The Meat

of the Matter," in *Cornbread Nation 2: The United States of Barbecue,* edited by Lolis Eric Elie. © 2004 by the Southern Foodways Alliance. Used by permission of the University of North Carolina Press [www.uncpress.org].)

University of Tennessee Press
Bad Man in the Mountains (Originally the foreword to Thomas G. Burton, *Beech Mountain Man: The Memoirs of Ronda Lee Hicks.*)

Wall Street Journal
Bringing the Jubilee (Originally "From Atlanta to the Sea.")
A Flag's Many Meanings

Weekly Standard
Our Celtic Fringe
Plus Ça Change, Y'all (Originally "A Solid South.")
(Both reprinted with permission of *The Weekly Standard,* www.weeklystandard.com.)

ABOUT THE AUTHOR

John Shelton Reed has written a dozen books, innumerable articles, and a country song about the South. His most recent books are about Southern barbecue and New Orleans in the 1920s. Two others, *1001 Things Everyone Should Know about the South* and *Holy Smoke: The Big Book of North Carolina Barbecue*, were written with his wife, Dale Volberg Reed. He has been chancellor of the Fellowship of Southern Writers and is cofounder and Éminence Grease of the Campaign for Real Barbecue (TrueCue.org).

He taught for some years in the Department of Sociology at the University of North Carolina, Chapel Hill, retiring in 2000 as William Rand Kenan Jr. Professor and director of the Howard Odum Institute for Research in Social Science. He was founding coeditor of the quarterly *Southern Cultures* and helped to found the university's Center for the Study of the American South. He is a lieutenant colonel in the Unorganized Militia of South Carolina and an Honorary Fellow of St. Catharine's College, Cambridge University.